Electronics Explained

Electronics Explained

A Handbook for the Layman

by
PETER LAURIE

FABER & FABER · London and Boston

First published in 1980
by Faber and Faber Limited
3 Queen Square London WC1N 3AU
Printed in Great Britain by
J. W. Arrowsmith Ltd Bristol
All rights reserved

British Library Cataloguing in Publication Data

Laurie, Peter
  Electronics Explained
  1. Electronic apparatus and appliances
  I. Title
  621.381   TK7870

  ISBN 0-571-11514-4
  ISBN 0-571-11593-4 Pbk

Contents

NOTE

While every care has been taken to ensure that this book is accurate and up-to-date throughout, the author and the publisher can accept no responsibility for any inaccuracies it may be found to contain or for any use or uses to which information or other material contained in the book may be put.

Introduction

The electron is the genie of the twentieth century: an immensely powerful, invisible magician, who affects every life and is understood only by a tight-lipped circle of initiated priests—the engineers—who cloak their expertise in jargon and equations to shield it from the unworthy. But it need not be like this. At bottom the electron is a simple fellow. His ways can be understood, his motions controlled by anyone who can understand, for instance, how a petrol engine works. However spectacular their functions, most electronic devices are less complicated than that.

Ideally, to grasp electronics, you should do it. The art is as much cookery as science: just as a vegetable garden follows logical rules, yet still needs green fingers to make it grow, so the fullest understanding of electronics is gained by handling the hardware. But this book, I hope, is aimed at a much wider audience of people who cannot spare the considerable devotion this kind of learning takes; because doing electronics is like learning to fly or sail or ride a horse—it is not done overnight. You do not cultivate the awareness of signs that show what is happening in these brightly coloured but uncommunicative little objects until you have spent many hours wrestling with them. So, what this book tries to do is to take the reader on a voyage in imagination—which he is welcome to follow on foot as well if he will as the terrain to be explored can be contained on an ordinary-sized table, and the fare is modest—by dissecting a dozen common devices, showing the principles on which they work, and how the components they are made of interact.

Elementary electronics divides nowadays into three broad areas: audio, radio and digital. However, these are far from watertight classifications, and they have many ideas in common. Digital electronics particularly, owing to the cheapness and complexity of the devices available, which are made by the hundred thousand for computing, is invading the other two areas by leaps and bounds. So I have made no strict attempt to keep them separate. In the end, I hope it will all become clear.

I struggled for a long time to try and make this book read in an orderly fashion from start to finish. In the end I gave up, because my own experience of learning electronics is that one proceeds in a sort of spiral, coming back over and over again to the same things, but with more understanding each time. Since there is no way of arranging the contents of a book in a spiral, the contents of this one may seem somewhat unconventionally arranged. I hope, though, that what the reader needs, he will find in it somewhere.

My thanks are due to Geoffrey Shorter of the staff of *Wireless World* who kindly read my manuscript, removed many blunders and made several valuable suggestions.

Part I: Audio

INTRODUCTION TO PART I

The obvious place to start our electronic journey is with its most familiar domestic embodiment: the record player amplifier. Whether it's lo-fi or hi-fi, the principles are the same, and in understanding it we shall cover a good deal of basic ground.

The process of picking signals off a gramophone record, amplifying them and transmitting them to the air as sound waves loud enough for the ear to hear takes place in four stages:

1 Turning the grooves on the record into electrical signals (in the pickup).
2 Amplifying these signals, and altering the tone if necessary (in the preamplifier).
3 Increasing the power of the amplified signal (in the power amplifier).
4 Turning it into sound waves (in the speaker).

Engineers call the first and last—pickup and speaker—'transducers'. Stages 1 and 4 are not really electronic, but one needs to know something about them, so we'll discuss them quickly now. The grooves in the record are tracked by a needle or stylus made of hardwearing sapphire or diamond, and shaped so as to fit without slap or wobble (see Fig. 1). If the record is stereo, the two walls of the groove are at right angles and have different wobbles in them, so the needle produces two

sets of electrical signal. There are two basic ways of turning the mechanical motion of the needle into an electrical waveform, i.e. either by compressing a piezo-electric crystal or by moving a coil of wire in a magnetic field.

The important electronic facts about a piezo-electric crystal are that it produces a strong, but rather low quality signal—on average about 10 mV (see p.110 for an explanation of units of measurement); and that it is also an insulator, so no direct current (DC) can flow through it. A crystal has an *impedance* (p. 117) of 1 MΩ or so.

A moving coil transducer produces a better quality signal at a lower voltage—about 1 mV—has an impedance of 40 kΩ, and, of course, since it is a coil of wire, passes a direct current.

At the other end of the amplifier is a speaker, whose job is to push air to and fro as nearly as possible in accordance with the wobbles on the disc and electrical output of the power amplifier (see Fig. 2). There are two basic types: electromagnetic and electrostatic. The commonest uses a coil of wire fixed to a horn mounted in the field of a permanent magnet. As a signal current flows in the coil, the horn is pushed to and fro, causing trumpets to sound.

There are two drawbacks: one is that the air pushed out of the front tends to rush round to fill the accompanying hole at the back, producing no net effect. The

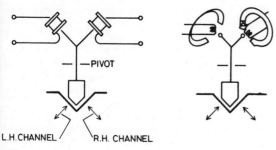

Fig. 1. Stereo playback from disc: the needle tip is moved in two directions at right angles by bumps coding the music waveform which are moulded into the record. The stylus, in turn, moves coils inside two magnets, converting the mechanical motion into small electrical currents.

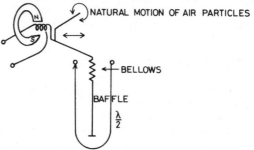

Fig. 2. Loudspeaker: current in the coil moves the cone which drives air to and fro. To prevent air leaking round the sides the speaker is mounted in a baffle which should be at least a quarter of a wavelength wide at the lowest frequency to be reproduced.

answer is to separate front and back by a *baffle*, which at its simplest is a sheet of acoustically opaque material.

If the baffle is a quarter of a wavelength wide, a particle of air has to move half a wavelength to get round it to the back of the speaker, and by the time it's got there, the cone has moved through half a cycle and it's time to be back where it started again. The result is a baffled particle and much better sound. Practical baffles are at the simplest a box lid with deadening material, and at the most complicated, amazingly intricate structures.

The other snag is that a big speaker cannot move fast enough to reproduce high notes, while a small speaker that can, can't shift enough air to give power to low notes. The answer is to have two or sometimes three speakers of different sizes—a tweeter for the high notes, a woofer for the low with filter circuits, called 'crossover networks' (p. 25), in the speaker to feed each one with the range of signals it handles best.

Another type of speaker uses two large sheets of metal which are held a small distance apart and charged with high voltage signal. The electrons on them attract and repel each other, producing excellent reproduction but at great expense, so they are not often seen. So we have the start and the end of the reproduction chain and in between we have to do two things: increase the voltage of the signal and also increase its power. How much voltage amplification or gain do we need?

Suppose we start with a magnetic pick-up giving about 2 mV of signal, in an impedance of 40 kΩ which means 100μW of power off the record (units explained on p. 110). We want to end up driving an ordinary speaker—which will almost certainly have an impedance of 8 Ω, with about 10 W of power—quite enough for the ordinary living room. 10 W into 8 Ω implies a signal of about 9 V (p. 110). The voltage gain is the output divided by the input, and is $9/0.002 = 4500$ times, i.e. 73 dB (p. 111).

In the simplest form, the preamplifier increases the voltage of the input signal by this 73 dB—or has the ability to—while the power amplifier increases its power to drive the low impedance of the speaker.

TRANSISTOR AMPLIFICATION

Here we digress to take in the principles of transistor amplification. In the process we shall cover the basic devices and ideas of audio electronics.

There are two main types of transistor: bipolar and field effect (FET). A bipolar transistor is a simple device with three terminals called *collector*, *emitter* and *base* (rather badly chosen names, incidentally, but we're stuck with them). It works like a tap: the amount of current flowing from collector to emitter is directly proportional to the current flowing into the base.

The *voltage* between collector and emitter has *no* effect.

Fig. 3. Currents in an npn transistor.

Fig. 3 shows an npn device in which the current flows like a valve—that is, the collector is connected to the + rail and the emitter to the − rail. Early transistors were pnp and upside down, which was most confusing (pnp devices are still available, but one tends to use them only for particular jobs which need voltage ju-jitsu). Npns are usually silicon, pnps usually germanium.

There are two salient facts about the bipolar npn transistor (see Fig. 4).

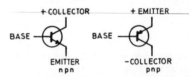

Fig. 4. Names of terminals in a bipolar transistor. By convention, the arrow in the symbol points to the negative rail.

1 The base is, if given the chance, *always* higher than the emitter (0.7 V for silicon; 0.2 V for germanium).
2 The collector current I_c is a fixed constant times the base current I_b. This constant, usually written β, is called the 'current gain'.

Since the base and collector currents flow out through the emitter the method in Fig. 3 of using a transistor is called, logically enough, 'common emitter'. There are other ways, which we will come to later, but this is far and away the most usual.

If the base current is big enough, the collector sinks all the possible current from its supply, and the device is said to be 'hard on' or 'saturated'. It is almost as if a wire connected collector to emitter. If there is no base current—because there is no voltage on the base to hold it 0.7 V above the emitter—then the device is hard off, and it acts like an open circuit. These two states are used in electronic logic.

For amplification of music or speech we need something in between the two, where the transistor acts vaguely like a variable resistor (p. 3). But before we look at an amplifier, let's consider the simplest transistor circuit, an emitter follower.

Suppose that the base is held by some other circuit at 5 V. The supply is at 10 V. The emitter settles—such is the nature of the beast—0.7 V lower than the base, and

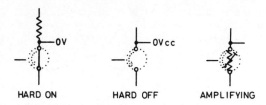

Fig. 5. When a bipolar transistor is hard on it acts much as if a wire connected the collector to the emitter. When it is hard off they are not connected at all; and when it is half way, or amplifying, it is as if they were connected by a variable resistor.

is therefore 4.3 V. Since the collector is tied to the positive rail, the collector–emitter voltage, written V_{ce}, is 10 V − 4.3 V = 5.7 V. But providing this is less than the maximum rating for the device in question (p. 8), this voltage has *no effect at all*. The emitter is connected to ground by a 500-Ω resistor. The current through this resistor—and also into the collector—is 4.3/500 = 8.6 mA (p. 107). Suppose that the β of this device is 100. Then the current into the base, I_b, must be 1/100th of this: $I_b = 0.086$ mA = 86 μA.

Suppose a signal of + 0.1 V now arrives at the base. For a moment the base–emitter voltage is 0.8 V. This opens the device up and lets more current flow from collector to emitter. This extra current piles up at the top of the resistor, so raising its voltage until things settle down again with the emitter 0.1 V higher at 4.4 V, and the base–emitter voltage once again 0.7 V. If the base voltage were to fall by 0.1 V the opposite would happen, with the emitter settling again at 4.2 V. In effect the emitter reproduces the signal voltage at the base. This is why the circuit is called an emitter follower: the emitter follows the base. Its signal is identical in size and phase.

'Well and good,' you may say, 'but what use is this? I thought we were to talk about voltage amplification, of which I see none.' You would be right. We come in a moment to amplification, but this is a useful step on the way. And, moreover, a useful circuit because it takes a weak signal and turns it into a strong one.

To see why this is so, go back to the emitter. A 0.1 V signal on the base raised the emitter by 0.1 V and drove 0.1/500 = 0.02 mA as signal current into the emitter resistor. By 2 above we know that this must have been caused by a signal current in the base 1/100th as large—i.e. 2 μA. As far as the signal source could see, 0.1 V on the base drove 2 μA of current into it. The base had an apparent resistance of 0.1/2.10 − 6 = 50 000 Ω, which is of course $\beta \times R_e$. In other words, the base could draw signal from a weak source without flattening it. By contrast, the output at the emitter is connected to ground by a 500-Ω resistor, and can supply quite a lot of signal current before it gets dented. An emitter follower acts as an impedance (p. 117) transformer.

Back to our record player. We want voltage gain, so consider the circuit shown in Fig. 6a. Notice carefully the difference: the *emitter* goes to ground, while the *collector* is connected to the positive rail through a resistor R_c. What happens now when we put a small voltage wave on the base? As it goes up, more current flows into the base, the device opens up, more current flows from collector to emitter, and the voltage at the collector *falls*. As the signal goes negative the device shuts down, less current flows, and the voltage at the collector *rises*. (The voltage across the resistor R_c must, by Ohm's law, be proportional to the current through it. Since the top is held at 10 V, the bottom must rise and fall.) It turns out that we can easily get the signal at the collector to be 100 × greater than the signal at the base. Notice that the output is in *opposite phase* to the input.

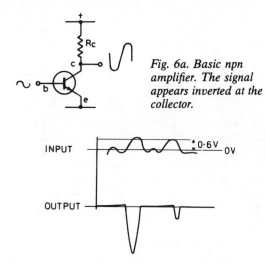

Fig. 6a. Basic npn amplifier. The signal appears inverted at the collector.

Fig. 6b. Without base bias, a transistor would only amplify input signals that exceeded 0.6 V.

So far, so good. There is, of course, a snag. As we have it, the average voltage on the base will tend to drift down to 0 V, and the device will only amplify on positive input peaks of more than 0.7 V. In Fig. 6b the input is high enough only twice. As a music amplifier this is no good. To get it to amplify all the time, we have to hold the base higher; we have to *bias* it. A usual sort of scheme is shown in Fig. 7.

The functions of the various parts are thus:

R_{b1} and R_{b2} bias the base so that the transistor conducts. They are usually set so that the emitter voltage is $(1/5 \times V_{cc})$ (this stabilizes the current through the device, and as we shall see later, p. 5, also stabilizes the gain). Let's take V_{cc} to be 10 V, and let's decide that the standing current should be 1 mA. V_e is 10/5 or 2 V. R_e must then be $2/1.10^{-3} = 2$ kΩ— nearest preferred value (p. 107), 2.2 kΩ. Let β be 300. The standing base current is 1/300 mA. Experience

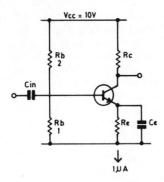

Fig. 7. Practical amplifier circuit. Notice the bias resistors for base, emitter resistor and decoupling capacitor.

shows that the current through the bias resistors should be about 10 times this for good stability = 0.033 mA. The two resistors together: $R_{b1} + R_{b2} = 10/0.033 = 300$ kΩ. The base has to be 0.6 V higher than the emitter, at 2.6 V. We thus have:

$$\frac{2.6}{R_{b1}} = \frac{10}{300.10^3} \quad \text{and} \quad R_{b1} = 78 \text{ k}\Omega$$

$$\text{and} \quad R_{b2} = 222 \text{ k}\Omega.$$

In practice one wouldn't bother making up these precise values; one would use the nearest preferred values: 82 kΩ and 220 kΩ (p. 107).

Now we come to the nub of the matter. As before, we have an amplified signal at the collector, which is opposite in phase to the base signal. The limits to this amplification are obviously set by the positive supply rail—the collector voltage can't rise higher than this—and the emitter voltage—it can't fall lower than that. It is usual to set the no-signal collector voltage half way between, so that with large enough input, the output bangs evenly against both limits—it is said to be symmetrically clipped; see Fig. 8. We can now settle a

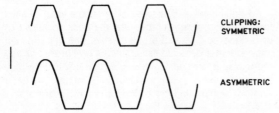

Fig. 8. If the input is enough to drive the transistor fully on or fully off the output will 'limit' or 'clip'. If this happens equally above and below the mean input voltage, the output is said to 'clip symmetrically'. If not, the clipping is asymmetric.

value for R_c. The collector voltage V_c has to be half way between 10 V and 2.6 V, i.e. 6.3 V. The drop across R_c is 10 V–6.3 V = 3.7 V, and the current

through it must be the same as the emitter current of 1 mA. It has to be 3.7 kΩ—nearest preferred value 3.9 kΩ. So the complete circuit is as shown in Fig. 9. As

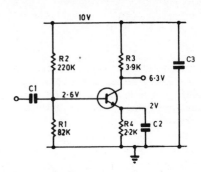

Fig. 9. Npn amplifier with resistor values (see text). Please note that values of kΩ use the abbreviation K and values of MΩ use the abbreviation M throughout the circuit diagrams in this book.

we shall see later, the voltage gain, ignoring C_e for the moment, is 1.7. The input impedance is 2.2 kΩ × 300 = 660 kΩ (p. 3) shunted by the base bias resistors which reduce it to something like 82 kΩ. The voltages shown are, of course, average values.

A most important element which we have not so far discussed is C_3. The amplifier works by taking current from the top rail and dumping it onto the bottom one. C_3 lets the alternating signal currents get back to where they started, so that the rails can maintain their unsullied purity of 10 V and 0 V. Without this *decoupling capacitor*, the amplifier will work badly and will upset other circuits fed by the same supply.

Emitter decoupling

Everything so far has been straightforward, with the exception of the mysterious C_e (C2 in Fig. 9). This is a most important component, and it is essential to understand it. Suppose for the moment that it does not exist, and R_e (Fig. 7) is the only path to ground from the emitter. When an upward signal arrives at the input, it drives current into the base which releases β times as much through the emitter. This tries to get to ground through R_e, but can't without raising the emitter voltage (p. 3). But it is precisely the difference in voltage between base and emitter that turns the device on and produces collector current and amplification at the output: this difference is now being reduced. From another point of view, we have *negative feedback* (p. 6). It turns out that the gain of the amplifier is simply R_c/R_e. We cannot get higher gain by increasing R_c because in the end that starves the transistor of current; we cannot get gain by reducing R_e because that lets so much current pass that the device breaks. A voltage gain of 1.7 times is hardly worth the trouble. What are we to do?

We bypass R_e with a capacitor which passes AC but not DC. The result is that if we put an alternating signal on the base it appears at the emitter but is shorted straight to ground by the capacitor. The emitter is *decoupled* (a nasty word, but engineers like it), and the amplifier gives its full gain, limited only by transconductance (p. 6).

What size of capacitor? A capacitor resists AC more strongly the lower the frequency. Its reactance in ohms (p. 112) is $1/2\pi \times f \times C$. If, say, the theoretical gain of the amplifier is 100, then, if we are to realize it, the reactance of the capacitor must be $R_c/100$. Since the reactance of the capacitor rises as frequency falls, we have to decide what the lowest frequency is that we want to amplify, and from that choose the capacitor.

Example: A transistor amplifier which can give a gain of 50 is needed to work down to 300 Hz as part of a communication channel. The emitter resistor is 1 kΩ, what decoupling capacitor is needed?

$$X_c = \frac{R_c}{50} \quad \text{or} \quad \frac{1}{2\pi \times 300 \times C} = \frac{10^3}{50}$$

So

$$C = \frac{50}{2\pi \times 300 \times 10^3} = 26 \ \mu F$$

This high value is typical of decoupling capacitors in audio amplifiers made of discrete transistors, which are often 100 μF. Fortunately they only have to stand 3 V or so, and therefore can be quite small.

Since C_e passes no DC, the direct current sees an amplifier with heavy negative feedback. This means that if the operating conditions change—usually due to β being altered by changing temperature—the voltages will rearrange themselves to minimize the effect. This makes for gain stability. On the other hand, AC sees an amplifier with the emitter connected direct to ground, which makes for high gain.

FEEDBACK BIASING

Another biasing system, which also illustrates the other main method of providing negative feedback, is shown in Fig. 10.

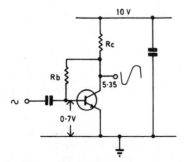

Fig. 10. Another method of biasing an npn transistor.

The resistor values are simple enough to calculate. Let's take the emitter current at 10 mA. The output voltage wants to be half way between the + rail, 10 V, and the emitter, 0.7 V = 5.35 V. R_c must be $5.35/10 \times 10^3 = 535$ Ω, nearest preferred 560 Ω. Since the emitter is at 0 V, the base must stand at an average value of 0.7 V. If we suppose again that β is 300, then the base must draw 10 mA/300 = 33 μA. The voltage across R_b is 5.35 V − 0.7 V = 4.65 V, and to give the required current, its value must be $4.65/33 \times 10^{-6} = 140\,909$ Ω; nearest preferred 150 kΩ.

This amplifier works well, is economical of parts, gives a wider output swing, but less gain because of negative feedback through R_b. (Remember that the input and output are opposite in phase and will therefore cancel out if given the chance.)

GAIN OF A TRANSISTOR

An obvious question, yet one that is seldom explicitly answered in books, is how to calculate the ultimate gain of a transistor amplifier.

Resolute on behalf of my readers, I set myself to examine this question in practice, having up to now managed to evade it. And I discovered why the answer is seldom given: because it is hard to tell exactly. However the results of my experiments are given below.

1 Gain is roughly proportional to emitter current multiplied by collector load: $G = kI_e \times R_c$
2 A small silicon npn audio transistor gave a k-factor of 20 at 3000 Hz.
3 A small germanium pnp gave 25.
4 A big germanium power transistor gave 2.

What does this mean in a typical amplifier stage? Let's have a positive supply of V_{cc}, the emitter held at $V_{cc}/5$ and the collector half way between, at $3V_{cc}/5$. The collector current is

$$\frac{V_{cc} - \dfrac{3 V_{cc}}{5}}{R_c} = I_e$$

so $R_c = 2V_{cc}/5I_e$ using $k = 20$: the gain is $20 \times I_e \times R_c = 20 \times 2V_{cc}/5 = 8 \times V_{cc}$. This is rather surprising, because it says that once you have chosen a supply voltage and decided to have the quiescent output voltage in the middle of the possible swing, the maximum gain is fixed at eight times the voltage of the supply. It makes little difference what type of transistor you use; for example, in the circuit of Fig. 9, $G = 8 \times 10 = 80$.

The gain, then, is $20 \times I_e \times R_c$. The '$20 \times I_c$' bit is a property of the device and is expressed in terms of a transfer conductance, 'transconductance' or 'mutual conductance', symbol g_m, which is just an expensive name for the number of amps of current you get out for each volt of input. (Notice that I/V, the definition of transconductance, is resistance upside down; and it is measured in mhos (ohms backwards), or more often in milimhos (or mmhos.)

It is a useful feature of the bipolar transistor that its output signal voltage is proportional to its standing emitter current,* for this means that we can tailor g_m to the figure we need. This is particularly helpful in minimizing noise (p. 76).

In practice transconductance is not a very useful figure for a bipolar transistor since it depends so much on the particular circuit (but see FETs, p. 12).

NEGATIVE FEEDBACK

So far we've assumed gain to be unlimited by anything else. In real life it almost always is—by negative feedback. This means simply that a small amount of the output is turned upside down and fed back into the input, with the following beneficial results:

1 Gain can be controlled by the amount fed back.
2 Stability is enhanced.
3 Distortion is reduced—because kinks in the output wave-form introduced by the amplifier go back in upside down and get unkinked.
4 However, input impedance is lowered and output impedance raised.

Let's examine this last point in the context of the amplifier we've already discussed. By analogy again with the emitter follower (p. 3), where the input impedance for both bias current and signal was $B \times R_e$, the DC input impedance is again $B \times R_e$, but the signal input impedance, Z_i, is $B \times X_c$. This will be much lower since C_e is there precisely to give a low reactance at signal frequencies. For instance at 1000 Hz our 24 μF bypass capacitor in Fig. 9 will have a reactance of 6.6 Ω, and the input impedance will be $300 \times 6.6\ \Omega = 1980\ \Omega$—a far cry from the 50 000 Ω of the emitter follower.

This effect—that negative feedback lowers input impedance—is not just an accident of this particular circuit. Let's consider any old amplifier which inverts the output, has natural input impedance of R_i and a gain of G. Let's give it negative feedback through a resistor R_f; see Fig. 11. (We're getting quite grown up

here and using a proper amplifier symbol. The − inside it is to show that the input is inverting. If it were non-inverting, the symbol would be + but then, of course, the feedback would be positive.)

Let's put a small positive voltage V_i on the input. It sees two paths: R_i to ground (p. 22), and R_f to a *negative* voltage V_o; see Fig. 12.

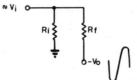

Fig. 12. The voltage state in Fig. 11: the input is small and positive, the output is negative, and the − terminal of the amplifier is 0 V.

Suppose that the overall gain (p. 22) is 100 ×. Then even if $R_f = 100 \times R_i$, the current through both paths will be the same, and the effective input impedance will be halved. In practice they are likely to be equal, so the effective input impedance will be 1/100th of what it was.

What saves bipolar amplifiers from having impossibly low input impedances (which large RF power devices do have) is the internal resistance of the base emitter diode (see also p. 77). In a small device this runs out at 2 kΩ, shunted by a couple of hundred pF (pronounced 'puff') to the emitter, and on to ground via C_e. This internal capacitance limits the high frequency gain of the amplifier just as C_e limited its low frequency gain. And finally the input is shunted by the bias resistors—but these should have high enough values so that no significant energy is lost in them.

How to measure base resistance

If you need to know the base resistance, here's how to do it. Having measured the β of the transistor, set up the circuit in Fig. 13. You will need the multimeter as an ammeter and a sensitive, high impedance, voltmeter (p. 12). By varying the 250 kΩ get three or four readings of I_c and V_{bc}. Convert I_c to I by dividing by β. Plot V_{be} against I_b as a graph. The points should plot as a straight line whose slope is the resistance.

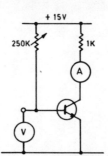

Fig. 13. Set-up for measuring base resistance.

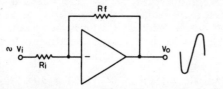

Fig. 11. An inverting amplifier with negative feedback through a resistor.

---

* The mathematically inclined can deduce this from the basic bipolar transistor equation linking I_c with V_{be}, the base–emitter voltage: $I_c = k \times e^{l \times V_{be}}$ where k, l are constants.

Direct feedback

Sometimes direct feedback is used from collector to base through a small capacitor, or a capacitor and coil combination, to suppress possible oscillation. When this is done in an RF amplifier, it's called 'neutralization', and is a nuisance because it reduces gain, see Fig. 14. In this case it is better to use a cascode.

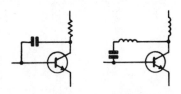

RF NEUTRALISATION

Fig. 14. Radio frequency amplifiers sometimes need negative feedback called neutralization to prevent oscillation.

There is also a *positive* feedback mechanism caused by internal capacitance between emitter and collector; see Fig. 15.

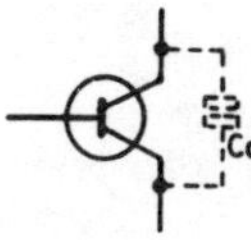

Fig. 15. RF oscillation is caused by positive feedback through the collector–emitter capacitance within the transistor.

A low voltage on the base causes a high voltage on the collector, which is passed to the emitter where it *increases* the base–emitter voltage, cuts the transistor off and raises the collector voltage more. This is used in some RF oscillators and can cause a high gain audio stage to oscillate. The remedy is better emitter decoupling to let the feedback run to ground, or less gain at high frequencies. 1000 pF between base and collector is the traditional remedy for audio work.

THE RF AMPLIFIER

Strictly speaking, perhaps, we should not discuss RF amplification (see Fig. 16) in a section on audio. But the principles are the same, and, as I explained in the introduction, there is no way this book can be completely logically arranged.

At radio frequencies we often use an LC resonant circuit as the collector load. While it may have an RF impedance of several kilohms, with corresponding gain, yet, of course, it presents no appreciable resistance to DC, so gain isn't limited by a reduced emitter current. It also has the advantage that it gives gain *only* at the resonant frequency (p. 118).

Two small points: since there's no collector resistance, the average collector voltage is V_{cc}, and the instantaneous voltage swings above and below the rail, due to the 'flywheel' effect of the resonant circuit. This heavy effect on the rail must be prevented from spreading to other circuits by a choke-capacitor filter for each RF amplifier. Small-signal amplifiers can get away with a resistor-capacitor filter. Secondly, a variable resonant capacitor is usually connected to ground so as to earth the rotor most effectively. It returns to the cold side of the coil via C_{cc}.

With the same bias voltages as before, the gain is: $20 \times I_e \times R_c$, with $I_c = (V_b - 0.6)/R_c$, and $R_c = QX_c$ (see p. 118). The useful feature of this is that gain is roughly proportional to base voltage, so we can easily control the performance of an RF amplifier with a potentiometer; see Fig. 17.

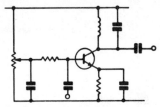

Fig. 17. RF gain can be controlled by altering emitter current. The easiest way to do this is to alter the base voltage with a variable resistor. Notice the resistor in the base lead to prevent the input draining away through the potentiometer decoupling capacitor. See Fig. 16 for a practical circuit.

A note on bias

Before we leave single transistor amplifiers we ought to notice that there are several biasing schemes. So far we have been talking about circuits which have a constant, standing current in the collector and emitter. This is fine for small signal work, and makes possible amplification of very small inputs. It is called Class A.

For higher powers the standing current is just a waste, so an npn transistor can be biased so it is just about to conduct. The smallest positive input will open it up. Naturally, negative signals will shut it down more, so for audio work it needs to be complemented by a similarly biased pnp device to cope with negative signals. This is called Class B.

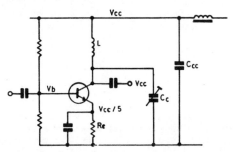

Fig. 16. A practical RF amplifier (without neutralization). Notice supply choke and decoupling capacitor.

In high power radio transmitters it pays to bias the output device—which is usually a valve, but the same principles apply—even harder off, so it only conducts on the peaks of positive inputs. The distortion that results is smoothed out in subsequent tuned circuits. This is called Class C; see Fig. 18.

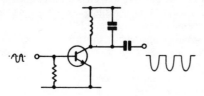

Fig. 18. A Class C amplifier with a tuned load. The transistor conducts on positive input peaks only, but the flywheel action of the collector load smooths the output.

A fourth system, practicable only at audio frequencies, aims at efficiency by switching the transistor either hard on or hard off. In either state little power is lost in the device. This switching is done at a much higher frequency than the highest audio frequency to be amplified. The resulting audio amplitude after smoothing in a simple low pass filter (p. 26) is proportional to the varying amounts of time that the output is high or low. This is called Class D; see Fig. 19.

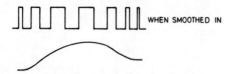

WHEN SMOOTHED IN

Fig. 19. Pulse width modulation. If the upper waveform is put through a low pass filter the lower one results.

TRANSISTOR TYPES

So far, all we have asked about our transistor is whether it's made of germanium or silicon, and its β. There are other useful things to know. The first is the broad class in which the device was made: these are audio, switching and RF. They are also made in low and high power forms (see Fig. 20).

It is important for best performance to use the right sort: a UHF radio device won't perform well as an audio amplifier, and an audio type probably won't work at all at 1000 MHz.* Switching transistors are going out of fashion with the availability of digital ICs (see p. 85), but they are occasionally useful.

There are literally thousands of types made. I find that these cover most low power applications: 2N2926 or BC109 for npn audio, and RF up to 3 MHz; BF173 for 30 MHz; BFY90 for RF up to 1000 MHz; 2N3702 for npn audio; BD131 npn and BD132 pnp for higher power audio.

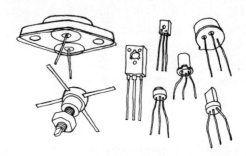

Fig. 20. A group of typical transistors. Top left: high power audio, with mica insulator. Lower left: UHF beam lead power transistor with stud and nut to heat-sink. Centre: medium power audio. Right-hand side: four miscellaneous low power devices.

HOW TO DECIPHER TRANSISTOR DATA

An essential tool is a good transistor data book. A good mail order house like Electrovalue will give the same data for the devices they stock in their catalogue. Let's look at the entry for the 2N2926 (a commonly used high gain audio transistor—almost identical with the BC 107 and 109) in Electrovalue's catalogue.

2N2926	
Vcbo max	18
Vceo max	18
Veb max	5
Ic max mA	100
Pt max mW	120
hfe (*hFE)	35–470
at IC mA	2
Icbo max nA	500
Noise factor dB	2.5 typ
fT typ MHz	120
Outline	TO98a
Price	

Fig. 21. Data sheet entry for typical transistor.

* Unfortunately this is not entirely true. Radio frequency signals—from broadcasting stations, TV transmitters, radio cabs and so on—can get picked up in the inputs to an audio amplifier, amplified in the first few stages and rectified in some base–emitter diode with the odd result that a record player that should be playing David Bowie gives out Radio Maroc instead. Most disconcerting. The same thing happens with baby alarms, door speakers and things like that. The answer is a judicious shunting of the input, as near to the first stage as possible, with low value capacitors. 100 pF would be a good start. But watch out for reduced high notes in what the amplifier ought to be amplifying.

Starting from the top, 'Vcbo max' tells you the maximum voltage which the collector may be above the base. Strictly speaking, one should allow for a situation in which the collector has a resonant load which can go to twice the rail voltage. This would mean that if the base were biased to $1/5\ V_{cc}$, then $2 \times (4\,V_{cc}/5)$ should not be more than 18 V; or V_{cc} should not be more than 11.25 V. In practice, transistors will stand quite a lot of overvoltage. 'Vceo max' says the same thing about the collector-emitter voltage, and since the emitter will be only 0.7 V lower than the base, the same calculation will do.

'Veb max' says how many volts the emitter may be *above* base (notice that it's 'eb', not 'be'). This means that the input to the transistor must not swing more than 5 V *below* its bias voltage.

'Ic max' specifies the maximum current that may be allowed to pass through the collector. Since this is very nearly the same as the emitter current, we can make absolutely sure by choosing the emitter resistor to pass no more than this with full V_{cc} across it. For instance:

$$V_{cc} = 12\ \text{V}, \quad R_e = \frac{12}{0.1} = 120\ \Omega.$$

This limitation is usually the important one; or, to put it another way, ignoring it usually results in a broken transistor.

'Pt max mW' says roughly how much power can be dissipated in the device and is found by calculating the voltage drop from collector to emitter (p. 4) and multiplying it by the emitter current. If one has observed the maximum voltage and current ratings, this one normally follows automatically. 'Pt' can only be a rough figure anyway, because the harm is done by the tiny transistor chip inside the case getting too hot. Just how hot it gets also depends on the rate at which the case dissipates heat, and that depends on the temperature of the surrounding air, and whether the device has a heat sink (p. 38).

That group of characteristics are often known as 'electrical'. The next group are more interesting, and tell you how this transistor will work better—or worse—than another one in the job you want done. 'hfe' is the current gain, otherwise known as β. This particular transistor is sorted by manufacturers into five h_{fe} groups and each device is marked with an appropriately coloured spot:

2N2926 h_{fe} groups:
Brown 35–70
Red   55–110
Orange 90–180
Yellow 150–300
Green 235–470

Unless you are doing something cunning with the noise factor (p. 76), there is no reason not to buy the green spot sort with the highest hfe. 'at Ic max' tells you the collector current at which hfe was measured. To us coarse practitioners this information is of no interest.

'Icbo max' says how much current will leak *out* of the base when it is reverse biased—that is, when the emitter is the maximum permitted voltage above it, which was 5 V. This transistor leaks 500 nA or 0.5 μA and the information is, again, only useful for noise calculations (p. 76). 'Noise factor' tells you how much more noisy the transistor is than a resistor of the same input impedance at the same temperature. Again, if you can make constructive use of that information, you don't need to read this book.

'fT' is very useful and tells you how good the transistor is at amplifying high frequencies. The table says that. fT is 120 MHz and that means that at 120 MHz the voltage gain of the transistor has dropped to 1 which means it does not amplify. A rough rule of thumb is that the maximum useful gain in common emitter (p. 4) is at one fifth of fT, in this case, 24 MHz. This means that although the 2N2926 is sold as a low noise audio device, it is actually quite useful for radio circuits as well up to the top of the HF band. No workbench should be without a handful of this useful and cheap device.

'Outline' refers the reader to another part of the catalogue which gives a base diagram and the dimensions of the standard package in which the device is sold; see Fig. 23.

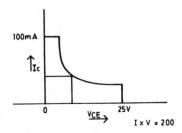

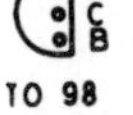

Fig. 23. *Underneath view of the commonly used TO 98 transistor package.*

PERMITTED OPERATING AREA

Fig. 22. *The operating area for a transistor. The collector current I_c in this case may not exceed 100 mA; the collector voltage V_{CE} must be less than 25 V, and the power dissipated in the transistor, $I_c \times V_{CE}$, must be less than 200 mW.*

Most, or even all of this information will be given in any respectable work of reference. Even though the symbols may vary, a little inspired telepathy serves to sort it out.

As time goes on, designers demand more information and manufacturers supply it more or less willingly.

The way to get it is to write to the manufacturer for a Device Data Sheet, which will usually be supplied free. An Applications Note, in the case of more complicated integrated circuits, will also suggest ways of using the thing, snags, neat circuits, and is usually worth reading just for its educational value.

RF Transistors

Even a rough theory of transistor behaviour at RF is quite complicated.* However, we can summarize roughly what happens at low frequency to a typical small transistor:

1 *Current* gain is independent of load resistance R_L, for common emitter, until R_L is about 10 kΩ, and then it falls off. In common base, current gain is 1, but it starts to fall off at much higher R_L.
2 *Voltage* gain increases with R_L for both common base and common emitter (but see p. 5, the limitation of average collector voltage).
3 *Power* gain is a maximum in common emitter when R_L is 50 kΩ; in common base at about 500 kΩ.
4 *Input* impedance is more or less independent of R_L at about 3 kΩ for common emitter; in common base it rises from about 30 Ω with low R_L to about 300 Ω when R_L is 1 MΩ.
5 *Output* impedance is constant in common emitter at about 90 kΩ; for common base it varies between 300kΩ with low input impedance to 3 MΩ for high. In practice it is usually shunted by the much lower emitted load.

All this is at low frequency. At high frequencies we have to take into account the internal base–emitter capacitance which shunts the base emitter resistance. This acts as an ordinary low pass filter to drain away the input signal above for the frequency where the reactance of the capacitor equals the resistance.

The input signal, and therefore the current gain, falls off at 6 dB, or halves, for each doubling of frequency above f_c' see Fig. 24. The gradient of the sloping part is, since the units are logarithms (Fig. 24) along both axes,

$$\frac{\log \beta - \log 1}{\log f_T - \log_{f_c}} = \frac{\log \beta - 0}{\log\frac{f_T}{f_c}}$$

And this = 1. So:

$$\log \beta = \log \frac{f_T}{f_c}$$

$$\beta \times f_c = f_T$$

To illustrate, take the BF 173 with h_{FE} 87, f_T 550 MHz. The turning frequency, where β starts to fall

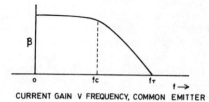

Fig. 24. The logarithm of current gain against the logarithm of frequency for a transistor in common emitter.

off, is given by

$$87 \times f_c = 550$$

$$f_c = 6.3\,\text{MHz}$$

which shows that f_T, as advertised, is a little misleading.

But in *common base* (p. 13), f_T is the point at which the current gain *starts* to fall. Which explains why common base still has its used for amplification at the frequency limits (p. 14); see Fig. 25.

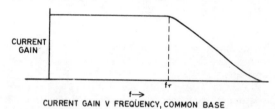

Fig. 25. As Fig. 24, common base. Note the higher turning frequency.

This all gives us a rough way of estimating input resistances and capacitances, which will be useful when we come to deal with RF power circuits in the next Part.

FIELD EFFECT TRANSISTOR (FET)

The FET is in many ways a more interesting and versatile device than the bipolar transistor. Older electronic engineers hailed it with delight, because it works just like a valve, instead of the messy, and to begin with, upside-down bipolar transistor (pnp devices came first). Like the bipolar, the FET has three leads: drain, source and gate, corresponding roughly to

Fig. 26. An N-channel junction FET (roughly equivalent to an npn transistor). The terminals are called: Drain, Source, Gate.

* See M. G. Scroggie, *Foundations of Wireless* (London, Iliffe Books, 1971), Chapter 12.

collector, emitter and base; see Fig. 26. *P*-channel FETs correspond to pnp transistors, but are rarely seen; see Fig. 27.

Fig. 27. A P-channel junction FET.

P CHANNEL

The main difference between an FET and a bipolar transistor is that the first is controlled by gate voltage and the second by base *current*. This makes the FET a much 'harder' device; it typically has an input impedance of 1 GΩ. This is good; but it gives less gain, which is bad. There are two types of FET, namely junction and insulated gate (p. 17). In a junction FET the drain-source structure is a bar of silicon, which also forms the cathode of a diode, while the gate is the anode. When the thing is working, the gate is always at a *lower* voltage than the source; i.e. $V_{GS} = -2$ V, say, and because this diode is reverse biased, negligible current flows into it.

The FET has two modes of operation:

1 When there is a small voltage between drain and source, the device acts as a resistor whose value depends on how negative the gate is to the source.
2 When there is a considerable voltage drain to source—as there would be in an amplifier circuit, the *current* that flows between them is dependent on the gate's negative voltage with regard to source, and is independent of the voltage from drain to source.

When the drain is tied to the source, $V_{GS} = 0$ V. If a reasonably large voltage is applied to the drain, a fixed current flows, called I_{dss} which is characteristic of that particular transistor, and will vary between different examples of the same device.

FET amplifier

See Fig. 28. No current flows into or out of the gate through R_1, so that can be large—say 1 MΩ. In effect,

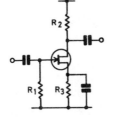

Fig. 28. A practical FET amplifier. R_3 must be adjusted to get gain.

this is the input impedance of the amplifier. It keeps the gate at an average of 0 V. The negative gate-source voltage, V_{GS}, is set up by R_3, which puts the source at a

positive voltage—2 V or so—according to its value and the source current. R_3 has to be chosen so this source current puts the drain at a proper operating voltage.

The snag about FETs is that each one is different, and you cannot specify resistances that will guarantee that the amplifier works. All you can do is make R_3 variable, and trim it till the device amplifies and clips symmetrically. A system that always works, but costs somewhat more, is to replace R_3 with a constant-current sink, drawing $\frac{1}{2}I_{dss}$. V_d can then sit at the value it likes; see Fig. 29.

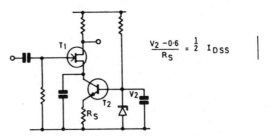

$$\frac{V_2 - 0.6}{R_S} = \frac{1}{2} I_{DSS}$$

Fig. 29. Automatic bias for an FET: T_2 sinks a constant current, set by the value of the zener diode and R_s.

Constant current sink

The base of T_2 is held at a constant voltage by the zener diode (p. 19). The emitter of T_2 is therefore at a constant voltage 0.7 V lower. Since R_s is fixed, a constant current flows through it and hence into the collector of T_2 and out of the source of T_1. It therefore makes no difference what the voltage is at T_1 source—the current out of it stays the same. Negative feedback arises here just as it did for a bipolar transistor (p. 3), and so the constant current sink circuit has to be bypassed by a capacitor if the FET is to give any gain. Or, of course, if we had another FET with I_{dss} one half of the first's, we could use that with gate and source grounded.

RF amplifier

FETs are useful at radio frequencies and this problem ceases to exist if the drain can sit at the positive rail, as it will if the drain load is a coil (see Fig. 34). Again, make the source current $I_{dss}/2$.

Source follower

Another use for an FET is as a high impedance source follower, which works very like the emitter follower

Fig. 30. FET acting as a source follower.

(p. 3); see Fig. 30. The voltage drop will be set up automatically and will depend on the device. The value of the resistor can be chosen to taste. A more elaborate version of this, used as a high impedance input for oscilloscopes and other measuring instruments, is shown in Fig. 31.

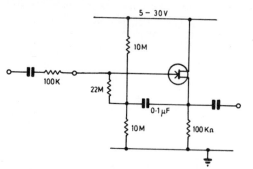

Fig. 31. A high impedance FET source follower for use as an oscilloscope input (reproduced by courtesy of Texas Instruments Ltd.).

The 100 kΩ resistor has no effect on the input because the gate impedance is so high: it merely protects the gate from reverse current flow. It's a good idea to do this automatically to every FET in non-RF applications. AC inputs are 'bootstrapped', i.e. there is in-phase, or positive, feedback to increase gain, by the 0.1 μF, and the input impedance to them is 1.5 GΩ. This has no effect on DC, or low frequency AC.

FETs can be used in long tailed pairs (p. 24); see Fig. 32.

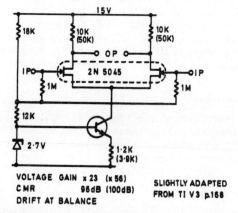

VOLTAGE GAIN x 23 (x 56)
C M R   96 dB (100dB)
DRIFT AT BALANCE

SLIGHTLY ADAPTED
FROM TI V3 p.168

Fig. 32. A long tailed pair of FET amplifiers using two matched devices in one package (reproduced by courtesy of Texas Instruments Ltd.).

It is important that the devices should be well matched for I_{dss}, and the best way is to buy them in a double device, such as the TI 2N 5045. Fig. 33 shows a simple voltmeter, which I use all the time.

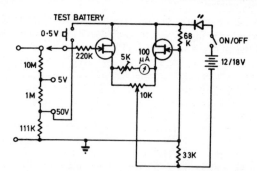

Fig. 33. A simple FET voltmeter using matched devices. The 5 kΩ variable sets the full scale deflection; the 10 kΩ sets zero.

The two devices act as a differential source follower: since one gate is held steady, the voltage between their sources is equal to the voltage at the input. This generates a current through the meter which then reads voltage—adjusted for correct full scale deflection by the 5 kΩ. Three voltage ranges are selected by SW/1:0.5 V, 5 V, 50 V. Zero adjustment is by the 10 kΩ. An LED tell-tale reminds one not to leave it on unnecessarily—and prevents reverse battery connections. A push button tests the battery. The zero adjustment can be used on occasion to offset the needle to centre scale.

FETs are particularly good as VHF and UHF amplifiers at the input of a radio receiver. They give good gain—slightly less than a bipolar transistor like the BFY90, but less noise and better stability. At low frequencies—up to about 250 MHz—the cascode circuit seems to be best; above that common gate. Common source amplifiers need neutralizing to prevent oscillation. Fig. 34 is an example. The negative

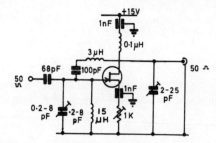

Fig. 34. An FET RF amplifier with neutralization (reproduced by courtesy of Mullard Ltd.).

feedback through the 3 μH inductor and 100 pF capacitor passes 10 MHz, and presents an impedance of about 1500 Ω at signal frequency.

Cascode

The cascode circuit ingeniously avoids two drawbacks to the straight common source version: instability and

Miller capacitance. Without neutralization, the amplifier in Fig. 32 would oscillate because of feedback between drain and gate. (At low frequencies the feedback would be negative (p. 5), but at high ones the phase shifts are unpredictable and can become positive.) It will also suffer from Miller capacitance: a tiresome effect which gives the gate an apparent capacitance to ground of its real value—which might be 2 pF—multiplied by the voltage gain of the amplifier—which might be 10—giving an effective input capacitance of 20 pF. Now 20 pF shunting 1 GΩ obliterates any signal with frequency higher than 80 Hz. In practice low frequency FET amplifier inputs are shunted to ground by the much lower input impedance of whatever drives them—otherwise they'd never work. And high frequency versions, as in Fig. 32, only work because Miller capacitance is tuned out by the 15 µH inductance. The cascode gets round both these problems by using two transistors: one in common source and the second in common gate.

Common gate

A digression here on common gate (and base) amplifiers. If we go back to the emitter follower, we remember that the bipolar transistor is worked by the *difference* in voltage between the base and the emitter. Similarly the FET works because of the difference between gate and source. As far as the collector or drain is concerned, the signal can be applied at either end. The FET is simpler to bias, so let's rearrange the amplifier of Fig. 28, as shown in Fig. 35. The bias

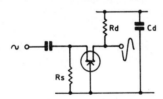

Fig. 35. An FET amplifier in common gate.

conditions are just the same, but the gate is held steady at 0 V for both DC and AC, and the signal goes on the source. The drain amplifies as before, but the input impedance is much lower—the signal gets to ground via R_s and through the FET, R_d and C_d, but stability is much better and gain goes on to much higher frequencies. (Naturally we do away with the source bypass capacitor since that would just earth the signal and we don't need one on the drain because it's tied to ground.)

Bipolar biasing doesn't lend itself so neatly to common base, but it can be done and is shown in Fig. 36. This time, base has to be decoupled because it's still 0.7 V higher than emitter. But again, the amplifier is more stable and gives gain to higher frequencies (see Fig. 25).

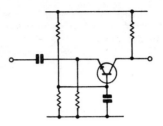

Fig. 36. A bipolar amplifier in common base.

Cascode amplifier again

Now we can get back to the cascode (originally a valve circuit, named, presumably, from *casc*aded an*ode*-cath*ode*). In Fig. 37 T_1 is in common source and drives

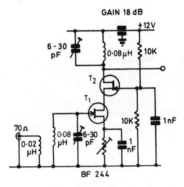

Fig. 37. A cascode FET amplifier for 240 MHz.

T_2 in common gate. But since the output impedance to T_1 is provided by T_2's source, and is low, T_1 gives little voltage gain. This prevents Miller capacitance and oscillation. T_2 looks more like Fig. 34 than Fig. 33, but this is because both its source and gate have to be a good deal above ground voltage in order to give T_1 room in which to work. Essentially, it is wired like Fig. 35. We will meet another version of this circuit on p. 17 in which the two transistors are amalgamated into one device.

Common base

Finally, for interest, a pure common base amplifier using resonant strip lines; see Fig. 38. These would have a characteristic impedance of 70 Ω (p. 57) and would be etched out of one side of double-sided copper clad board, with the width of the inductors adjusted to the thickness of the board (see p. 122). It would be most important to keep the transistor lead lengths down and better to use one of the flat packages (p. 8).

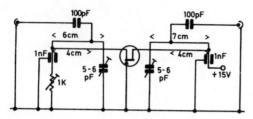

Fig. 38. An FET common gate amplifier using strip line resonators tapped down to match input and output impedance to co-ax line, at 470 MHz (reproduced by courtesy of Mullard Ltd.).

TABLE 1	
V_{gs}, (V)	I_d, (mA)
2.5	0.57
2.0	2.06
1.5	3.7
1.0	6.0
0.5	7.0
0.0	8.5 $(=I_{dss})$

Measurements on FETs

An FET amplifier can usually be got to go by tweaking the source resistor. (Use a variable for setting up, and replace it with the nearest preferred value to the best setting.) But sometimes it is nice to know the two parameters that define the characteristics of a particular device: I_{dss} and the pinch-off voltage on the gate, V_p, at which no appreciable current flows from drain to source. (Strictly, at which the drain current is the same as the gate leakage current. But since this is nA and quite beyond my powers of measurement, we'll ignore this nicety.) I_{dss} is easily measured; see Fig. 39. The 1 kΩ resistor is just to prevent accidents.

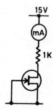

Fig. 39. Set-up to measure I_{dss}, the drain current with gate and source connected together.

There is no simple way to measure V_p directly because ordinary ammeters show no current long before V_p is reached. But it can be calculated from the basic FET equation using I_{dss} and one value of I_d and V_{gs} got from the circuit shown in Fig. 40. Here, for instance, are results I got from a BF 244:

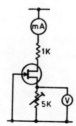

Fig. 40. Set-up to measure pinch-off voltage (see text).

The FET equation is:

$$I_d = I_{dss}\left(1 - \frac{V_{gs}}{V_p}\right)^2$$

rearranging:

$$V_p = \frac{V_{gs}}{1 - \sqrt{\dfrac{I_d}{I_{dss}}}}$$

using the underlined values in Table 1:

$$V_p = \frac{1.5}{1 - \sqrt{\dfrac{3.7}{8.5}}}$$
$$= 4.4 \ V$$

The gain of an FET amplifier

It is quite easy, using simple calculus, to work out what happens to I_d when a small signal δV_{gs} arrives at the gate and therefore get the gain A_v. The sums are not particularly interesting and take up a lot of space: this is the result:

$$A_v = R_d \times I_{dss} \times 2 \times \frac{V_{gs}}{V_p}$$

V_{gs} here is the average value—obviously it varies with signal. If you pick V_{gs} so the quiescent source current is $\frac{1}{2}I_{dss}$, then this boils down to

$$A_v = R_d g_m$$

g_m is again the transconductance (p. 5) and tells us how much current the device passes for an extra volt on the gate when it's properly biased. Obviously, to get the voltage output, you multiply g_m by the value of the drain resistor R_d. Since g_m is amps per volt it is the reciprocal of resistance. Engineers measure it as 'mhos' ('ohms' backwards). Or, rather, mili-mhos. For the BF244 used to get Table 1, V_{gs} to give $I_d = \frac{1}{2}I_{dss} = 4.25$ mA would be about 1.2 V. If we insert this into the equation for gain, with $R_d = 3.9$ kΩ (to make things comparable with the bipolar amplifier in Fig. 9),

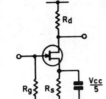

Fig. 41. Common source FET amplifier.

we get

$$A_v = 3.9 \times 10^3 \times 8.5 \times 10^{13} \times 2 \times \frac{1.2}{4 \cdot 4}$$

$$= 3.9 \times 10^3 \times 4.1 \times 10^{-3} \ (g_m = 4.1 \text{ mA/V})$$

$$= 16$$

In practice you don't have to go through the rigmarole of measuring these currents and voltages. The manufacturer's data sheet quotes an average g_m for the type (sometimes called Y_{fs}) in mmhos, and you get a rough gain figure from that.

The gain value we find here, 16, compares rather badly with the gain in Fig. 9 of 80. This is typical of FETs, which give less gain but better stability than bipolars.

Specification of an FET

In a catalogue or manufacturer's data sheet you will find something like this, the figures for the BF244B:

V_{ds} max:	30 V
V_{dg} max:	−30 V
I_g max:	30 mA
P_t max:	360 mW
I_g reverse max:	−5 nA
V_p or V_{gs} cut-off, max:	−8 V
I_{dss} @ $V_{gs} = 0$:	25 mA max
Y_{fs} or g_m	3–6.5 mA/V
Package:	TO 92c

The first four are just the same as the absolute max ratings in the bipolar table on p. 8. They tell you how not to bust the device, but since FETs are almost always used for small signal work, there will seldom be any temptation to. 'I_g reverse' tells you how much current leaks out of the reverse biased gate—this is needed for noise calculations (p. 76) and also to set the maximum value for the gate bias resistor: −5 nA across 1 MΩ produces 5 mV of unwanted bias which is unlikely to upset any but the most finicky circuit. 'V_p' we have discussed; 'I_{dss}' must, by definition, be

measured at $V_{gs} = 0$, but it is kind of them to remind us; 'Y_{fs}/g_m' no longer holds any secrets, 'Package' again refers us to another page where we see that the thing comes wrapped as shown in Fig. 42.

SOURCE
GATE   UNDERNEATH
DRAIN

Fig. 42. Terminals of BF 244.

To test an FET, connect ohmeter leads to drain and source (remember polarity) leaving gate free: the resistance should show 1 kΩ or so. Touch gate to drain and it should fall. Then, leaving the positive lead on the drain, put the negative lead on gate (n-channel). A very high resistance should show. Do not get this the wrong way round, because the gate will only stand a small forward current.

FET AS RESISTANCE

As we mentioned earlier, when there is a *small* voltage across drain-source, an FET acts as a resistor whose value is controlled by V_{gs}. This varies from 1 MΩ at cut-off, to 1000 Ω for a BF244 at +0.5 V, and much lower for more expensive devices made specially for this application.

It is quite simple to use an FET to build a dynamic-range compressor, a kind of circuit that is used in recording, broadcasting, telephone equipment to compress the amplitude range of speech or music; see Fig. 43. The gate takes up a voltage equal to the

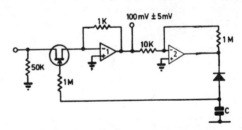

Fig. 43. FET used as a variable resistance in a speech compressor.

rectified negative swing of the output. If this goes more negative than the source, the FET's resistance increases, the gain of amplifier 1 falls (p. 22) and output returns to the desired value. The bigger the output, the smaller a proportion of it will be the 0.6 V variation needed to give full FET control, and therefore the better the regulation.

Since the resistance of the FET is controlled by its gate-source voltage, the signal passing through it contributes. If it is large enough it too will change the source-drain resistance. With a sine wave input, this produces a characteristic distortion in which peaks are amplified more than troughs; see Fig. 44.

Fig. 44. Characteristic distortion of a sine wave input by circuit in Fig. 43.

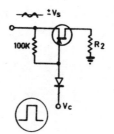

Fig. 45. Series chopper using an FET.

A more sophisticated system would use an op-amp rectifier with gain to amplify the control current rather than the actual signal. In this way distortion would be reduced.

The lowest resistance for a cheap FET is, say 1 kΩ. With a 1 MΩ feedback resistor, amplifier 1 has a gain of 1000 and an output of 1 V peak to peak. Suppose we want an output signal of 100 mV. The FET's resistance must be 10 kΩ to give this gain. Amplifier 2 has an input of 100 mV peak to peak and will limit at an output of 5 V peak to peak (with a 10 V supply). So its maximum gain can be 50. A BF244's resistance can be varied from about 1 kΩ to infinity with a 0.5 V range on the base. 15 V at the output of Op-amp 2 is 10 mV at the input, so we can control the output of the circuit to within 10 mV in 100 mV.

The time constants (p. 33) are set by C and the feedback resistor round Op-amp 2. For a speech compressor we want a fast attack time and a slow decay—200 ms or so, to cover the gaps between words. Attack is governed by C charging up through the output impedance of the amplifier—which is probably about 500 Ω. C discharges to the virtual earth (p. 22) at the negative input through the feedback resistor: say it is 500 kΩ, then to give 200 ms C has to be 0.4 μF. This will charge up in 0.2 ms—which is quick enough.

Information in speech is conveyed almost entirely by frequency variations—amplitude changes give charm and colour but no more. For the best use of SSB transmitters it is obviously best to do away with any quiet passages. This can increase the effective power of the transmitter—which is judged by its ability to put the quietest parts of speech into the receiver—a hundred times. We could do that by shortening the delay time constant, so that the compressor tracked the volume variations between and within syllables. A better method is to amplify the signal and then clip it to remove any amplitude modulation. If done at audio frequencies this process produces unpleasant higher harmonics (p. 60), so it is best done at RF where the harmonics are inaudible and can easily be filtered out.

CHOPPERS

If we ignore the intermediate values of an FET's resistance, we can think of it as a voltage controlled switch. Circuits using the device like this are called 'choppers'. In Fig. 45 the control voltage V_c must be greater than $+V_s$ on the upward swing, and less than $-(V_s + V_p)$ on the downward. The signal voltages are V_{ds} because the device is either off or fully on. The difficulty with these circuits is that the edges of the switching waveform cause spikes in the internal

capacitances of the FET, so it may be necessary to shunt them with a low value capacitor across the output. Also it helps to switch with a sine wave rather than a square wave. The diode prevents the FET conducting in reverse through the gate. Another arrangement is the shunt chopper, which by itself works no better than the series version. But for the best possible performance use both;* see Fig. 46.

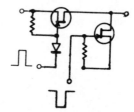

Fig. 46. Series-shunt chopper. The devices must have antiphase drive.

Two *n*-channel devices need antiphase drive. Use drive from collector and emitter of unity gain amplifier, or one could use a *p*-channel FET for the shunt chopper and drive them both with the same signal; see Fig. 47.

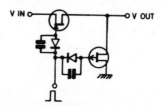

Fig. 47. Series-shunt chopper using N- and P-channel device with common drive.

MOSFETs

A most useful type of device is the MOSFET—Metal Oxide Silicon Field Effect Transistor. This is like an ordinary FET in most ways, but with some differences. The principal one is that the isolation between gate and drain-source bar is achieved not by a reverse biased junction, but by an extremely thin insulating layer of metal oxide. There is thus a huge input impedance—of the order of hundreds or thousands of GΩ, with very low input capacitance. The capacitance between

* See *Semiconductor Circuit Design VIII* (Bedford, Texas Instruments, 1974), pp. 175–89.

source and drain is also very low, with corresponding advantage in VHF and UHF circuits.

The drawback to MOSFETs has been so far that the gate impedance is so high that static electricity on the fingers could puncture the gate insulation before it is connected into a circuit. However, the new devices have back-to-back zener diodes with a breakdown voltage of about 11 V and negligible extra capacitance between the gate and source; see Fig. 48.

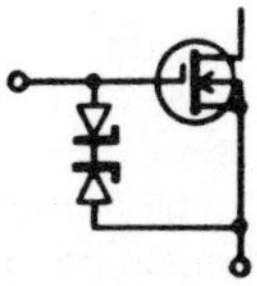

Fig. 48. Protection zeners on gate of insulated gate FET (IGFET).

Thus, whether the static charge on the gate is positive or negative, one diode will break-down and the other will conduct forward to keep the gate voltage within safe bounds, usually about ±11 V. That said, it must also be recognized that MOSFETs are not as robust as junction FETs.

MOSFETs are made in 'enhancement' and 'depletion' types. In the depletion sort, the channel conducts without gate bias; forward bias increases channel conductivity, reverse bias reduces it. The enhancement type does not conduct with zero bias (referred to source), and must be forward biased to produce conduction. The two types have the symbols shown in Fig. 49.

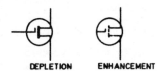

DEPLETION   ENHANCEMENT

Fig. 49. Depletion and enhancement IGFETS (the latter is seldom seen).

In the ordinary way, one has to deal with depletion types, and their biasing is very similar to the ordinary FET described on p. 11. That is, the gate must have a lower voltage than source for amplification and the extent of this voltage varies from device to device.

A most useful feature of some of the newer MOSFETs is that they have two gates; see Fig. 50. In

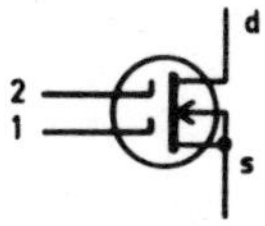

Fig. 50. Dual gate IGFET; the zeners (see Fig. 48) are there in most devices, but not shown.

effect the device is a pair in cascode (p. 13). Gate 1 needs to be biased slightly negative: −0.5 V to −1.5 V is usual, and gate 2: 2 V–4 V positive with regard to source. This second gate has several useful functions: it

can be grounded to AC by a capacitor and the gain of the device controlled by a direct voltage on it.

A great advantage of the MOSFET for RF amplifiers is that the drain to source capacitance is so low that the device will usually not oscillate even at 400 MHz and neutralization is not needed (see Fig. 51).

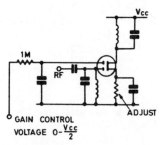

Fig. 51. RF amplifier with gain control using dual gate IGFET. Because the drain-source capacitance is low, neutralization is not needed.

Another application is as a mixer (see Fig. 52a). Here RF is applied to gate 1, grounded through a secondary coil as usual, and the local oscillator (LO) to gate 2. If the LO voltage swings between 0 V and + 3 V or so, it can be coupled direct to gate 2. Although it needs a relatively high voltage, the power drain is negligible owing to the gates' high impedance. To cope with device variability, the source resistor and one of the bias resistors should be adjusted for best results.

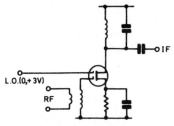

Fig. 52a. Dual gate mixer.

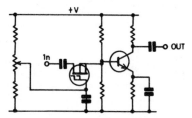

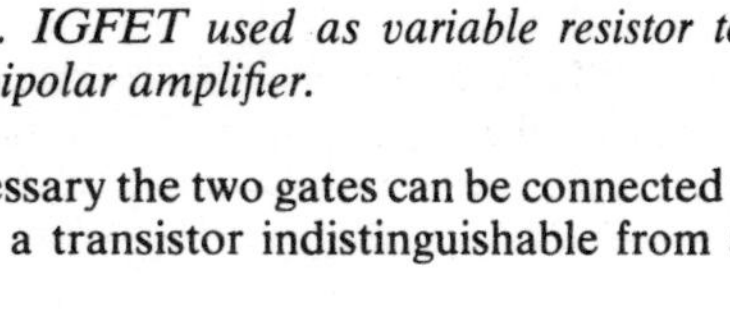

Fig. 52b. IGFET used as variable resistor to control gain of bipolar amplifier.

If necessary the two gates can be connected together to make a transistor indistinguishable from a single-gate MOSFET. Either with gates separate or together, MOSFETs act as voltage controlled resistances, just like ordinary FETs.

One can easily build a voltage controlled attenuator, as shown in Fig. 52b. Choppers are just the same as for FETs, remembering to include the pinch-off voltage in the maximum swing that can be handled.

Any FET with its gate/s connected to its source passes a constant current, usually something between 2 mA and 10 mA, independent of the voltage across it; see Fig. 53. As V_{sg} becomes greater, the current

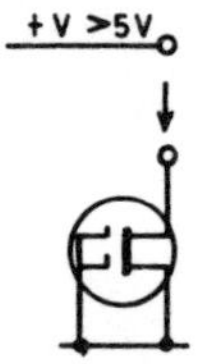

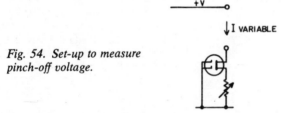

Fig. 53. Set-up to measure I_{dss} of dual gate IGFET.

decreases. A variable 'constant current diode' (in contrast to the constant voltage zener diode, p. 19) can be made as shown in Fig. 54. Of course, a junction FET would do just as well.

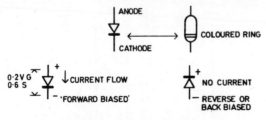

Fig. 54. Set-up to measure pinch-off voltage.

DIODES

The diode (see Fig. 55) is the oldest semiconductor device and, as the 'cat's whisker' of the old crystal set, antedates even valves by many decades. It acts as a true valve for electrons: they travel more easily one way

ANODE

CATHODE

COLOURED RING

0·2 V G
0·6 S   ↓ CURRENT FLOW

'FORWARD BIASED'

+
      NO CURRENT

–   REVERSE OR
      BACK BIASED

Fig. 55. Diode characteristics.

than the other. It has two terminals, called academically the anode and the cathode, and they are almost unique among electronic components in being sensibly marked: one end always has a coloured ring and that

end is the cathode. The graph of voltage against current is shown in Fig. 56.

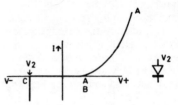

Fig. 56. Current through a diode plotted against voltage across it.

At A the device is strongly forward-biased with the anode positive and the cathode negative—and conducts easily. As the voltage across it drops, the current falls away in a curve. At B = +0.6 V for a silicon device (0.2 V for germanium) current stops. This is the threshold voltage necessary for conduction. To the left of B there is no significant current until we get to C where the barrier breaks down or 'avalanches'. The diode—with enough reverse bias—will conduct again, with a fixed voltage drop across it. This is a useful property.

Nothing is perfect. The imperfections of real diodes are these:

1 A voltage drop when forward biased.
2 Internal resistance—which impedes the flow when conducting.
3 Internal capacitance—which lets signal through when not conducting.
4 A leakage current when reverse biased—negligible for silicon, often substantial for germanium.

The basic uses for the diode are therefore:
1 To rectify a current; see Fig. 57. This is one method of AM radio detection (see p. 64). The drawback of

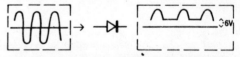

Fig. 57. Half cycle rectification by a diode.

this simple arrangement is that the first 0.6 V of the wave is wasted in getting the diode to conduct: better if we hold the voltage across it at, say 0.58 V, so it's very

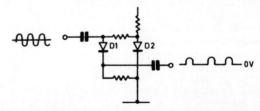

Fig. 58. Bias system to eliminate the 0.6 V forward bias needed in Fig. 57.

nearly conducting; see Fig. 58. A current through D_2 sets up a bias across D_1 so that it conducts nearly all of the positive waves.

2 To rectify mains, or voltage transformed mains to get DC for power supplies. The forward drop is unimportant and can be allowed for in the transformer; see Fig. 59. The diode lets the positive peaks through, and

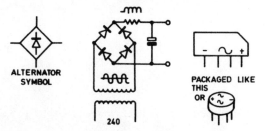

Fig. 59. Mains rectification—the 0.6 V can be ignored.

the capacitor smooths out the bumps. The resistor, one ohm or so, prevents overloading of the diode or transformer while the capacitor charges up. A better arrangement uses four diodes and is called a bridge rectifier; see Fig. 60. This turns the negative half peaks

Fig. 60. Four diodes in a 'bridge' give full wave rectification, with two common packages.

upside down and makes them positive: you get more power, and the ripple on the output is now 100 Hz instead of mains 50 Hz, which makes the smoothing capacitor twice as effective.

3 As a voltage source. When a diode is forward conducting you know there's 0.2 V or 0.6 V (or 1.2 V or so for LEDs) across it, see Fig. 61, according to type

Fig. 61. Forward voltage drop across a diode.

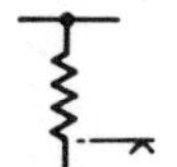

and this can come in handy (see Fig. 135). Also, when it is reversed biased, 'broken down' or 'avalanching', there is some other, much higher, voltage across it. Although most diodes will do this, you buy specially made ones called zener diodes,* which are specified by the voltage across them and the power they will dissipate. For instance in a 9 V, 400 mW zener as shown in Fig. 62, R must be at least 136 Ω in this circuit, otherwise the zener will explode. Actually 44 mA is far too much: 2 mA or 3 mA would be ample to get a

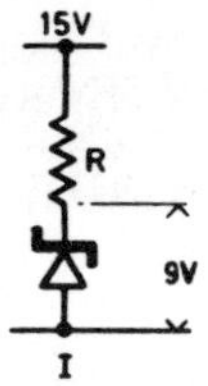

* So-called after its inventor's name.

Fig. 62. Voltage drop across a zener.

steady voltage for most small-signal purposes. Zeners come in a wide range of powers but small ones are usually used to create a reference voltage, and an amplifier relates it to the practical problem. If you're stuck for a zener, the base-emitter junction of most transistors will do the trick; see Fig. 63. The collector can be cut off or tied to the base.

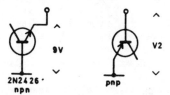

Fig. 63. Npn and pnp transistors can be used as zeners.

4 As a variable resistance. Going back to the graph on p. 56 we see that the line between A and B is curved. This means that as the forward bias drops, the current drops too, but faster. In effect the diode is acting as a resistance which increases in value as the bias falls. We can use this to attenuate—or reduce—a signal by feeding a variable direct voltage through it; see Fig. 64.

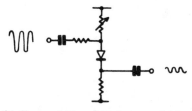

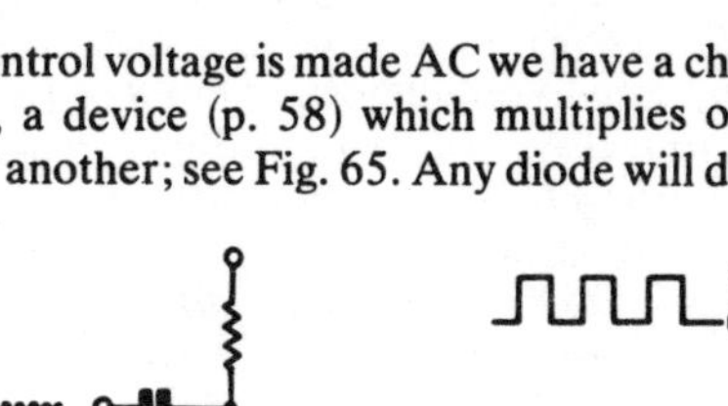

Fig. 64. Forward biased diode as variable resistor.

If the control voltage is made AC we have a chopper or a *mixer*, a device (p. 58) which multiplies one wave form by another; see Fig. 65. Any diode will do this (as

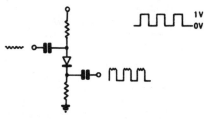

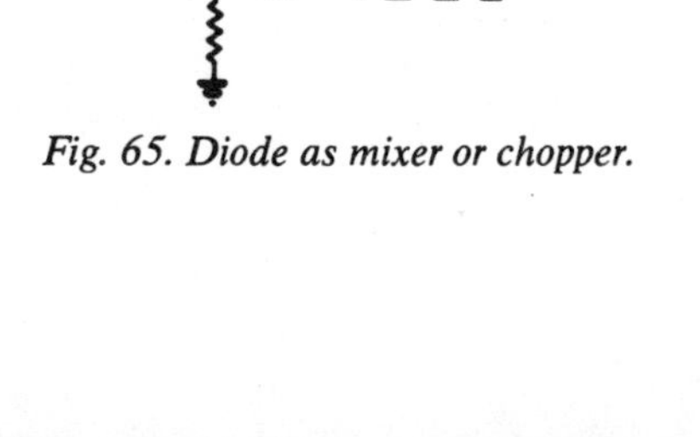

Fig. 65. Diode as mixer or chopper.

long as its junction capacitance isn't so big it lets the signal through anyway) but a special type called PIN or (*p*-intrinsic-*n*) is particularly good and is used for controlling VHF and UHF signals. For instance, a BA379 gives 2.5 kΩ off, 6.5 Ω on at 10 mA, with only 0.3 pF leakage capacitance.

5 As a variable capacitance, a 'varicap' or 'varactor'; see Fig. 66. Most of a diode's internal capacitance is

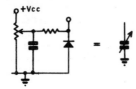

Fig. 66. Variable capacitance diode.

caused, as it were artificially, by the cloud of mutually repulsive electrons in its junction. We can alter the size of this capacitor by altering the reverse bias to squeeze or expand the cloud. This is a most useful property and means that we can have a variable capacitance controlled remotely by DC rather than the mechanical capers of the old vane type variable (p. 113).

A special sort of diode called 'tunnel', or 'Esaki' after its cunning Japanese inventor, acts a bit like a zener: as the reverse voltage across it rises, so does the current, but then it starts to fall, and after a dip rises again; see Fig. 67. Between points A and B the device

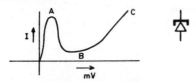

Fig. 67. Tunnel diode symbol and operating curve.

has *negative* resistance—it's almost the electronic engineer's ideal: 'a straight piece of wire with gain'. If properly handled it can therefore be used as an amplifier at UHF where it gives high gain and little noise, as an oscillator, or in various switching circuits which exploit its ability to 'latch' like a self-switching relay.* Attractive as it sounds, the tunnel diode is hard to get and tricky to use, but interesting.

A light emitting diode (LED) is a useful device to use as a tell-tale or to illuminate a light sensitive transistor, see Fig. 68a. Electronic car ignitions are fired by a rotating vane shading such a device.

When forward biased an LED lights up: it needs 10 mA–20 mA, according to size, and has a forward voltage drop of about 1.5 V. So for a 15 V tell-tale, see Fig. 68b. Or, if the circuit draws little current (p. 12) see Fig. 68c. This also prevents damage due to

Fig. 68a. LED packages.

Fig. 68b. LED as 'power-on' indicator.

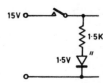

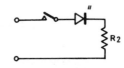

Fig. 68c. LED as indicator and reverse polarity preventer.

reversing the power supply. Newly available: power LEDs that can be used for rectification.

A Schottky diode is a particularly fast switching device with high reverse break-down voltage. It is used in a sub type of Texas Instruments '74 series TTL logic gates (p. 87). And as individual devices—sometimes called 'hot carrier' diodes—in high quality RF mixers (p. 19) because they are less noisy than ordinary RF diodes.

Buying diodes

A typical manufacturer's or supplier's data sheet specifies:

> PIV—peak inverse volts
> I_F—maximum forward current
> V_z—zener voltage (if applicable)
> IFS—maximum forward surge current
> I_r—reverse leakage current in μA
> V_F—forward voltage drop—sometimes more than 0.2 or 0.6

But for most purposes you order 'general purpose' or 'RF' according to the frequency you want to handle. Silicon diodes are 'hard' and more used for low frequency and switching work; germanium are 'soft' and best for RF. A 'junction' type will usually have a substantial internal capacitance; a 'point contact' will

---

* For a full account see G. R. Jessop, *VHF–UHF Manual* (London, RSGB, 1971), pp. 525 *et seq*; and P. Hawker, *Amateur Radio Techniques* (London, RSGB, 1974), p. 8.

not. 'Gold doped' implies high speed, and this type will therefore have a low internal capacitance.

So much for our long diversion over the active devices of modern electronics. Together with the three basic passive devices—coils, capacitors and resistors—banished to the back of the book because we know something about them already, we now have almost everything needed to build or understand modern circuits.

Back to the original objective of this section, a record player amplifier.

AUDIO AMPLIFIER

Nowadays it is hardly worth the bother to build a complete amplifier out of separate transistors, resistors and capacitors when circuits almost as good in performance are available in integrated circuit (IC) packages needing only a few extra components and costing less than the separate bits. See, for example, *Sinclair Radionics* and many similar kits. However, it is nevertheless instructive to look at an audio amplifier designed round non-specialized integrated circuit (IC) devices called op-amps, because on the way we shall learn something about amplifier design and also about this very important class of IC. The audio amplifier described here was designed by Richard Mann for Texas Instruments* by whose kind permission it is reproduced.

The 'op-amp' started life as an operational amplifier; a circuit element designed specifically for the early analogue computers. Early op-amps were made of separate components; now they come in minute IC packages, but the principles are the same. They are called 'operational' because they were—and still are—used to perform operations like add, subtract, integrate, differentiate, form log x, e^x and so on, on the voltages which represent numbers in this type of computer.

Op-amps

This background has produced a device with some, at first, apparently odd features. It has two power supplies—one positive, usually between 3 V and 15 V, and the other equal, but negative. Unless there is some special reason, the power supplies are not shown in circuit diagrams. It has two inputs: one inverting, marked −, and one non-inverting marked +. It has one output (Fig. 69). It may also have terminals for frequency compensation and offset adjustment, which are less important. In a state of rest, both inputs and the output will be at 0 V, ground potential. *It is important not to confuse op-amp circuits with ordinary npn tran-*

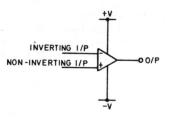

Fig. 69. Operational amplifier: two inputs, two power supplies, one output.

sistor ones where the negative supply and ground are usually the same.

The voltage that is amplified by the device is the *difference* between the voltages on the inverting and non-inverting terminals. If they go up or down in unison, then this *common-mode* voltage has no effect. (Of course, life being what it is, it has some effect, but not much.) The ratio between the output due to common mode and output due to the same input voltage as a difference between the two terminals is called *common-mode rejection ratio* (CMRR) and is somthing like −90 dB (1/30 000, p. 111).

The built in voltage gain is usually enormous. The popular 741, with which we shall be mostly concerned, has an 'open loop' gain of 200 000 times or 106 dB. Open loop means gain measured with no negative feedback, an essential method of reducing gain to managable proportions. The input impedance is high—at least 250 kΩ—and the output impedance low at 200 Ω.

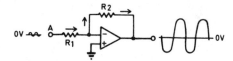

Fig. 70. Inverting amplifier.

Fig. 70 shows a very common use of an op-amp: to amplify the voltage of a small signal. We assume its average value is 0 V (to bias the −input) and that it is 0.2 V pp. The + input is grounded. The amplifier will amplify the difference between the two inputs, which is just the voltage at A. Freeze the action when A is 0.1 V positive. A current will flow from A through R_1 to the − input. The input impedance of both terminals is something like 2 MΩ, so not much current actually disappears into the device. This positive voltage at the − input makes the output go negative. Because the output is negative, a current flows from the inverting terminal through R_2 to the output, and the output will move negative until the current away from the input through R_2 balances the current into it through R_1. Because the internal gain of the amplifier is so huge the voltage of the inverting input changes an

* *Semiconductor Circuit Design VII* (Bedford, Texas Instruments, 1973), pp. 159–72.

imperceptible amount from 0 V to produce the output swing V_o. So we have a balance at the − terminal: $0.1/R_1$, the current in from A is equal to the current out through R_2, which is V_0/R_2. Therefore:

$$\frac{0.1}{R_1} = \frac{V_o}{R_2}$$

The actual voltage amplification of the whole circuit, which must be less than the open-loop gain of the op-amp because of negative feedback through R_2, is $V_o/0.1$, and equals R_2/R_1.

Suppose R_1 is 1 kΩ, and R_2 1 MΩ, then we have, by Ohms Law

$$\frac{0.1}{10^3} = \frac{V_o}{10^6}$$

or,

$$V_o = 0.1 \times \frac{10^6}{10^3} = 10^2 \text{ or } 100 \text{ V}$$

Of course the output can't go more positive than the positive rail, or more negative than the negative—and in fact won't go within 2 V of either in this type of op-amp, so that with a 0.1-V input and 15-V rails the output will look like Fig. 71. This is called clipping, and

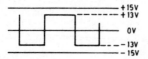

Fig. 71. Clipped input: signal highs and lows are 2 V or so from rail voltages.

sounds terrible if it happens in an audio system such as the one we're trying to design. With this amount of gain, the maximum input the amplifier will handle is

$$\frac{13}{1000} = 0.013 \text{ V}$$

But still, the gain of an op-amp with negative feedback is simply R_2/R_1. When R_1 and R_2 are the same or both absent, the amplifier has a gain of 1. This sounds nonsensical, but it can be useful to reduce an impedance, which is all very simple and nice. However, there is one very odd and interesting thing about this circuit. Because of the opposite effects of the input and output at the − terminal, acting through R_1 and R_2, the − terminal is always at the same voltage as the + input, in this case 0 V, and acts, in effect, as if it were itself an earth. It's called a virtual earth, and will soak up almost any signal you care to put on it. So the input impedance of the whole amplifier is R_1, in this case 1 kΩ, which is also nice and easy.

It isn't any use using a higher value for R_2 than 1 MΩ because it won't deliver enough current to satisfy even

the modest demands of these high impedance inputs. So the maximum gain is set by how low you can get R_1, and that depends on how low the impedance is of the circuit or device that produces the input. In this case we're interested in using a magnetic pick-up with an impedance of, say, 50 kΩ. If we make R_1 equal to that we get maximum power transfer. (It is a basic theorem of electronics, proved in innumerable texts, that least power is lost when output and input have the same impedance.) The maximum gain we can get with such a high impedance input is $10^5/50.10^3 = 20$, which is not too hot. However, in order to get more gain we'd do better to use the high impedance of the positive terminal and make the op-amp into a non-inverting amplifier. In Fig. 72 R_1 goes straight to ground, and

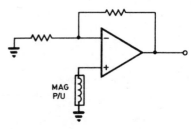

Fig. 72. A magnetic pick-up is just a coil of wire, so it can connect the non-inverting input to ground.

because ground has, one hopes, a very low impedance, it can have a low value: say, 100 Ω. R_2 is again 1 MΩ, and the + terminal is connected to ground through the coil of wire in the magnetic pick-up. Vibrations of the stylus produce a voltage in the coil, which goes straight to the + terminal, whose effective impedance is actually 2 MΩ multiplied by the gain. As before, the op-amp amplifies the difference between the voltages on its two terminals, which is $V_{in} - 0 = V_{in}$. The gain is:

$$\frac{R_2}{R_1} = \frac{10^6}{100} = 10\,000$$

If we were dealing with a crystal pick-up, which cannot connect the + terminal to ground, then it would be necessary to earth it with a resistor as shown in Fig. 73.

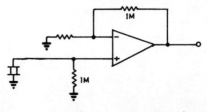

Fig. 73. A ceramic pick-up won't conduct electricity, so the positive terminal must be grounded with a resistor.

Non-inverting gain

WHY IS THE GAIN STILL R_2/R_1?

With the signal at the + input we have a non-inverting
amplifier; see Fig. 74. But the − input still plays an

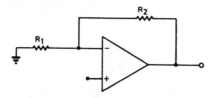

Fig. 74. Non-inverting amplifier.

essential part. We found the gain for the inverting
amplifier easily enough; what is it this time? R_2, R_1
produce negative feedback by sending back a proportion of the output voltage to the − input where it is
subtracted from the + input. Suppose the overall
gain of the amplifier, V_o/V_i, is represented by A_v.
The fed-back portion of the output is $V_o \times R_1/R_1 +
R_2$. The output, V_o, is the open-loop gain, A_o, multi-
plied by the difference between the inputs:

$$V_o = A_o(V_i - V_o) \times \frac{R_1}{R_1 + R_2}$$

which gives

$$A_v = \frac{A_o(R_2 + R_1)}{R_1(A_o + 1) + R_2}$$

Modern op-amps have a large A_o. If R_1 is small
compared to R_2, R_1, A_o is still much larger than R_2, so
the gain simplifies to:

$$A_v = \frac{R_2}{R_1}$$

For practical purposes one can take the gains of the
inverting and non-inverting amplifiers to be the same.
At the risk of being tedious, here is another reminder:
when you first start using op-amps, it's easy to fail to
make them work because of confusion over the
ground. Both inputs must have some way of settling at
0 V, otherwise the output will swing to one rail or the
other and stay there. A good preliminary check is to
make sure that +, −, and the output are all at 0 V
without signal. If not, something is wrong.

Long-tailed pair

The insides of op-amps are complicated, but we need
to understand their basic circuit: the *differential
amplifier* or 'long-tailed pair'; see Fig. 75. This is an
important circuit which appears all over the place.
Imagine that both bases are biased in the normal way,

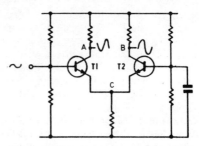

Fig. 75. Two transistors wired as a differential amplifier:
an interesting and important circuit.

so that the emitters (naturally at the same voltage) are
at 1/5th rail, and the collectors are half way between
that and the top rail. Suppose that the base of T_2 is held
steady, and a signal is applied to the base of T_1. As T_1
base goes up, more current flows through the device,
the collector voltage falls, and we get an inverted,
amplified output at A. Also, because more current
passes through T_1, point C rises in voltage. (R_3 is *not*
decoupled to ground by a capacitor. If it were, the
circuit would not work.) This raises T_2 emitter against
its base, which is equivalent to the base falling, so T_2
conducts less current until point C falls to its old
voltage. But because T_2 is conducting less, point B rises
producing an amplified (in phase) copy of the input to
T_1 base or the output of T_1 inverted. It is important
that T_1 and T_2 are matched for β. The less well the
emitter resistor—from C to ground—conducts signal,
the better the circuit works. It is often replaced by a
constant current sink (see Fig. 29) or an FET (Figs 51
and 52).

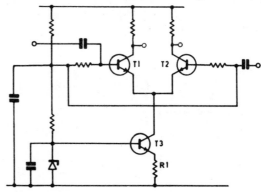

Fig. 76. A refined version of Fig. 75: T_1 and T_2 are
biased from the same potential divider, and the common
emitter resistor is replaced by a constant current sink—
T_3.

Suppose now that T_2 base has a signal applied to it,
the result at A and B will be an amplified version of the
difference between it and the signal on T_1 base. Hence
the name 'differential amplifier'. But this is not all. If

both signals rise or fall together, the effect largely cancels out at A and B. This is called 'common-mode rejection' (CMR). It is most often caused by a change in temperature on the transistors which, if hotter, causes them to conduct more current. This gives more gain, which in turn makes point C rise in voltage, which then reduces the base emitter voltages and so reduces the current flow. Thus a differential amplier is fundamentally insensitive to temperature variations. If a signal is applied to T_1 base while T_2 base is decoupled to ground but can have its voltage altered, we can shift the average voltage of the amplified signal at A or B (see Fig. 76) so that we can use it to bias a following stage, or compensate for input bias, or to move a display, as it might be on a cathode ray tube (CRT), up and down or to and fro.

Finally, as one transistor draws more current, the other draws less, so the total stays almost constant. The effect of the circuit on the positive rail is much less than for a single transistor amplifier—another advantage given by the long-tailed pair, which makes them much easier to cascade for high gain and therefore makes it possible to cram half a dozen into a tiny IC package. In Fig. 76 transistors T_1 and T_2 are biased through equal resistors to a chain which also sets T_3's emitter voltage and therefore the current through R_1. If R_1 is variable, we can control this current and therefore the gain of T_1 and T_2. Notice that T_3 emitter is *not* decoupled because we want as little AC amplification as possible from it.

Once again: it is most important that T_1 and T_2 should have similar βs. If you are building a long-tailed pair out of separate devices, take a dozen or so and measure their βs, and select two with the closest values. But the best way is to buy them ready packed in an IC. Fig. 77 shows the useful CA3028: it comes in an eight-pin round pack or DIL.

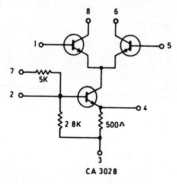

Fig. 77. *The internals of the CA3028, which can be wired as Fig.* 76.

Limiting

A limiter is an amplifier which eliminates amplitude variations in a signal by having enough gain so that the upper and lower swings of the output are bounded by the supply rails or the saturation of the transistors. It is necessary in FM receivers to eliminate AM noise (p. 82). There are many circuits to do the job. A simple

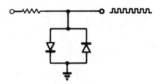

Fig. 78. *Two diodes limiting a signal.*

way is to use a pair of diodes (see Fig. 78) providing the smallest input swing is greater than the forward conduction voltage of the diodes. A long tailed pair is better; see Fig. 79. Here, by way of a change, the upper

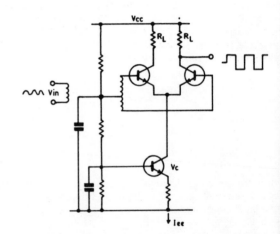

Fig. 79. *Overdriven differential amplifier as a limiter.*

bases are biased and driven through the centre-tapped secondary of a transformer. If the input is big enough, the outputs will clip, and because the output of one side is reproduced inverted on the other, either side clips very symmetrically—which would otherwise be tricky to arrange. R_l has to be big enough so that the collector voltage cannot fall to its low saturation value—more or less the emitter voltage of the bottom transistor.

The proper value for the load resistors is:

$$\frac{V_{cc} - V_c}{I_{ee}}$$

If a tuned load is used (p. 25) the reactance can be twice this. It would be worth shunting it with a resistor to make sure the optimum value is not exceeded, see Fig. 80.

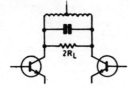

Fig. 80. Tuned output for Fig. 79, with resistor to limit Q.

Voltage adder

Since the − input of an op-amp is at 0 V and behaves like earth, we can connect several signal sources to it through resistors, confident that they will not interfere with each other; see Fig. 81. R_1, R_2, R_3 etc can have

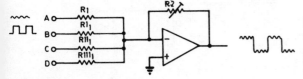

Fig. 81. Since the voltage at the negative input of an op-amp is 0, voltages can be added there and amplified without affecting each other.

different values, and the signals through them will be amplified proportionally. The gain of the whole addition can be changed by R_f, the feedback resistor. Circuits something like this are used in recording studios to mix inputs from different microphones. (Note that to audio engineers 'mix' means *add*. To radio engineers, it means *multiply*.) Since there are no capacitors in series with the signal, a voltage adder will work down to DC and can be used for shifting the level

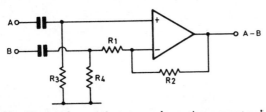

Fig. 82. A voltage subtractor—alternating current only.

of an alternating signal, or for adding two static voltages.

If signal is applied to both inputs, the device amplifies the *difference* between their voltages at any one time. In other words it subtracts one voltage from the other; see Fig. 82. If one wanted to add two groups of voltages separately and subtract one group from the other, it would be necessary to use three amplifiers because voltages can't be added at the + terminal as they can at −; see Fig. 83. All the resistances are the same, so there is no gain. The second amplifier is necessary to re-invert the first group of voltages. This circuit also shows how several op-amps can be strung together in cascade (a snag can arise if more than one has high gain—see p. 31).

Frequency filter

We can take advantage of the time dependent properties of resistance and capacitance together (p. 33) to give op-amps a variety of useful properties. Frequency

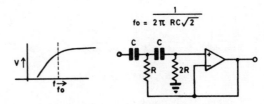

$$f_0 = \frac{1}{2\pi\,RC\sqrt{2}}$$

Fig. 84. Op-amp wired as high pass filter.

filters are handy. Fig. 84 is a high pass, with the cut-off frequency given by:

$$F_c = \frac{1}{2\pi RC}$$

R should be around 10 kΩ. Low pass (Fig. 85): F_c given by the same equation. The input must be tied to ground by a resistor: 20 kΩ, 39 kΩ would do. The gain of these filters falls off 12 dB every time the frequency doubles (per octave), or 40 dB per decade because of two RC sections. One section would give 6 dB per octave and three sections could give up to 18 dB per

Fig. 83. A circuit to add three voltages and subtract the sum from the sum of three other voltages.

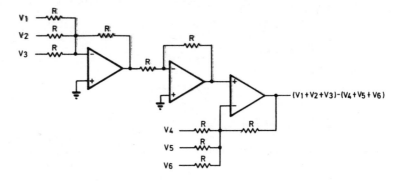

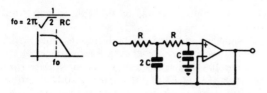

$$f_0 = \frac{1}{2\pi\sqrt{2}\, RC}$$

Fig. 85. Op-amp wired as low pass filter.

octave, and so on. However, stability becomes difficult and multisection filters need careful design. A bandpass filter is shown in Fig. 86. The circuit symbols are as

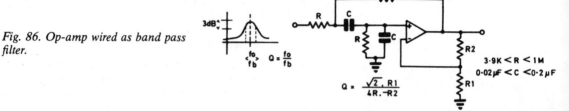

$$Q = \frac{1}{R_1 + R_2} \times \frac{C_2 \times R_1 \times R_2}{C_1}$$

$$f_c = \frac{1}{2\pi C_1 C_2 R_1 R_2}$$

R: 50 kΩ–1 MΩ

C_2: 1 μF–10 μF

C_1: 40 nF–100 pF

$R_1 + R_2 = R$

Fig. 86. Op-amp wired as band pass filter.

$$Q = \frac{\sqrt{2}\,.\,R_1}{4R\,.\,{-}R_2}$$

$3 \cdot 9\mathrm{K} < R < 1\mathrm{M}$

$0 \cdot 02 \mu\mathrm{F} < C < 0 \cdot 2 \mu\mathrm{F}$

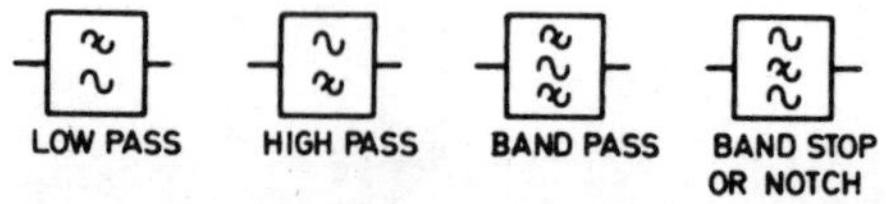

This can be used as the feedback element for an amplifier giving a tunable bandpass filter. Follow it with the full-wave rectifier (p. 30) to make an analysis of the amplitudes of different frequencies in speech sounds. The results (see Fig. 90) are quite interesting

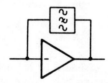

Fig. 87. Filter symbols.

shown in Fig. 87. A notch filter is one that cuts out a particular frequency, and can simply be made by putting a band pass filter in an amplifier's negative feed-

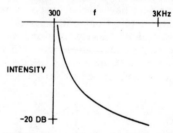

Fig. 90. Distribution of intensity against frequency in speech.

and show surprisingly little variation between men, women and children.

Fig. 88. Band pass filter made by putting notch filter into feedback.

Integrator

If negative feedback is through a capacitor, the amplifier becomes an integrator; see Fig. 91. If the

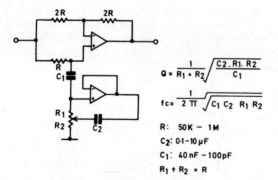

$$Q = \frac{1}{R_1 + R_2}\sqrt{\frac{C_2\,.\,R_1\,.\,R_2}{C_1}}$$

$$f_C = \frac{1}{2\pi}\sqrt{\frac{1}{C_1\,C_2\,R_1\,R_2}}$$

R: 50K – 1M

C_2: 0·1–10 μF

C_1: 40 nF – 100 pF

$R_1 + R_2 = R$

Fig. 89. Notch filter.

back; see Fig. 88. A tunable notch filter is shown in Fig. 89.

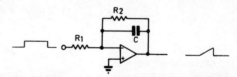

Fig. 91. Integrator: the output voltage is a measure of the area under the input voltage. Since the capacitor passes more negative feedback at high frequencies, it's also a low pass filter.

input is a square wave, the output is triangular. The *height* of the output peaks is proportional to the *area* under the square waves. Or, of course, one may just want a ramp voltage, and this is an easy way of generating it. The time constant (p. 33) is $R_1 \times C$. The snag with this circuit is that since the input actually draws current, eventually the output will drift to one rail or the other and stick there. Either there must be some provision for connecting the − input and output together occasionally to zero the integrator, or a high value resistor R_2 must be used. An interval timer is shown in Fig. 92. S_2 connects the input and output

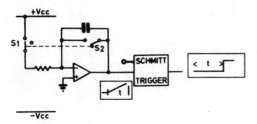

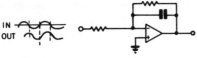

Fig. 92. Delay circuit: the integrator charges up from the + rail. When the output equals a reference voltage, the Schmitt trigger switches, to give a delay $t \sim R \times C$.

together. It is ganged with S_1: when it is opened, S_1 connects R to the + rail and starts to charge the integrator. After a time the output has risen enough to fire the Schmitt trigger (see p. 28). The switches have to be reversed before the cycle can begin again.

If a sine wave is fed into the integrator, its integral, a cosine wave, comes out. But this is a sine wave with a 90° phase shift; see Fig. 93. This trick, shifting a signal

Fig. 93. The integrals of sine is cosine, which is the sine wave shifted by 90°.

by 90°, is one that is often needed (p. 72). Unfortunately this circuit gives different gain at different frequencies—because of varying feedback through the capacitor.

Instead of a ramp, we may want a voltage that goes up in steps (p. 95). Packets of charge from a square-wave generator are fed into an integrator through a diode; see Fig. 94. A double integrator is shown in Fig. 95.

$$R_1 \times C_1 = 4R_2C_3, \ R_s \times C_2 = R_1C_4, \ R_2C_2 = R_3C_3$$

This gives the effect of two integrators in series, but better since it has a DC feedback path through the R_3s. It might be used to integrate the output of an accelerometer twice to give distance travelled. If a is

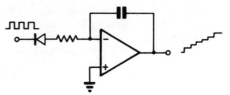

Fig. 94. An integrator fed with current pulses will produce a step voltage.

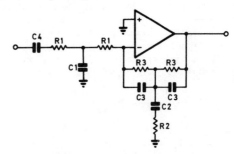

Fig. 95. A double integrator.

the acceleration at any time t, then velocity is $\int_o^t a \, dt$ and distance gone $\iint_o^t a \, dt \, dt$.

Logarithmic amplifier

In analogue computers a logarithmic amplifier is used to multiply numbers represented by voltages; see Fig. 96. It makes a useful dynamic range voice compressor

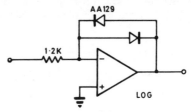

Fig. 96. Logarithmic amplifier—germanium diodes work best.

for a radio transmitter. As long as the input voltage is less than 0.2 V the diodes do not conduct, there is no feedback, and gain is high. Above 0.2 V the diodes conduct more and more strongly until the gain falls to 1. The result is compressed audio.

In Fig. 97 we do the opposite—form the anti-logarithm. The two together, with adding and gain

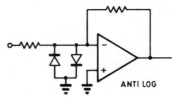

Fig. 97. Antilog amplifier.

amplifiers in between, can multiply functions by each other and raise them to powers. Now, of course, these things are usually, though not always more easily, done digitally. If we use an FET in the feedback path of an op-amp, we can get square and square root functions directly.

Positive feedback

So far, all our circuits have used negative feedback. Sometimes we simply want to know whether one voltage is higher or lower than a second—a situation that often arises in recovering digital signals from a transmission line or radio path. One circuit for this is the Schmitt trigger; see Fig. 98. When B is higher than

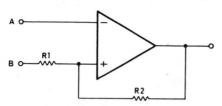

Fig. 98. Schmitt trigger—this time the feedback is positive.

A the output switches to the + rail; when it is lower, it switches to the − rail. Just how much higher or lower it has to be for switching to take place is determined by R_1 and R_2. Assume that A is 0 V, B is slightly negative at V' and the output is high. The situation is equivalent to that shown in Fig. 99. R_1, R_2 act as a potential

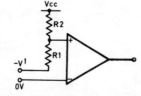

Fig. 99. Voltages as the trigger switches.

divider: when $V_{cc}/R_2 = V'/R_1$ the + terminal will also be at 0 V, and when V' falls a fraction further, the output will start to go negative. Helped by positive feedback through R_2, it will switch violently to the negative rail.

Since $V_{cc} \div V' = R_2/R_1$ we can think of this too as the 'voltage gain' (p. 22).

$$V' = \pm V_{cc} \times \frac{R_1}{R_2}$$

V' is the uncertain area in the middle called the 'hysteresis voltage'. The input has to rise above this voltage for the output to go negative, and below it for the output to switch positive.

A 741 amplifier will work, but the internal compensation (Fig. 135) slows down the switching. A 748 is

better, and in this application it needn't have a compensating capacitor.

We've assumed that A is held at 0 V. This is not necessary: A can have an alternating voltage and the trigger will switch as A becomes positive or negative

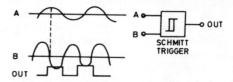

Fig. 100. The reference voltage can vary too: here the trigger switches as A is positive or negative with regard to B.

with regard to B; see Fig. 100. Evidently, hysteresis is least when R_2 is infinite and R_1 is 0. See Fig. 101, a voltage comparator, which needn't necessarily have

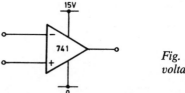

Fig. 101. Op-amp as voltage comparator.

split supplies. With an open-loop gain of 100 000 the 741 will switch to the rails on 75 μV difference. But of course, the circuit lacks the locking action of positive feedback.

Schmitt triggers can be had as ICs in the popular logic families, but their hysteresis is fixed (see also p. 32 for COSMOS possibilities). A Schmitt trigger in fashionable environmental example (see Fig. 102): in a solar roof installation it's necessary to compare the temperature of water on the roof with that in the hot

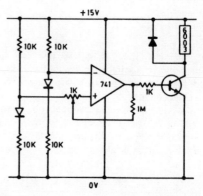

Fig. 102. Circuit to control a solar panel: the op-amp compares the voltage drop across two diodes to measure temperature. Its output operates a relay through a transistor.

water tank. A couple of ordinary diodes will serve as temperature sensors since the forward voltage drop across a silicon diode alters by 2.10^{-4} V per °C. So, if, for instance, one wanted the trigger to switch on a 1 °C difference with a 15-V supply, then the hysteresis would have to be 2.10^{-4} V and

$$R_1 = 10^6 \cdot 1 \frac{2.10^{-4}}{15} = 13 \ \Omega$$

Note that both inputs are around +0.7 V, but because of the common mode rejection of the op-amp this has no effect on the output. Hysteresis—and therefore the sensitivity of the circuit to temperature differences—can be adjusted by the potentiometer. The pump motor is switched by a relay, turned on by a small transistor (make sure the relay's impedance is high enough to protect the device). The diode across the relay protects the transistor against possible switching spikes.

Window comparator

Two Schmitt triggers wired in opposite senses feeding an AND gate (p. 85) make a window comparator which goes high when the two voltages are within a set amount of each other and is otherwise low; see Fig. 103. In period A, the Y voltage is rising but is less than the reference voltage X. The output of ST 1 is low, and of ST 2 is high. Shortly after Y passes X—just how shortly depends on the hysteresis—the output of ST 1

goes high, and ST 2 goes low. If they have different hystereses, both outputs will be high for a short time. They are combined in a COSMOS AND whose output is low unless both inputs are high. The result is the pulse as required.

Delta modulator

Fig. 104 is an example of a Schmitt trigger in a type of 'delta modulator' used to convert an analogue signal—as it might be voice—into a switched form:

The integrator output is a ramp which goes + or − according to the state of the Schmitt trigger. Suppose it is plus-going. The ST compares it to the audio input: when the ramp exceeds the audio by the hysteresis voltage V', the ST switches and the integrator output starts going negative. It continues until it is V' less than the audio, and the ST switches again. The integrator tracks the audio, and the ST output can be used to control a frequency shift radio signalling system, or could be converted into a digital form. At the other end of the link the signal is fed into another Schmitt trigger to recover wave-form C, integrated to get B and smoothed to get an approximation to the original audio A.

Precision rectifier

The drawback to a simple diode rectifier (p. 18) is the 0.7 V forward voltage drop. If we use a diode in the

Fig. 103. A window comparator: the Schmitt triggers, ST1 and ST2, are wired in opposite senses and have slightly different hystereses so that as voltage Y increases, ST1 goes positive shortly before ST2 goes negative. The two are combined in an AND gate to produce a pulse as X and Y become equal.

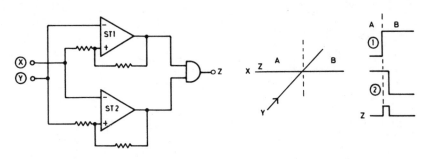

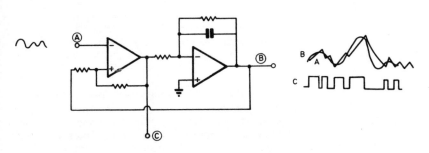

Fig. 104. A form of delta modulator: to turn voice into a digital signal audio is applied at one input of a Schmitt trigger. The trigger output C is integrated to produce B which is used as the other input to the trigger. The effect is that B tracks A: each reversal of direction is represented by a change of state at C, and this is the digital signal.

negative feedback path of an op-amp this drop will be off-set; see Fig. 105. This gives half wave rectification, right down to 0 V; see Fig. 106. Fig. 107 shows full

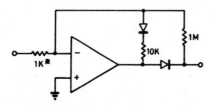

Fig. 105. Half wave positive rectifier. The voltage drop across the diodes is absorbed in the op-amp feedback, so that rectification is complete down to a low voltage.

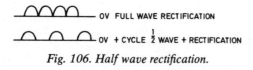

Fig. 106. Half wave rectification.

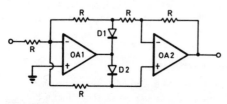

Fig. 107. Full wave rectifier. Omit either diode for half way rectification.

wave rectification. If we make R_1 less than R, we get a rectifier with gain—often a useful trick.

A sensitive audio signal detector can be made using this circuit and a Schmidt trigger or the comparator. If it is preceded by a high Q band pass filter (p. 26), we have a detector which will respond to a very small band of audio frequencies—useful, say, for switching things with a whistle. This is how ultrasonic TV channel remote controls work.

Peak programme detector

This circuit (see Fig. 108) charges the capacitor up to the peak voltage applied to the input—say a passage of

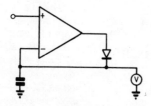

Fig. 108. Audio peak voltage meter. The integration time is set by the size of the capacitor.

music—and stays charged to that voltage for a time depending on the value of C and the current drawn by the voltmeter and the − terminal. A circuit like this drives the meter on a tape recorder that indicates the proper recording level.

Audio output buffer

And this brings us at last to audio amplification. The problem is that to get enough power to fill a room with music, using low voltages appropriate to transistors, we must have speakers with low impedances. Driving them requires a power amplifier, and these are a subject in themselves.

When the 200 Ω output of an op-amp is too high—say to drive a small 8-Ω speaker, it can be reduced with a transformer; see Fig. 109. A more powerful arrangement is shown in Fig. 110, with two transistors

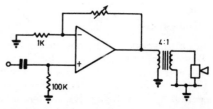

Fig. 109. Low power audio amplifier using an op-amp and transformer to match speaker impedance to amplifier output.

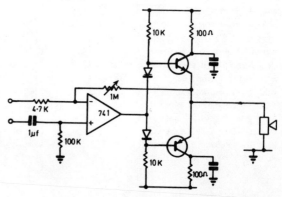

Fig. 110. Op-amp with transistor output stage. The diodes compensate for base–emitter voltage drop, and the transistors work as emitter followers over the positive and negative cycles. Feedback is from the transistor outputs.

in class B (p. 7). The diodes, obviously, are the same type—germanium or silicon—as the transistors, and serve to turn them just on. The 100-Ω resistors prevent the transistors busting if the output is short circuited. They should be well decoupled. Feedback is taken from the final output—this helps to smooth out the inevitable slight hiatus as the transistors switch on and off around 0 V. This makes a neat little monitor amplifier for the bench, driving a 70-Ω speaker. With a two-sided supply, the speaker goes straight to ground without a capacitor; with a single-ended supply it must be protected by an electrolytic capacitor which has 1/10th, say, of its impedance at the lowest frequency you intend to handle (300 Hz for communications equipment, 50 Hz for mid-fi, see Fig. 111). If we

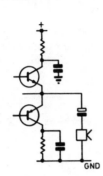

Fig. 111. Double emitter-follower output stage. The transistors are npn and pnp and work over the positive and negative half cycles respectively.

reckon that the op-amp's output impedance is 500 Ω and that its supplies are ± 18 V, then it can deliver a maximum current of 18/500 = 36 mA. If the output transistors have β of 60, they can deliver a maximum of 2 A, or an rms output power of 15 W (p. 110). However, a circuit handling so much current would need a better biasing system than this (p. 38).

Types of op-amps

The commonest and most useful op-amp in current use is the 741; see Fig. 112. It's made by several manufacturers, and appears in catalogues numbered SN72741

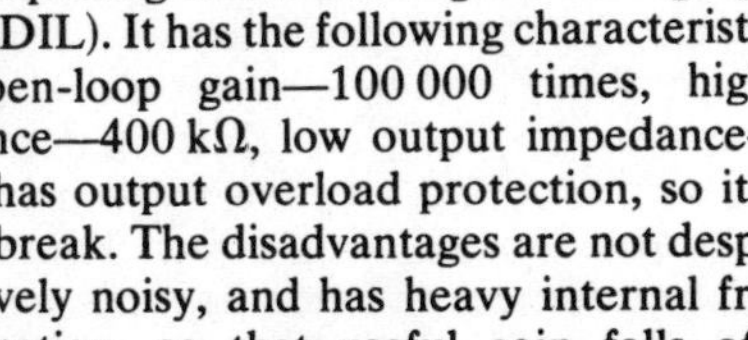

OFFSET NULL — 1   741   8 — N/C
− IN — 2   TOP   7 — +V
+ IN — 3   6 — O/P
− V — 4   5 — OFFSET NULL

Fig. 112. Pin assignments for the 741 op-amp. The 748 is the same, but needs 10 pF or so between pins 1 and 8.

(TI), CA741 (RCA) μA741CP etc. It is also available in several packages. The one to get is the eight pin Dual in Line (DIL). It has the following characteristics: very high open-loop gain—100 000 times, high input impedance—400 kΩ, low output impedance—200 Ω app. It has output overload protection, so it is quite hard to break. The disadvantages are not desperate: it is relatively noisy, and has heavy internal frequency compensation, so that useful gain falls off above 100 kHz. An uncompensated version, the 748, is available. To prevent it oscillating a capacitor of

10 pF–30 pF must be connected between pins 1 and 8 (see p. 33).

Although in theory the quiescent voltages of the plus and minus inputs and the output should all be 0 V, in practice—life being what it is—there may be a few mV difference. If necessary the offset null pins can be used to adjust the input and output voltages to exact equality. They work as shown in Fig. 113. In practice this

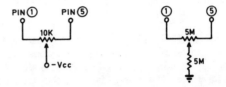

Fig. 113. If offset null is needed to adjust the output no-signal voltage precisely to the input, this is how it is done. Left: 741; Right: 748.

would only be necessary for the most accurate work or if one wanted to cascade two directly-coupled op-amps for very high gain—in the latter case the offset of the first might make the second limit. I've used dozens of 741s and never needed offset null.

Supplies should nominally be in the range of ± 15 V down to ± 5 V, though I have had 741s working happily off a single sided supply of 5 V. The output swings from about 2 V below the + rail to 2 V above the − rail. This needs bearing in mind when mixing op-amps and discrete transistors, because signal levels in the second case often swing right to one of the rails, and this may cause difficulties.

SN72747 is a dual 741 in a 14 pin DIL. There are now dozens of other IC amplifier types available, for higher frequencies, higher powers or other specialities. IC audio amplifiers which give acceptable quality outputs at a couple of watts are useful in communication radio receivers. It is always worth browsing through manufacturers' and suppliers' catalogues, but because the 741 is made in such huge quantities, it is the cheapest.

Op-amp power supplies

The 'normal' supply for most op-amps is a double rail, usually ± 5 to 15 V with earth at 0 V. Equally usually, such a supply isn't easy to arrange, and one often has to make do with a single rail. However, it isn't hard to make a fake ground, as shown in Fig. 114. Here the + terminal is 'grounded'. The thing to remember is that the ground must have a low impedance compared with the input. Since the + terminal of 741 has an impedance of at least 250 kΩ at the lowest working frequency, this is easy enough—but remember that ungrounded signal at the + terminal will be amplified by the gain of the circuit.

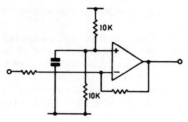

Fig. 114. Dummy ground for inverting amplifier when only one supply voltage is available.

A grounded − terminal is more tricky (see Fig. 115), because the effective input impedance here is R_1, which may be fairly low to give high gain. R_b and X_c must have even lower impedance if the circuit is to work properly.

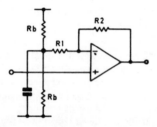

Fig. 115. Dummy ground for non-inverting amplifier.

On occasion the two inputs of the conventional op-amp are a nuisance and one just wants single input amplification with the least number of external components. One of the simpler COSMOS gates will often do the trick: an inverting buffer or a NAND; see Fig. 116. Gain is R_2/R_1—though R_1 can be set by the

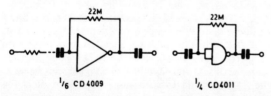

Fig. 116. Inverting op-amp amplifiers made from COSMOS logic gates: 1/6 CD 4009 buffer, 1/4 CD 4011 Quad NAND ('1/6' means one gate out of six on the chip, etc.).

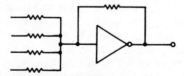

Fig. 117. A COSMOS amplifier can work as a voltage adder (see Fig. 80).

output impedance of the preceding stage. Again, just like an op-amp, signals can be added at the input terminal; see Fig. 117. A two input NAND can be used as a mixer; see Fig. 118.

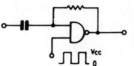

Fig. 118. A NAND gate wired as a switch or mixer. A positive voltage on the lower input enables the output.

Four inverters in cascade will give 100 dB of gain—capacitors shunting the feedback resistors will give up to 24 dB of high frequency roll-off per octave; see Fig. 119.

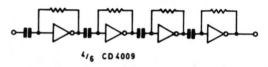

Fig. 119. Four buffer amplifiers in cascade give 100 dB of gain. Feedback capacitors can limit the upper frequency response.

Two inverting gates, or one non-inverting, make a Schmitt trigger (see Fig. 120), which switches on an

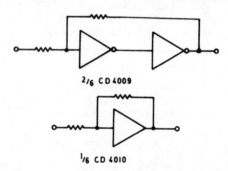

Fig. 120. Two inverting buffers make a non-inverting buffer and can be wired as a Schmitt trigger.

input voltage difference of $\frac{1}{2}(R_1/R_2) \times V_{cc}$. (The little circle at the output of the 4009* specifies an inverter.)

So, to get back to the audio amplifier on page 39, the first op-amp is the pre-amplifier. It has several jobs. Firstly it must give a modest amount of gain to the input signal so that it will be larger than noise voltages (p. 76) arising in later stages. Second, it must match the input to differential signal-sources—magnetic or crystal pick-up, tape, radio etc. Third (in this case, but not in all) it must remove very low frequencies caused by turntable rotation in a 'rumble filter'. Fourth it must 'equalize' for different sources. As we'll see, not all

---

* The shorthand: '1/6 CD 4009' etc means that one is using one of the six available gates on this particular IC. If no use can be found for the other five, their inputs should be tied to ground, and the outputs left floating.

signal sources produce an output which is the same size at different frequencies. The pre-amp has built in filters that remove intrinsic distortions. These arise because the medium has poor noise or dynamic range characteristics. However, before we can understand how op-amp 1 does these things, we need to know a little about frequency filtering.

More filtering

The fundamental problem in filtering is to distinguish between waves of different frequencies—to encourage one, discourage another. The simplest way to do this is to measure the time intervals between successive peaks or troughs, and the simplest electronic clock is made by charging up a capacitor through a resistor; see Fig. 121. If we suddenly connect point A

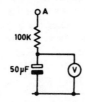

Fig. 121. An electronic watch: when a capacitor charges up through a resistor, the voltage across it is a measure of time.

to a 10 V supply, and watch the needle of the high-impedance voltmeter, we'll see it rise: quickly at first, then more slowly as it gets to the 10 V mark—which, in theory, it never reaches. To begin with the capacitor is empty and the electrons, pushing through the resistor, collect in it as fast as the impedance of the supply will let them. Then, as they accumulate, they begin to resist new electrons coming in—because like charges they repel each other. The sign of this is a rising voltage at the top of the capacitor: as it fills up more and more with electrons, and its voltage approaches 10 V, so the voltage difference across the resistor gets vanishingly small, and so does the current through it—which will finally fill it up, see Fig. 122. Mathematicians will recognize an exponential curve here.

Fig. 122. Plot of voltage against time for Fig. 121. The voltage across the capacitor tends towards 10 V but never quite gets there.

When you do the sums—which we shan't bother with—it turns out that resistance multiplied by capacitance; $R \times C$, gives the time in seconds it takes the voltage to reach 63.2 per cent of the final value—in this case 5 s to reach 6.32 V. So here we have a sort of stop watch: you could calibrate the voltmeter dial in seconds and use it to time shortish foot races. But for the moment we want it to distinguish between frequencies.

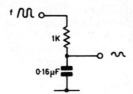

Fig. 123. The same circuit is also a low pass filter, since high frequencies drain to earth through the capacitor.

Let's look at Fig. 123. If we put a constant tone 1 V peak-to-peak (pk-pk) at a frequency of, say, 1 kHz, on the input, we find that it's $\frac{1}{2}$ V pk-pk at the output, because at this frequency the reactance X_c (p. 112) of the capacitor is just 1 kΩ, that is it acts as a 1 kΩ resistor, and so it forms a voltage divider, for example as shown in Fig. 124. The reactance of a capacitor: that

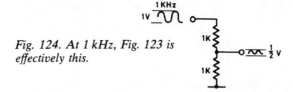

Fig. 124. At 1 kHz, Fig. 123 is effectively this.

is, the resistance it presents to AC, varies inversely with frequency. The higher the frequency, the lower the reactance, the less the resistance. The equation is

$$X_c = \frac{1}{2\pi \times f \times C} \ \Omega$$

Compare this with the reactance of a coil, p. 114.

At 2 kHz the reactance of the capacitor is *half* as much, so the circuit is roughly equivalent to Fig. 125

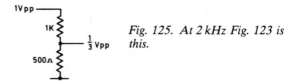

Fig. 125. At 2 kHz Fig. 123 is this.

(only roughly, because there is also a phase shift, p. 113. But for many purposes we can ignore it). As the frequency goes up, the output gets less. Conversely, in the other direction, as the frequency becomes less, so the output becomes greater; at 500 Hz the reactance of the capacitor is 2 kΩ, the output is $\frac{2}{3}$ V, and the graph is as shown in Fig. 126. We've built a *low pass filter* whose

Fig. 126. Plot of voltage out against frequency for Fig. 123.

critical frequency, f_c, is 1 kHz. (Strictly speaking, at the critical frequency the output is 3 dB down, not 6 dB as here.) Both these simple filters rely on the changing impedance of a capacitor at different frequencies compared with the fixed impedance of a resistor. Since the impedance of a capacitor is proportional to $1/f$, it is evident that if you double the frequency you halve the impedance; or, if you halve the frequency you double the impedance. Similarly, ten times the frequency gives a tenth the impedance. So all the 'roll off' of these filters is in proportion to the multiplication or division of the frequency. The usual way of putting it is to say that the roll off is 6 dB (2 times) per octave (doubling of frequency) or 20 dB per decade. If we had two identical low pass filters in series, the roll off would be 12 dB per octave, or 40 dB per decade.

If the resistor and capacitor are interchanged, we have a *high pass* filter; see Fig. 127.

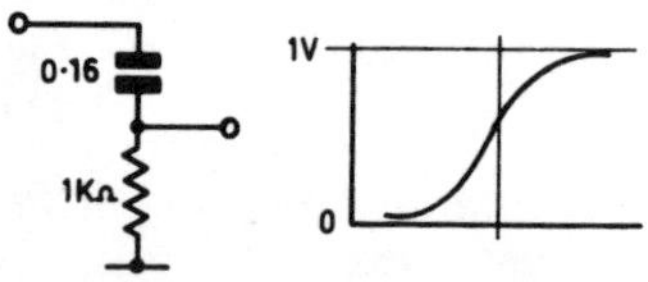

Fig. 127. A high pass filter.

There is a catch about these simple little graphs: since we're talking about *ratios* of voltage and *ratios* of frequency, they either have to be plotted on logarithmic paper, or we have to remember that it's log V up the y axis, and log f along the x axis. The reason why f_c is measured at 3 dB down—or up—is that for many purposes in electronics, a 3-dB increase or decrease

(corresponding to multiplying or dividing by $\sqrt{2} = 1.414$) is hardly noticeable, so it can be taken as the beginning of the filter's effect.* To get faster roll offs it is necessary to cascade RC filters. It is possible to do this directly; see Fig. 128. However the impedances tend to get out of hand and it is better to build an op-amp or two into the circuit and use feedback techniques (p. 25).

We can now look at the filters around the pre-amp at the beginning of the record player amplifier; see Fig. 129. Reading from left to right, we start with three input terminals for radio, magnetic pick up and tape. The first needs no frequency shaping, the other two need standard treatment specified by industry agreements. The first element is the rumble filter, a high pass circuit with a critical frequency of 100 Hz that has halved the amplitude of input signals by 30 Hz. The 47-kΩ resistor is part of it and this also provides the bias for the positive input of op-amp 1, and matches the impedance of a magnetic pick-up. There are two negative feedback paths, the first of which is through 100-kΩ and the 1-kΩ resistors. However, signals through these resistors are shunted to ground by the 100 pF capacitor, so they have effect only at DC. As we saw previously, the negative input will sit at the same voltage as the + input, 0 V, and so will the output.

Signal feedback is through the three circuits switched by SW 2—appropriate for radio, mag p/u and

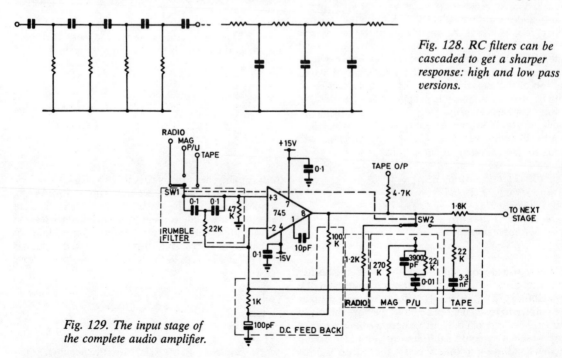

Fig. 128. RC filters can be cascaded to get a sharper response: high and low pass versions.

Fig. 129. The input stage of the complete audio amplifier.

---

* For example: the ear can just detect a 3 dB change in the volume setting of a record player or a radio, but it makes no great subjective difference.

tape in turn. The radio input needs no frequency shaping, so the feedback is simply a 1.2-kΩ resistor. The magnetic p/u has to match this curve, and the combination of resistors and capacitors shown in Fig. 130 does the trick. The filter for tape has to compensate for the high frequency emphasis given by tape

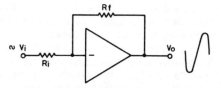

Fig. 130. An inverting amplifier with negative feedback through a resistor.

recorders. It gives more feedback at high frequencies and so less gain. This particular circuit is right for DIN $8\frac{1}{2}$ ips. The dotted line between the switches means they are ganged together. The op-amp is a 748, a version of the 741 that lacks an internal capacitor for stability (see p. 31) and therefore needs 10 pF externally to prevent oscillation—worth it for higher slew rate (p. 31). The tape o/p can go straight to a separate amplifier. The next stage is fed through a 1.8-kΩ resistor. The first stage raises the signal level to about 50 mV, getting it out of the noise (p. 76) and setting it up for tone control in the circuits round op amp 2.

STABILITY, BANDWIDTH AND SLEW RATE

The ideal op-amp has infinite gain and infinite bandwidth: real ones don't—and if they did they would oscillate. To prevent this it's necessary to have some sort of negative feedback through a capacitor. In the 741 the capacitor is built in; in the 748, and most others, you have to wire it in. The capacitor prevents the amplifier oscillating, but it also: (a) imposes a limited bandwidth of frequencies over which the amplifier will work; and (b) restricts the slew rate, the speed in volts per microsecond at which the output can change. For example, take the 741, which has a bandwidth of 1 MHz. As is usual with manufacturer's data, this is the most optmistic way of putting things: the frequency at which the gain is 1. However, we're not interested in unity gain, we want something like the amplifier's full and impressive performance, of 200 000 times, and this starts to give out at about 100 kHz. Now the time between a trough and a peak at this frequency is 5 μs. In that time the amplifier's slew rate of 0.5 V/μs lets the output move 2.5 V, which is not quite the output one might have hoped for. If we want the maximum permitted possible swing of ±16 V, then the output can't shift from bottom to top in less than 32/0.5 s which is 64 μs and which corresponds to a frequency of 15.6 kHz. Even that won't sound too good because the output can't track a sine wave properly at this frequency; see Fig. 131.

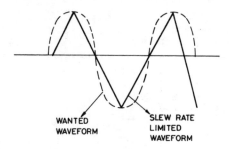

Fig. 131. If the input frequency is too high, the amplifier's output is limited by its slew rate to a triangular wave form.

Fortunately high frequency sound waves don't normally need large amplitudes because the ear's sensitivity increases logarithmically with frequency. But certainly slew rate, which affects the ability of an amplifier to reproduce sharp sounds such as drum beats and cymbal clashes, is becoming more important in modern music reproduction.

Filters

After the pre-amp comes the tone control—usually represented on the outside by two knobs, one to emphasize or reduce treble, and the other to do the same for bass. A graph of what they do might look like Fig. 132 (actually this applies to the complete amplifier

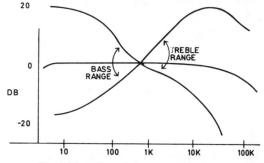

Fig. 132. Effect of the tone control stage.

whose circuit is on p. 39). When the two controls are at their mid positions, the gain curve is flat except for a droop starting at 10 Hz at the low and at 10 kHz on the high side. (Since these are on the limits of normal hearing, it doesn't much matter.) The bass control can alter the gain at 10 Hz by up to 20 dB either way—which is a factor of 10 times, with proportionately less at higher frequencies. At 1 kHz, neither control has any effect; above it bass has no effect, but treble gives ±15 dB at 13 kHz. It has less effect than bass, but the ear is more sensitive to it.

How does the tone control stage work? It is actually two filter circuits in parallel, arranged round the same

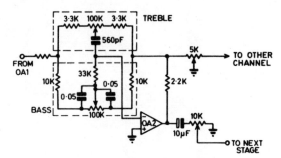

Fig. 133. Wiring of the tone control stage.

op-amp, this time a 741; see Fig. 133. To go back to our simple RC filters of p. 34, if we varied either the resistor or the capacitor, we could make a tunable filter, but since variable capacitors with a higher value than about 500 pF are hard to build, it's easiest to vary the resistance. If we then put these two in series, we'd have something like the tone control we need; see Fig. 134.

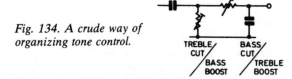

Fig. 134. A crude way of organizing tone control.

In practice this simple circuit is less than ideal for a number of reasons, and a slightly more complicated set up is used, arranged as part of the feedback of an op-amp. Fig. 135 is a simplified version of the treble

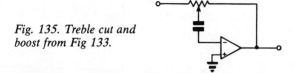

Fig. 135. Treble cut and boost from Fig 133.

control in the amplifier on p. 39. The 3.3-kΩ resistors in Fig. 133 act as end stops to the potentiometer. Negative feedback to the amplifier passes through a 100 kΩ potentiometer which alters the relative values

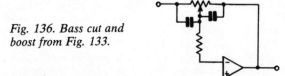

Fig. 136. Bass cut and boost from Fig. 133.

of R_1 and R_2 (Fig. 70) and therefore the gain. The negative terminal is in series with a capacitor, and therefore the higher the frequency the more effect the gain control has.

The bass control is the inverse, using the same op-amp; see Fig. 136. The gain control potentiometer is shorted by capacitors, so the lower the frequency, the less they pass, and the more effect it has. This type of tone control circuit was originally designed by Peter Baxendall, an ingenious gentleman whose name quite often crops up in audio engineering.

There are a couple of other minor points. There are actually two of these circuits, one for each channel, but to keep the tone controls in unison both 100-kΩ pots are double ganged, two for each side. The balance control goes to the same point in the other channel, and shorts more or less of each side's output to ground. The volume control is a double gang logarithmic pot to match the ear's logarithmic sensitivity, and taps the output down. The capacitor prevents a slight offset error in the first two amplifiers being magnified to such an extent that the final output is permanently held against one rail or the other. Since the tone control stage gives little gain, the 10 μF tantalum will be subjected to a maximum of 0.5 V back voltage—which it can stand (p. 112).

The third stage is op-amp 3 connected as an amplifier with two transistor stages to buffer its output and give some more gain; see Fig. 137. It starts with a switchable scratch filter—a low pass filter circuit which, when working has rolled off the rail to 1/3 of what it was at 10 kHz. Naturally, in the process, it does bad things to the treble—which is why it can be switched out. There is a modern hi-fi gimmick consisting of a circuit which detects a scratch by its sharp wave front, switches it out of the amplifier and fills the hole with sound played a few milliseconds before and stored in a delay line. It is said that one can score a record with a knife and play it apparently unharmed. We don't show this circuit here but perhaps the diligent reader will be able to design one by the time he has struggled to the end of the book.

Op-amp 3's negative feedback is from the final output rather than the immediate output of the op-amp. This is quite normal; what is not is the way the final pair of transistors—heavy duty power types—are connected as amplifiers rather than emitter followers like T_4 and T_5. In the usual way the final stage just follows the output of the preceding voltage gain stages to give a reduced output impedance and more power. Here, because of the limited slew rate of op-amp 3, some extra gain is made up in the final stage. However this is immaterial.

The output transistors can be divided into three chunks. A simple version of the top half of the output circuit would look like Fig. 138. Because of the unvarying 0.6 V drop between base and emitter, the output of the transistor follows the output of the op-amp but 0.6 V lower and at a lower impedance—because the transistor can supply more current than the op-amp. It's called an emitter follower. If we *raise* the output of the op-amp by 0.6 V by using a diode as a

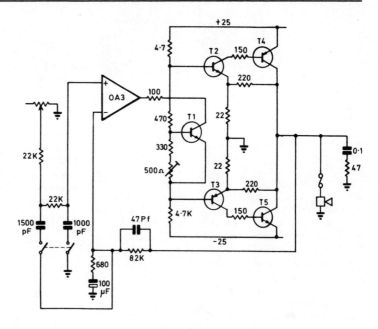

Fig. 137. Output of the complete audio amplifier stage with switchable scratch filter at the input to op-amp 3. T_1 biases T_2 and T_3 work as emitter followers, T_4 and T_5 are wired as amplifiers to give a little gain. See below.

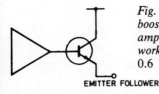

Fig. 138. A crude way of boosting the output of an op-amp. The transistor will only work for outputs greater than 0.6 V.

EMITTER FOLLOWER

sort of voltage step ladder, we can get it at exactly the same voltage level; see Fig. 139. A diode is a one way valve—but here we're not interested in the one-wayness, but in the voltage drop across it (see p. 18).

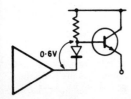

Fig. 139. A diode lifts the signal 0.6 V so that the transistor works down to 0 V.

This circuit will increase the power of positive peaks. An exactly similar circuit, using the other type of transistor—pnp instead of npn (p. 2)—will deal with the negative peaks; see Fig. 140. Since the output of the transistors is exactly like the output of the op-amp we can take the feedback from it, and this will help control distortion in the transistors. The 100-Ω resistors are simply to prevent the transistors overloading when they're turned hard on. Notice that since the quiescent voltage of the output is 0 V, we can connect the speaker to it direct without having a big blocking capacitor. I have an amplifier with these values permanently under my bench with input and volume

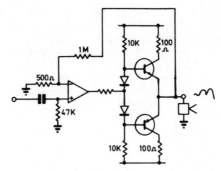

Fig. 140. To work with negative signals the booster stage needs a pnp emitter follower as well. Negative feedback comes from the final output. The 100-Ω resistors are to protect the transistors.

control on a bracket at the back—very handy for listening to odd things.

But we digress. If the diodes weren't in Fig. 140, the amplifier would not work for 0.6 V either side of 0 V; see Fig. 141. It turns out that a better way of doing the

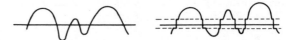

Fig. 141. A push-pull output stage like Fig. 140 is apt to suffer 'cross-over distortion' around 0 V. Diode biasing, as in Fig. 140, is apt to be inaccurate, particularly as temperature changes.

same voltage offset job is to use a V_{BE} multiplier circuit. (V_{BE} is engineers' shorthand for the 0.6 V

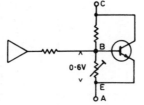

Fig. 142. A better biasing system: the 'V_BE multiplier'. See text for explanation.

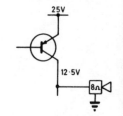

Fig. 143. Power dissipation in an output transistor: in this case 12.2 V × 1.56 A = 19.5 W.

between base and emitter); see Fig. 142. The theory is simple enough: the two resistors form a voltage divider, which divide the voltage CE in the ratio CB/BE. The voltage across BE has to be at 0.6 V. When V_{CB} gets too high, so does BE—this opens the transistor and dumps current from C to restore the status quo. The voltage across the whole, from C to E, can be made to vary in proportion by altering resistor BE. This makes it possible to adjust both transistors T_2 and T_3 so they turn on exactly at 0 V and so eliminate cross-over distortion.

So far, so good. We have accounted for T_2 and T_3—emitter followers which increase the power of the output. They might give us 0.5 W: to upset the family if not neighbours we need at least 10 W, and this is provided by the last stage, which uses bigger power transistors. These could be wired as emitter followers too, and are in most designs. Here they're upside down—the pnp device is at the top—and work as amplifiers just like the circuit in Fig. 6a. (It is most important to remember the difference between an amplifier, where the output comes from the collector and the output is *out of phase* with the input; and an emitter follower where it's in phase and there is no voltage gain, see p. 3). The extra resistors R_{28}–R_{33} give some negative feedback (p. 6) and generally prevent disasters.

The effect of the V_{BE} multiplier is to hold the output devices just open, so they draw a trickle of current even when there's no signal (about 20 mA is enough), and are ready to reproduce the slightest whisper, however small. But as they get hotter, so their V_{BE} falls at the rate of 2 mV/°C (this is standard for silicon devices and makes them useful thermometers), and so the V_{BE} multiplier turns them harder and harder on. They have no resistors to prevent inordinate consumption, so they draw more current, get hotter, draw more . . . kapow! This can be avoided by glueing the V_{BE} transistor to the heat sink of one of the output devices, so that its V_{BE} will fall in exactly the same way, so reducing the standing drive and preventing this unhappy fate, which is called *thermal runaway*. Heatsinks are one last essential for the circuit for the following reason. Suppose the top output transistor finds itself in the situation shown in Fig. 143—as it well might. The voltage on the speaker at this instant is 12.5 V. The speaker has an impedance of 8 Ω, so the current into it, through the transistor is 12.5/8A = 1.56 A. There is a voltage drop of 12.5 V across the transistor, and

1.56 A through it, so it is absorbing 12.5 V × 1.56 A = 19.5 W, which appears as heat, and if not radiated away, will melt the device. Thus we must mount the output transistors on elaborate fins to keep them cool and happy.

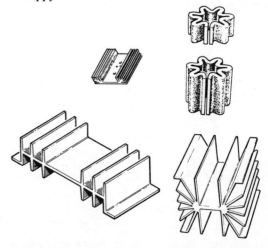

Fig. 144. Heat sinks: top right—clips for small metal-case transistors; others for bolting onto power transistors (see. Fig. 20).

A heatsink (see Fig. 144) is specified as needing to be so many °C above its surroundings to dissipate 1 W. For example, type TV4 gets rid of 0.06 W/°C. If we reckon that 70 °C is hot enough for a transistor, and that room temperature is 25 °C, then this sink will get rid of 2.6 W. In this case we have to get rid of 20 W, and therefore need a heat sink with an index of 2.25 °C/W.

Small transistors usually have insulated cases, can often be bolted direct to the case or chassis and get rid of enough heat that way. Larger ones need help. Since heat is generated at the collector, most power transistors have their cases and collectors in one piece to help heat to escape. Consequently the case usually has to be insulated from the chassis or heat sink. To this end mica washers are available and usually supplied with power devices. Heat flow will be improved by a smear of silicon grease. Larger devices are usually in T03 cases which need a special mica, plus insulating bushes for the bolts. (The plastic plug at the top of a ball point pen is just the right size: drill it out.)

The complete amplifier is shown at Fig. 145.

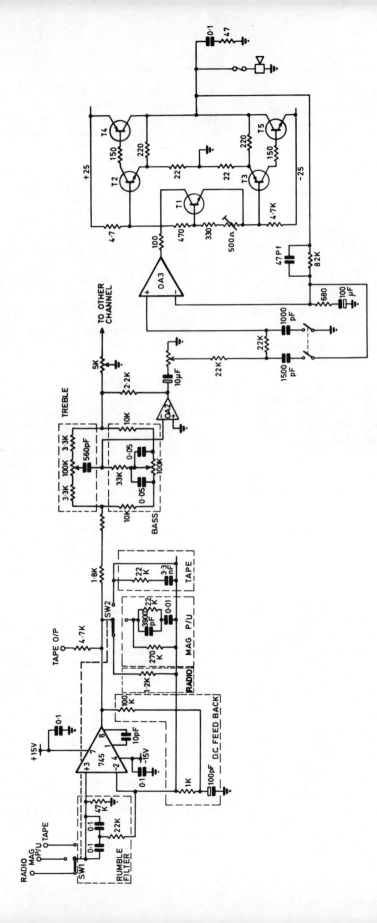

Fig. 145. The complete amplifier (reproduced by courtesy of Texas Instruments Ltd.).

'Hi-fi'—some reservations

Two of these amplifiers, connected together at X and Y, with two-gang pots on the volume and tone controls, make a perfectly adequate hi-fi stereo amplifier giving 30 W per channel with a considerable saving in cost over the purchase price of a ready made one.

Quality in audio reproduction demands quality in each link of the chain. The amplifier is the easiest to make acceptable. This design gives 0.1 per cent distortion between 30 Hz and 15 kHz—that is, if you feed in a pure sine wave at any frequency in the operating band, and filter that frequency from the output only 0.1 per cent of the input power will appear at other frequencies. To improve this to, say, 0.01 per cent would be very expensive and quite unnoticeable.

To get good music reproduction the things to spend money on are, in order of importance:

1 A good magnetic pick-up and an arm that presses it to the record with the right force. Change the needle often.
2 Good speakers. For living room listening, 'monitor' speakers of the sort used in broadcasting and recording control rooms are the best value for money. They are good without expensive flashiness.
3 A good turntable. But all it has to do is to turn the record round $33\frac{1}{3}$ times a minute. This is not hard.

If you are not deaf, and you are doing your listening in an ordinary sized room, you don't need more than 10 W–30 W of output power. (This figure depends rather on the efficiency of the speaker design. Reflex speakers make plenty of noise with 10 W, a small closed box speaker that has to be heavily damped to get a flat response might need 30 W.) Moreover, much of the trouble the designers of your gear have gone to to get perfectly flat frequency response from the pick-up, amplifier and speakers is wasted because of the resonances in the room. Take a room with the dimensions 8.65 m (10 ft) × 13.7 m (15 ft) × 8.2 m (9 ft). The 8.65 m (10 ft) dimension resonates at roughly 100 Hz with harmonics at 200, 300, 400, etc. The other two dimensions have their own fundamentals and harmonics. The corners are perfect reflectors and resonate to each other along the diagonals with another set of frequencies. The speaker has images in each of the four walls, ceiling and floor; its output beats at different frequencies with all six. The amount of soft furniture such as carpets and curtains, and the number of people in the room, makes a profound difference to the reverberation time. The result is a most peculiar frequency response that alters as you move about the room at any one time, and changes from day to day as people and things move in and out.

All this makes even mono 'hi-fi' something of a joke—though in fact you get used to the acoustics of a particular room and your brain removes the worst of the effects. Ordinary stereo using speakers, which aims at building up a three dimensional image of the original sound source by feeding each ear with a different signal is hardly likely to work because the signals are bounced off the walls like squash balls. I must confess that I can only just detect ordinary domestic stereo, and it adds nothing to my enjoyment of music. Stereo headphones, which make it possible for the recording engineer to reproduce the signals he wants unimpeded by room acoustics, are spectacular, but in the long run they are restrictive, antisocial and tiring.

It is unfortunate that the audio business has to peddle expensive gimmicks to survive, but at least one can arm oneself with a little relevant knowledge and look on their wilder claims with self-defensive cynicism. 'Ye shall know the truth, and the truth shall make ye free' says St John. Half the point of a book like this is to dispel illusions and combat humbug—a commodity which is extremely prevalent in all departments of the electronics industry.

MUSIC SYNTHESIS

A booming branch of audio electronics is the synthetic construction of music and electronic processing of signals originating from 'acoustic' instruments. Although it is easy enough to generate tones which are equal to the nominal frequency of musical notes, it turns out to be difficult to imitate the precise coloration of particular instruments. Still, on the other hand, synthesizers can produce effects which no conventional instrument can, and few pop records now are without them. A synthesizer essentially consists of a keyboard like a piano's but with less range—forty-nine or sixty-one notes are usual—covering four or five octaves. As each note is pressed a sine wave is generated of appropriate frequency—A above middle C, for instance, is 440 Hz. (In practice there are often three or more oscillators running at the same nominal frequency to give richness to the sound.) This note is then amplified or attenuated, has its waveform shaped, is modulated with other notes, and is finally mixed with other outputs and recorded on tape—or turned into sound waves through an amplifier and loudspeaker. The business has become quite a science of its own, so we can do no more here than outline the basic principles. For those who want to go deeper into it, there are several books and kits available, and it would probably be much more satisfactory to start that way than try to design one's own synthesizer from the ground up.

A voltage controlled sine wave oscillator like the circuit on p. 42 would be useful. Its output can be squared by clipping in a high-gain amplifier (p. 4), made triangular by integrating the square wave (p. 27), or saw tooth by integrating only on positive or negative waves; see Fig. 146.

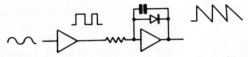

Fig. 146. Audio waveform processing, much used in pop music to make weird sounds. Here a sine wave is amplified to square and then integrated on half cycles to make a triangular waveform.

Tones often need shaping to imitate the dying away of a struck or bowed string. This can be done using a damped oscillator—one with just not enough positive feedback. Its output, rectified, gives an exponential curve; see Fig. 147. This exponential wave can be used

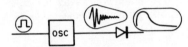

Fig. 147. Simulation of the die-away note of a string instrument. An oscillator with not quite enough positive feedback is set ringing by a pulse; the oscillations die away exponentially and are rectified to produce a decaying voltage to control an amplifier.

in a gain controlled amplifier (p. 15) to control the wanted tone. Moreover, one tone can modulate another, using gain control. The modulating tone can be sine wave, or shaped to produce a number of odd effects. A voice can be modulated in the same way. White noise is used to imitate wind, which can be generated by amplifying the output of a zener diode; see Fig. 148. An effect called 'glide' is produced by

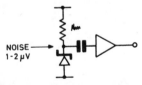

NOISE →
1-2 μV

Fig. 148. Current through a zener fluctuates randomly over a small range of voltages: the signal can be amplified to produce white noise. ('White' implies equal voltages at high and low frequencies. 'Pink' noise has the high frequencies cut out; 'Blue' noise the low. The colours are analogous with energy distribution in the visible spectrum.).

letting the control voltage drift up or down from one note to the next, so that the output sound swoops from one frequency to the next. Reverberation can be generated by having a microphone and loudspeaker in a small brick room, or by clamping them to a sheet of steel—which is more compact but less satisfactory. Echoes can be produced by re-recording with spaced out heads, and attenuating the signal between them; see Fig. 149.

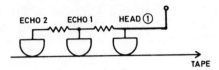

ECHO 2   ECHO 1   HEAD ①

TAPE

Fig. 149. Echo on tape with multiple heads.

Outputs of all these processes are mixed together using voltage adders and re-recorded to produce the final track. Since oscillators are expensive, it is usual for a synthesizer to have one or more master circuits, whose frequency is controlled by the note pressed. Either the key is connected to a resistance ladder, so it selects an appropriate voltage, or it generates a binary number which is later converted into an analogue voltage. At first sight it seems odd that only one note can be produced at a time, unlike conventional musical instruments which are capable of generating dozens. But this is no great handicap in practice since a piece of music can easily be built up by re-recording or 'over-dubbing'.

AUDIO OSCILLATORS

The *unijunction* is a specialized sort of FET whose two principal terminals—called, confusingly, Base 1 and Base 2, are joined by a bar of silicon. In the normal state this bar has a high impedance, but when the voltage on the third terminal—the emitter—rises above a critical fraction η—usually 0.6—of the voltage across the bases, the device fires. The inter-base resistance drops to a few tens of ohms, and the emitter impedance, which was extremely high, also drops. One can use a unijunction to make a crude voltage controlled relaxation oscillator which produces a ramp voltage at the emitter, a negative pulse at Base 1 and positive pulse at Base 2; see Fig. 150. V_1 must, of

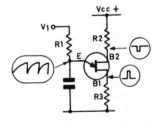

Vcc +

V_1 R1   R2   E   B2   B1   R3

Fig. 150. Unijunction oscillator.

course, be higher than $\eta \times V_{BB}$ otherwise the thing will never fire. If the base pulses aren't wanted, R_2 and R_3 can be left out. If voltage control isn't wanted, R_1 can go straight to V_{cc}. The frequency is roughly:

$$\frac{1}{R_1 \times C}$$

Another approach to a VCO uses a TTL quad NAND gate 7401; see Fig. 151. When A output goes

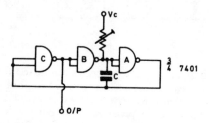

Fig. 151. Variable frequency oscillator using three TTL NAND gates.

high, it charges up the capacitor through its own impedance. When the capacitor is charged up, it allows C input to go high, B input goes low. A input goes high, A output goes low. Current injected from a control voltage through a 100-kΩ resistor at A input readily controls the frequency over a 30 per cent range. This will run up to 20 MHz and maybe beyond.

A COSMOS version

See Fig. 152. With $C = 1$ nF and $R_x = 0.4$ m MΩ the frequency was 14 kHz. $R_s = 800$ kΩ stabilizes the frequency against V_{cc} variations.

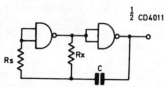

Fig. 152. Oscillator using two COSMOS NAND gates.

A voltage controlled version

See Fig. 153. When V_{cc} is 15 V, the frequency was 20 kHz with $V_a = 0$ V, and 41.6 kHz when $V_a = 15$ V. The whole circuit can be made using a CD 4007 IC which contains two complementary pairs and an

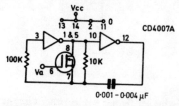

Fig. 153. Voltage controlled oscillator using the two complementary pairs and one buffer on a 4007 chip— with pin connections. This will run at up to 100 kHz. (Courtesy R.C.A.).

inverter (pins numbered). A Schmitt trigger, with negative feedback through R_1 is used to charge up C and start the amplifier switching the other way; see Fig. 154. If the hysteresis is low the period will be roughly $E = CR_1$.

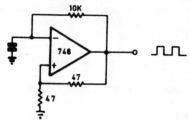

Fig. 154. Op-amp oscillator. Since the device switches from rail to rail, frequency compensation for the 748 is unnecessary.

The Wien bridge oscillator

The frequency can be varied by making the R_s a ganged pot. R_1 is usually a thermistor whose resistance reduces with current to stabilize the output. It can also be a FET acting as a resistor, biased by a rectified portion of the output. A quadrature oscillator is another type of oscillator, this time producing a sine and cosine output which have a 90° phase shift between them (90° = 'square' = 'quad'); see Fig. 155. The zeners stabilize the output.

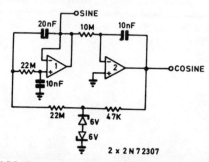

Fig. 155. Sine and cosine oscillator—use SN72307 or op-amps with FET input (reproduced by courtesy of Texas Instruments Ltd.).

Phase shifts

This brings us to an explanation of '90° phase shift'. One of the great simplifications of electronics is that every kind of varying waveform—music, singing, talking, the sound of marching feet or the wind in the grass—can be taken to be made up of sine waves of different amplitudes and frequencies. (This is mathematically correct, as Fourier showed with his Analysis.)* A sine wave looks like Fig. 156. This is a graph of

* For a good explanation, see: R. Feynman, *Lectures On Physics I* (New York, Addison-Wesley, 1963), pp. 50–52.

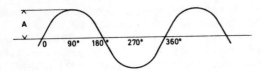

Fig. 156. Sine curve showing phase angle.

sin ϕ as ϕ goes from 0° to 360°. It repeats every 360° or 2π radians. A 90° phase shift simply means moving the whole wave forward or back; see Fig. 157. A 180° shift

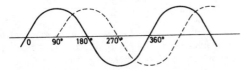

Fig. 157. Sine (solid) and cosine (dashed) curve with phase angles.

turns the whole thing upside down. A 270° shift forward is the same as a 90° shift backwards. And obviously, one can have any shift in between.

How to do it? Any frequency filter also alters phase (p. 113); see Fig. 158. Go back to the resistor and

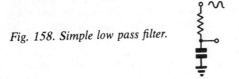

Fig. 158. Simple low pass filter.

capacitor stop-watch on p. 34. When we connected the top of the resistor to a voltage source V_s so that current started to flow into the capacitor, it took a certain amount of time before the voltage in the capacitor even reached 0.632 V. If we make V_s vary in a sinusoidal way, it's obvious that the peaks at the output are going to lag behind the peaks at the input (see Fig. 159) simply because there can't be a peak at

Fig. 159. Low pass filter showing phase difference of input and output.

the output until the capacitor has charged up, and that takes a certain amount of time. Of course, before it has fully charged, V_s is starting to go low, so it never gets fully charged up before it too has to start going low. The angle ϕ of the phase shift is given by: $\tan \phi = X_c/R$. Remembering that the reactance X_c, of the capacitor is $1/(2\pi f \times C)$:

$$\tan \phi \text{ becomes } \frac{1}{2\pi f \times R \times C}.$$

A single sideband selective shouter

It is a sad fact that much of electronics is solutions looking for problems, and the power of modern devices and techniques rather outweighs the ingenuity that is applied to them. This gadget, however, might prove interesting, and at any rate illustrates how the building blocks described in this last section can be used to solve a practical problem. (The same idea is to be found in US Patent 3398810 of 1968.)

The human ear is sensitive only to frequencies below about 15 kHz. Sounds above that range are supersonic. However, if we imagine two sound trains—one at, say 20 kHz and the other at 21 kHz, it is likely that they will be mixed in the ear and produce the sum and difference frequencies so that the owner of the ear will hear a 1 kHz tone. If we arrange that the difference of two supersonic tones is a voice signal, and project the two tones with directional loudspeakers so that they cross only where the person is that we want to talk to, we have a selective shouter. It might be very handy for telling magicians what card the straight man is holding up, or for briefing witnesses in court with failing memories who are wilting under cross examination. The possibilities are, if not endless, at least intriguing. However, it will only work if the voice signal on the 20 kHz carrier is single sideband. Then, mixing it again with the original carrier—or indeed any tone within 100 Hz or so of the carrier—will reproduce the original audio (plus a component at twice the carrier frequency which will be definitely inaudible and can be ignored).

Single and double sideband

This is as good a place as any to talk about sidebands, although they crop up most often in radio work (p. 53). The principle is simple. If you have one frequency A and mix it (multiply it by) another frequency B you get two frequencies out: $A + B$, $A - B$. So in our case, if A is 1 kHz, and B is 20 kHz, the result of simple mixing is two tones: 19 kHz and 21 kHz. They are called the 'lower' and 'upper' sidebands respectively, and the whole thing is called 'double sideband with carrier'. This is what emerges from an ordinary AM radio transmitter. The carrier of, say, 1 MHz has been mixed with an audio signal of, say, 2 kHz and produces two radio frequencies: 998 000 Hz and 1 002 000 Hz. They are so close together that they pass through the radio amplifiers as one, and because their amplitudes vary identically, a diode rectifier (p. 18) recovers identical audio signals from them.

The sums are quite simple: call the audio frequency A, and the carrier C. Then their amplitudes at any moment are $\sin(2\pi A \times t)$ and $\sin(2\pi C \times t)$ which can be multiplied together: $\sin(2\pi A \times t) \times \sin(2\pi C \times t)$.

This can be simplified using the formulae:

$$\sin(X+Y) = \sin X \times \cos Y + \cos X \times \sin Y$$

$$\sin(X-Y) = \sin X \times \cos Y - \cos X \times \sin Y.$$

Adding:

$$\sin(X+Y) + \sin(X-Y) = 2 \sin X \times \cos Y$$

So:

$$\sin A \times \cos B = \tfrac{1}{2}\sin(A+B) + \tfrac{1}{2}\sin(A-B)$$

and

$$\sin(2\pi A \times t) + \sin(2\pi C \times t)$$

$$= \tfrac{1}{2}\sin 2\pi((A+C) \times t) + \tfrac{1}{2}\sin 2\pi((A-C) \times t)$$

Hence the upper and lower sidebands which contain the sum and the difference frequency. Most of the time you don't have to do the trigonometry, but just add and subtract the frequencies each time you mix. However, in complicated systems there are tricky moments when a whole sideband gets inverted and this shows up in the trigonometry but not in the simple sums.

The snag is that the ear does not work like a diode. To recover the audio, we have to feed it with the carrier C as well and rely on further mixing within it. A further snag is that if you mix double sideband (DSB) with the carrier, even if it is exactly the right frequency and in phase with the original carrier, you get the audio out from each sideband—but opposite in phase—so it cancels out and you hear nothing. If you get the injected carrier frequency slightly wrong, or even out of phase a bit—as it may well be here owing to the geometry of the set up—you get a horrible scrambling noise. So to make the selective shouter work, we have to get rid of the carrier and one sideband, leaving $A+C$ (if we keep the USB). Then mixing with frequency C will indeed produce the audio. We can see this by working out the further sidebands:

$$C \times (A+C) = (A+C+C) + (A+C-C)$$

$$= (A+2C) + (A)$$

$A+2C$ will be around 40 kHz and quite inaudible, leaving A, which is what we wanted.

The shouter again

We therefore have to generate a single sideband audio signal on a carrier at 20 kHz. In principle there are three ways of generating an SSB signal or, in other words, removing the carrier and one sideband from an AM signal. Firstly, we get rid of the carrier in a balanced mixer (p. 48) and then filter off one sideband. This is difficult to do even at this low carrier frequency, because it means building a filter that passes, say, the upper sideband at the lowest voice frequency, 20 300 Hz, and reduces the other at 19 700 Hz just 600 Hz away—by a factor of at least

100. At radio frequencies it can be done using crystal filters (p. 80), but it isn't easy any time.

The second system is more elegant. The carrier and audio are each shifted 90° in phase (p. 43), mixed and added according to the scheme shown in Fig. 160. The upshot is that one of the sidebands is doubled and the other cancels out.

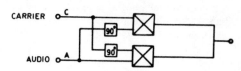

Fig. 160. Generation of single sideband by mixing twice with 90° phase shift. The circuit of 163 could be used to produce the audio shift. Or see Fig. 164.

The trigonometry is quite simple: We start with two frequencies $\sin a$ and $\sin c$ ($a = 2\pi ft$ where f_a is a frequency in Hz). We mix one, say $\sin a$, with the other shifted by 90°:

$$\sin a \times \cos c = \tfrac{1}{2}(\sin(a+c) + \sin(a+c))$$

We mix $\sin c$ with the other shifted 90°:

$$\sin c \times \cos a = \tfrac{1}{2}(\sin(a+c) - \sin(a-c))$$

Add these two together and we get $\sin(a+c)$, the upper sideband; subtract them and we have $\sin(a-c)$, the lower sideband. The snag, as we shall see, is in the phase shifting.

Since $\tan 90° = 0$ we can't generate this shift in one go with real capacitors and resistors. However, it's enough in principle to do two 45° shifts: $\tan 45° = 1$ which means that $R = X_c$; see Fig. 161. This is fine if

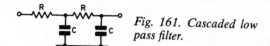

Fig. 161. Cascaded low pass filter.

we want to phase shift one frequency f, the critical frequency (p. 26) of the filter. We could use something like this for the carrier—though, as we shall see there are better methods—but for the voice, which ranges between 300 Hz and 2700 Hz just for communication quality, this simple network would be no good at all. If it was right at 300 Hz it would be wildly out at 2700 Hz and vice versa. Or, if we thought of using the integrator on p. 27, we'd get a 90° shift, but the amplitudes would alter so that there wouldn't be proper cancellation of the unwanted sideband.

This is one of those problems that only the professionals can solve, and then with some difficulty. The circuit shown in Fig. 162 is pinched from a complicated surround sound system due to Michael Gerzon (*Wireless World*, August 1977, p. 69). It produces two similar outputs 90° apart with unity gain. The resistors and capacitors should be 1 per cent accurate (except for the ones marked with an asterisk which can be 5 per

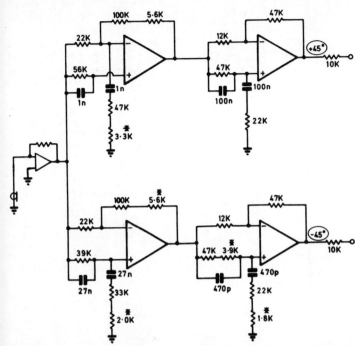

Fig. 162. Precision circuit to produce
90° phase shift over audio frequencies.

cent). It would be worth spending some money and doing it right since this circuit would just be acceptable for amateur band SSB since the outputs are within $\pm 1\frac{1}{3}$ per cent of a 90° phase shift over the range 30 Hz to 16 kHz. Restricted to the communications band of 300 Hz to 2.7 kHz it should do much better.

In some ways an easier method is to mix the audio A with a fairly high frequency M, about 500 kHz, and then shift that by 90°—or twice 45°. Since the ratio of 500 300 Hz to 503 000 is only 1 : 1.0054, a single 45° shift in each direction will do the trick with acceptable accuracy. The shifted frequencies can then be mixed back down to audio taking the phase shift with them; see Fig. 163.

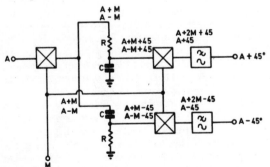

Fig. 163. Accurate 90° phase shift produced by mixing audio with a much higher frequency M, shifting that in simple RC networks, mixing down again, and filtering out 2M.

C is chosen so that $X_c = R$ at the average of the two extreme frequencies—501650 Hz. With 1 per cent components in the phase shifters, one would expect the unwanted sideband to be at least 37 dB down; with one resistor adjustable, it should be possible to do much better.

Until accurate balanced mixers became available as cheap ICs, such a roundabout method would be hardly worthwhile; now it may well be easier to go to these lengths than to build an accurate wideband phase shifter.

The 'third', or Barber Weaver, method[*] is a refinement of the second. Instead of trying to shift the whole audio band by 90° without changing its amplitude (p. 27) which is, in principle, impossible, and in practice difficult, the audio is mixed twice with a pilot tone P of about 1600 Hz which is shifted 45° forwards and backwards. The upper sideband is removed in a multi section section audio filter and the two resulting lower bands are mixed again with the carrier, shifted 45° in the same way; see Fig. 164.

The final cancellation depends on the fact that $A - P - C - 90°$ is the same frequency as $A - P - C + 90°$ but always 180° out of phase with it, which means the two waves are always equal and opposite and so obliterate each other. The effective carrier frequency here is, of course, $C + P$. The proper working of the circuit depends on good cancellations, and that depends on the mixers having identical gains and the filters having identical roll-offs. This is not so easy. It would be nice if we could use a single filter switched between the two

* See *Radio Communication Handbook* (London, RSGB, 1976), pp. 6–82.

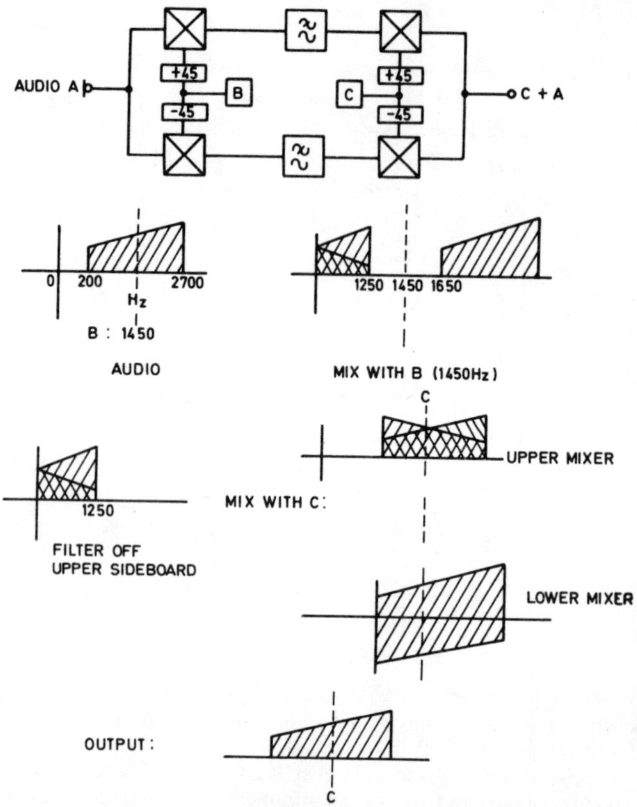

Fig. 164. Phase shifting a fixed frequency is easier than shifting a variable one: the Barber Weaver method of generating SSB using pilot P, and carrier C, frequencies each shifted plus and minus 45°. However, the filters have to be very steep.

paths (see Fig. 165), so that SW1 and SW3 are on together while SW2 and SW4 are off and vice versa. Obviously this switching would have to be done at some high frequency D – say 30 kHz—so as not to interfere with the audio. The snag is that the filter, which cuts off at around 1.5 kHz, will 'see' a 30 kHz frequency and will pass just the two audio components added. In other words, a switch is a mixer and its output is, as you would expect, D + the input frequency, D – the input frequency.

In electronics, as in life, you get nothing for nothing and the filters which have to pass 1250 Hz and reduce 1650 Hz by at least 100 are not really much easier than the 90° phase shifter for the whole audio band that we looked at for method 2. And you need two of them.

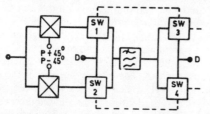

Fig. 165. The effect of using one filter in Fig. 164 and switching the two audio signals into it alternately. See text.

Still, Fig. 166 is a circuit which will do the trick. (The techniques necessary for designing multi-stage audio filters like this are explained in *Rapid Practical Designs of Active Filters* by Johnson and Hilburn, Wiley, 1975.) So much for the audio. Now to shift the carrier. The easiest way to do this is by using digital techniques (see p. 85 et seq.).

Suppose we start with an 80 kHz square wave A. It won't necessarily be absolutely square—that is the ups and downs are exactly the same length, so we'll divide it by 2 in a circuit that switches alternately high and low on positive going voltages (p. 90); see Fig. 167. This gives an accurate square wave B, because each up and down is the length of a complete cycle of the 80 kHz wave. Invert the 40 kHz wave C and then divide the original and inverted versions again by 2: D and E. Both D and E are 20 kHz, but D leads E by a quarter of a cycle or 90°. The block diagram is shown in Fig. 168. The only source of inaccuracy is *propagation delay* in the inverter (which will make the lower output lag the upper by slightly more than 90°, see p. 88). It will be good enough if the error is no more than 0.6° which makes the unwanted sideband sine 0.6° = 1 per cent or less of the wanted one. The period of a 20 kHz wave is 50 μs; 0.6°/360° of it is 83 ns. A COSMOS B (e.g. 4069) gate has a propagation delay of 30 ns, so we can use this useful logic family.

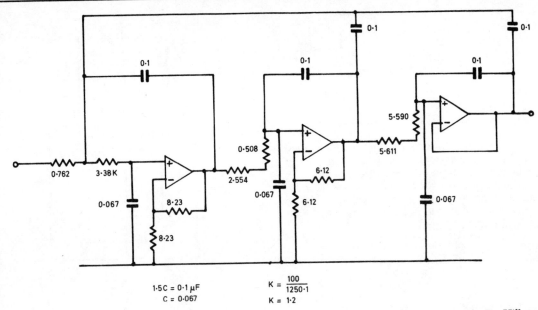

$$1 \cdot 5C = 0 \cdot 1 \,\mu F$$
$$C = 0 \cdot 067$$

$$K = \frac{100}{1250 \cdot 1}$$
$$K = 1 \cdot 2$$

Fig. 166. An audio filter suitable for Fig. 164: cut-off frequency 1250 Hz. Designed using: Johnson, D., Hilburn, J., Rapid Practical Design of Active Filters (New York, Wiley, 1975).

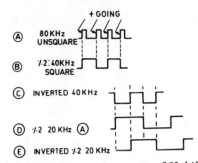

Fig. 167. Using ÷2's to make a square, 90° shifted wave from an unsquare one: A, 80 kHz unsquare; B, divided by 2 it is 40 kHz square; C is B inverted; D is B divided by 2; E is C divided by 2. D and E are 20 kHz 90° shifted.

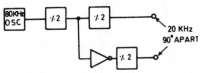

Fig. 168. Block diagram of circuit to realize Fig. 167. Use TTL or CMOS according to speed needed.

Mixing

All that remains for the SSB generator is to mix the audio and carrier together. As we have already noticed, mixing two frequencies means multiplying the size of one at each instant by the size of the other. The easiest way to do this is in an amplifier whose input is one frequency and whose gain is controlled by the other. The cascode was an example of this (p. 13). Its gain was proportional to the current through the two transistors, and that was controlled by the voltage on the bases. We could alter this by varying the 10-kΩ resistors, but it could just as well have been done by putting a substantial signal on the upper base; see Fig. 169. You can get cascode IGFETs, two transistors in one package which are particularly good at this at high frequencies (p. 17).

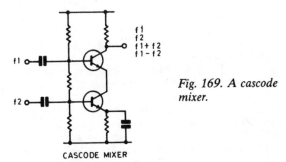

Fig. 169. A cascode mixer.

You can mix two signals in one transistor; see Fig. 170. Again, the gain of the thing is proportional to the current through it and that is controlled by the voltage across the emitter resistor, which we alter by applying f_2. Notice that the emitter bypass capacitor (p. 5) is absent—otherwise it would just short f_2 to ground.

The drawback to both these circuits in their jumbled outputs which contain f_1, f_2, f_1+f_2 and f_1-f_2.

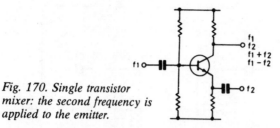

Fig. 170. Single transistor mixer: the second frequency is applied to the emitter.

However, a balanced mixer, based on the long-tailed pair (p. 23) will cancel out f_1 because it appears as + at one collector and − at the other. f_2 will appear, though, because it affects both collectors equally; see Fig. 171. (Remember that even though the signal is applied to only one base of a long tail pair, it is transferred inverted to the other base.)

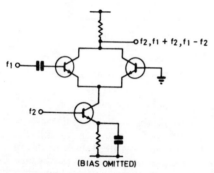

Fig. 171. A long tail pair mixer (bias omitted).

Double balanced mixer

By folding two of these together in a 'double balanced' mixer, we can also eliminate f_2. Fig. 172 is Texas Instruments' SN76514, a particularly handy IC because all the resistors are built in. It can be run from a single ended supply of 15 V max. (connect pin 4 to pin 12 to set up the bias voltage) or from split supplies (in which case connect pin 4 to ground). Two external components are needed; these are dc coupling capacitors at pins 10 and 9, which must have low impedances at RF and LO respectively. (This means that if one uses it to mix two audio frequencies, then the decoupling capacitors must be much larger than if one were mixing two radio frequencies.) If they are to pass audio, they should be tantalums with low leakage so as not to upset the bias voltages. The input impedances are 600 Ω for RF and 50 Ω for LO. The best results are got with about 200 mV input at pin 5. An account is given in *Semiconductor Circuit Design III*, pp. 113–25. Mullard have a similar type of device, TCA240, Plessey have the SL1640C etc., RCA have matching double long tailed pairs in a single IC which just need external resistors.

To see how the circuit works (Fig. 173), imagine + inputs at both RF and LO. Because of the long tail pair

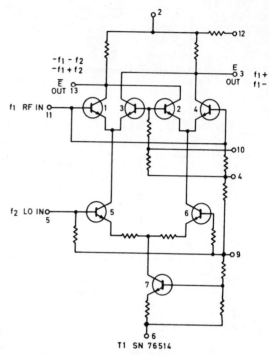

Fig. 172. A double balanced long tail pair mixer: the SN76514 by Texas Instruments.

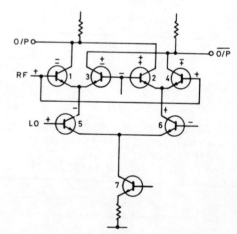

Fig. 173. How the circuit in Fig. 172 cancels out signal and carrier. See text.

operation, − inputs appear at bases 2, 3 and 6, + outputs appear at collectors 2, 3 and 6, − outputs at collectors 1, 4 and 5. The outputs on the two lower transistors 5 and 6 are transferred direct to the outputs of the upper transistors so that collectors 1 and 2, which are connected together, have −RF, −LO and +RF, and +LO respectively, which also cancel out, leaving only the difference products (not shown) upright and inverted on the two outputs. Transistor 7 is wired as a constant current sink to make the long tail pairs work properly. Because all the transistors are made at the same time on the same chip of silicon they can be accurately matched, so that these cancellations actually do happen. It would be possible, but difficult, to build such a circuit from individual components.

For the selective shouter we need two such mixers whose outputs, when added, should produce the SSB signal. Generation of SSB for radio is not much different, except that one would use a higher carrier—say 0.53 MHz instead of 20 kHz. Once the SSB signal is established on a 500 kHz carrier, it can be shifted by mixing again to any desired frequency. Naturally two sidebands will again be produced, but they will be 2×0.5 MHz apart, instead of the 600 Hz of the original problem, so it will be easy to get rid of the unwanted one. We also need a microphone preamplifier to deliver a reasonable signal to the phase shifter; see Fig. 174. The microphone here could be an

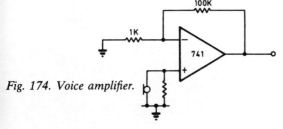

Fig. 174. Voice amplifier.

ordinary telephone earpiece—a robust and useful magnetic device with an impedance of about 2000 Ω. (Loudspeakers operate as microphones and vice versa, so beware of quiet PA systems. And a simple surveillance modification to a telephone uses the earpiece as a microphone which operates even when the receiver is on the hook.)

To get the best use out of the limited frequency spectrum in radio SSB, it is important to minimize alterations in loudness in the voice signal. Transmitters therefore use gain controlled amplifiers, or voice

compressors (p. 27), or 'VOGADS' (Voice Operated Gain Adjusting Device). The Plessey 1626C gives about 80 mV of output whether the input is a shout or a whisper. It also cuts off the unwanted parts of the voice spectrum below 300 Hz and above 2700 Hz.

After the phase shifter, we need a power amplifier. One channel of the stereo amplifier, using the 'radio' input, would do—with the tone controls set to treble boost. Or, if one were building specially, just from the gain control on.

Lastly, we need a directional speaker. It is a basic law of radiation—and this applies to radio and radar as much as to audio—that to get a narrow beam you need a large aperture aerial (or, in this case loudspeaker).

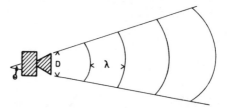

Fig. 175. The spread of a beam of sound from a loudspeaker is given by $\sin \theta = \lambda/D$.

The spread of the beam in radians (see Fig. 175) is roughly λ/D, where λ is the wavelength and D the aperture of the emitter. In degrees:

$$= \frac{360}{2\pi} \times \frac{\lambda}{D}$$

Suppose we want the beam to be 1 yard (0.91 m) wide at a distance of 30 yards (27.42 m). The spread in radians (for yards) is therefore $1/30 = 0.0333$. The wavelength in air of a 20 kHz wave is roughly 0.6 in. (15.2 mm), so we have $0.6/D = 0.0333$ or $D = 18$ in. (45.72 cm). A speaker this wide would be too massive to radiate 20 kHz, so we need a synthetic aperture using two or more tweeters,* fed in phase, and

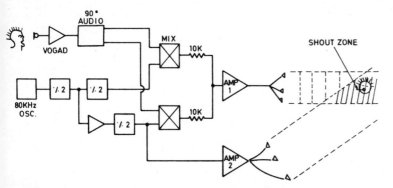

Fig. 176. Block diagram of the Selective Shouter.

* Radio astronomers do the same trick in reverse: using many small aerials spread out over large areas to get a narrow angular resolution.

arranged 18 in. (45.72 cm) apart. The limit to how many we can have is set by the output impedance of the amplifier which is 1 Ω. This is equivalent to eight of the 8 Ω speakers in parallel, or 9 times as many of the little 70-Ω speakers.

The feed wires need to be the same lengths to preserve the same phase. We need two such power amplifiers and arrays, one for the SSB signal, and one for the pure tone. The final system is shown in Fig. 176. All this assumes that the ear will act as a mixer. And there is the possibility that 20 kHz in large doses might damage it. I take no responsibility for any of that.

Part II: Radio

INTRODUCTION TO PART II

Since radio goes anywhere, it makes the world a village hall. Given the will, every one of the world's billion people could speak at once—a black whispering gallery rocking with the shouts of multitudes. So the useful radio spectrum is controlled in great detail by governments following the rules worked out by the International Telecommunications Union at Geneva, founded in 1865, and an unusually successful example of international co-operation. It controls the radio spectrum from 10 kHz to 275 GHz (1 GHz is a thousand million cycles a second)—in terms of wavelength this is the range from 3000 m, or a mile and a half, to 1 mm.

This spectrum is divided into eight bands, ranging from Very Low Frequency (VLF) to Extra High Frequency (EHF). Each band covers a decade of frequency or wavelength, and ranges from 3 to 30 of whatever it is in Hz. Thus the HF (short wave) band stretches from 3 MHz to 30 MHz. This particular frequency band corresponds to an important physical peculiarity which we will come to in a minute, which forces the rest of the spectrum to arrange itself round about. But the 3 to 30 accident is another happy, though trivial one, because the speed of light is 3.10^8 m/s, and so such a band of frequencies corresponds to a decade of wavelengths from 100 to 10. The bands vary widely in their uses and naturally their applications reflect this, though compounded with a good deal of historical accident. The basic differences between them lie in their modes of propagation, with the complication that high frequencies can carry much more information than low ones.

The low frequency waves are propagated either by ground wave, or in the duct between the earth and layers of the upper atmosphere. VLF runs from 3 kHz (the part of the band below 10 kHz is not used at the moment though the USN is experimenting with very low frequencies using buried aerials tens of miles long in an attempt to find a totally reliable way of communicating with Polaris submarines) to 30 kHz. Before the first war it offered the only vehicle for round the world communications. It needs vast aerials, so big that the world's VLF stations are famous objects in their own sphere, and are some of the largest manmade structures. There is a VLF station at *Rugby* which transmits an extremely accurate time signal for laboratories as well as command signals for the Royal Navy's *Polaris* submarines, *Criggion* on the Welsh borders—built during the war to give Churchill and Roosevelt a scrambled telephone link (German intelligence was able to read their traffic with little trouble), and *Anthorn* near Carlisle, used to relay radar warnings of missile attack from *Fylingdales* to the US air defence HQ at Colorado Springs. In America there are transmitters at *Jim Creek* in Maine, in Hawaii, and at *Boulder*, Colorado. Current interest in VLF is almost entirely military because these frequencies penetrate up to 30' of water and so allow communication with submarines which do not have to surface an aerial, and because they are relatively unaffected by nuclear bursts in the upper atmosphere—which tend to mess up HF communications. The Americans have a worldwide hyperbolic navigation system (mainly for their *Polaris* boats), which works at VLF and is called *Omega*. Generally speaking, in times of nuclear strife, any VLF station is likely to be high on the opposition's target list and is not therefore a good thing to be neighbours with. Propagation of VLF is so regular that each transmitter has its pole on the opposite side of the globe, where the waves come together again in phase. *Rugby's* pole is south of New Zealand.

The low and medium frequencies run from 30 kHz to 3 MHz, and are the ranges in which radio first developed commercially. Consequently there is a rare hotch-potch of uses in these bands, not all of which one would retain if the whole thing were being started again. Unfortunately, however, radio bands preserve themselves just as street lines do in old cities: new equipment is introduced piecemeal into new slots. So, although most national broadcasting networks would like to move into VHF, they are tied down by the millions of MW receivers there are in the world. These frequencies give daytime ranges of 100 miles, and at night are reflected erratically by the ionosphere over distances up to 1000 miles. This is why the MW band is so crowded at night. This band has most national broadcasting networks (more than half the stations

TABLE 2

Name	Frequency, f	Wavelength, λ (m)	Propagation	Range	Purpose
ULF	<3 kHz	>10^5	ground wave	worldwide	strategic command
VLF	3–30 kHz	10^5–10^4	ground wave	up to worldwide	strategic command, long range navigation, time signals
LF	30–300 kHz	10^4–10^3	ground wave	1000 km	navigation, broadcasting
MF	300 kHz–3 MHz	10^3–10^2	ground wave some reflection from ionosphere	100–1000 km	broadcasting, fishband, navigation
HF	3–39 MHz	10^2–10^1	reflection from ionosphere, some ground wave	10 000 km–100 km	sound broadcasting, long range point-to-point communication for fixed and mobile users, OTH radar
VHF	30–300 MHz	10^1–10^{-1}	Line of sight, penetrates ionosphere	5–100 km	broadcasting, sound and TV; short range mobile users—air land and sea, air navigation aids, some satellite communication
UHF	300 MHz–3 GHz	10^{-1}–10^{-2}	line of sight, penetrates ionosphere	5–100 km	same as for VHF
SHF	3–30 GHz	10^{-2}–10^{-3}	line of sight, penetrates ionosphere	30 km line of sight microwave links—10^6+ km in space	microwave links, radar, deep space communication, radio astronomy
EHF	30 GHz+	<10^{-3}	line of sight, penetrates ionosphere	same as for SHF	same as for SHF

Note: $\lambda = 300/f(\text{MHz})$ m.

operating on pirated frequencies), long range navigation aids such as Decca, Loran and Consol, and umpteen ship and aircraft radio beacons. Ideally the band is best suited to coastal navigation and communication. Local marine radio—the 'fishband'—stretches from 1.8 MHz to 4 MHz.

The HF band, from 3 MHz to 30 MHz, is the traditional jewel of the spectrum, but now beginning to look a little antique. Discarded contemptuously to the amateurs by the American legislation of 1912 as being of no use to anyone, they rapidly proved it to be the most useful of all. The point is that these frequencies are refracted downwards by charged layers in the ionosphere and so hop round the world bouncing alternately off land and sky. With patience you can raise New Zealand on 5 W, but regular working is much more difficult. Ship's radio officers in the Indian Ocean often spend two days clacking away with their morse keys and 1.5 KW to raise Britain's central station for the Merchant Navy at Portishead.

Communication in this band is more of an art than a science, for the maximum usable frequency (MUF), that is the one that gives the strongest signal between two points for the least transmitter power, varies from hour to hour, day to day, and year to year, as well as with one's position on the globe.

Demand for HF communication is now such that channel spacing is down to 2.5 kHz, getting near the minimum for voice. That gives 10 800 speech channels in the band which is not much for the whole world, particularly since any point-to-point link will have to be assigned three or five frequencies so it can keep within the maximum usable frequency curve during its many variations. But the number of channels is multiplied by crafty juggling: fixed transmitters and receivers have highly directional aerials so that they may give gain in the chosen direction and less everywhere else. It is then possible to assign the same frequency to two links pointing in different directions on opposite sides of the world. HF stations tend to be large, expensive and complicated, with computer control and automatic monitoring of telephone or voice quality and automatic frequency changes according to programmes prepared months ahead.

There have been many detailed improvements in HF technique in recent years; multiplexing several voice and telegraph channels together saves bandwidth while more accurate frequency standards, and frequency synthesis techniques keep transmitters on tune. Single sideband transmission too, though more expensive, greatly reduces bandwidth at both ends (p. 58). The permitted error in a high power transmitter is now 15 Hz in 1 MHz—just about equal to the average channel spacing over most of the HF band.

Wideband cables and satellites have taken a great deal of point-to-point work off the HF band, but there are always more applicants than there is room, and a good deal of unseemly jostling and piracy. For instance, the inland British monitoring service, run by the Ministry of Posts and Telecommunications, deals with 100 complaints of interference a month.

The cold war still goes on in the HF band: one use, very popular with governments, is international broadcasting. Disguise it how you will, the result is propaganda, and the unwary Briton who is caught by the BBC's overseas service is likely to suffer a nasty jolt. The plummy, moustached voices, the dignified understatement, and, to the critical mind, the reckless slanting of the news in favour of Government views, flings one back into the jingoistic dream world of wartime newsreels. Worldwide, there are some eighty external broadcasting stations operating, many of them in the HF band beamed to some other victim corner of the world. Voice of America is a huge organization, aimed mainly at Russia and her satellites. The British Broadcasting Corporation (BBC) has a chain of transmitters through the middle and far east. It is interesting that one of the more powerful transmitters in Britain is the Foreign Office's Aspidistra station at Crowborough in Sussex, built during the war for subversion of German troops (see Sefton Delmer's, *Black Boomerang*). Aspidistra would pretend to be a German army pirate station, broadcasting cheering items to front line troops like: 'The smallpox epidemic among children in the homeland has now been contained due to the heroic efforts of German doctors and nurses. The death rate last week was only 20 per cent'.

Although radio has been around for half a century or more,—and vast sums have been spent on it, and many clever people have made it their life's work, and arguably the last war was won by supremacy in the aether—there is still much to be known, even in the much exploited HF band. The British, Americans and Russians have been experimenting for some years with HF radars that detect rockets and aircraft thousands of miles away, far over the horizon. An early OTH (over the horizon) radar was installed at Orfordness in the late 1960s to watch the Russian rocket launching site at Plesetsk. It was so powerful that radiation hazard monitors were installed on the site, no-one was allowed outside sheltered buildings while the set was transmitting, and aircraft were forbidden to come nearer than 4 miles. It was closed in the mid 1970s. The Americans have sets in Cyprus and Japan to watch Russian and Chinese missile tests in the desert heart of Asia. The USAF is phasing out its system of early warning radars along its coast and the DEW line across Canada, and is replacing them with far fewer of these immensely long-range stations, supplemented by Airborne Warning and Control (AWAC) aircraft, which carry powerful centimetric radars.

Although textbooks tell us that HF signals are propagated by bouncing from earth to ionosphere, there are other less explored modes. Sometimes signals get trapped in a duct, hurtle right round the world and come back with a loss of only 6 dB. There is a low layer technique, again explored by the Americans, which offers secure communications in the D layer about 25 miles up: the signals are launched and recovered from highflying balloons. During the Korean war the military found that if they hurled enough power at the ionosphere a little would be scattered forward to be heard 800 miles further on, whatever the state of the ionosphere. So these systems used enormous aerials and megawatts of power. The frequencies are still allocated around 39 MHz but little used.

Above the HF band is VHF, first regulated by the Cairo conference of 1938. Here the band planning is more sane though there are occasional bizarre conjunctions like the police and fire services in Britain on the same band as VHF broadcasting, so that many transistor radios can listen to their messages. A lot of this band is taken up with television because the amount of information in a TV picture needs at least 6 MHz bandwidth to carry it. If TV were transmitted at the lowest possible frequency, the signal would vary from 0 Hz to 6 MHz, which would be impossibly difficult for the receiver, and would mess up the useful radio bands below HF. So, since the Q of a practical receiver is about 7, it follows that the minimum carrier for TV is $7 \times 6 = 42$ MHz, and the channels follow at roughly 8-MHz spacing, allowing for a sound carrier and guard bands between them, up to 800 MHz or so, in the UHF band. At these frequencies propagation is essentially line-of-sight with less bending and more shadows towards the top of the band. The British Independent Broadcasting Authority, for example, in replacing its forty-seven VHF stations, had to build 500 odd at UHF to get the same coverage. The band is much used for mobile links—police, radio taxis, aircraft, the military; a recent estimate put the number of users in the UK at 100 000, and in the USA it is perhaps 10 000 000. The Home Office has constructed and operates an elaborate network of VHF communications which embraces all the emergency and local authority services, with gas, electricity and water, and links them if necessary to secret underground headquarters for use in time of revolution or nuclear war.*

Although propagation at VHF and above is essentially line-of-sight, the ability of the ionosphere to reflect radio waves does not vanish suddenly as frequency increases. On about two days in 100 temperature inversions act as waveguides, and American police messages come booming out of TV sets tuned to BBC1 in Britain. UK amateurs working on 70 and 144 MHz bounce their signals off the aurorae, clouds of sporadic E and meteor trails, to get contacts as far away as Scandinavia and southern Europe.

Functionally, VHF and UHF are much the same until one reaches about 800 MHz. At this point the technology starts to change. Up to now the wavelengths have been much larger than the components used, and but for change of component values, a circuit working at VLF is much the same as one at UHF. However, above this frequency circuits are etched out of copper clad boards or built of pipe. Transistors and valves begin to run out of gain at SHF, so signals have to be generated by magnetrons, klytsrons or bulk-effect semiconductor devices and amplified by travelling wave tubes. It becomes difficult to receive amplitude or phase modulated radio signals and instead innumerable forms of pulse coding are used.

At 2 GHz there is a final brute force fling at long distance communication with scatter from the troposphere, a low layer in the atmosphere. If enough power is shot at the horizon some is scattered forward in this layer and comes to earth at the next horizon, 800 km further on (see Fig. 177). There are a number of these stations around the country: four 20-m dishes in pairs, back-to-back. In Europe most of them are part of the NATO link ACE HIGH from Iceland to Turkey.

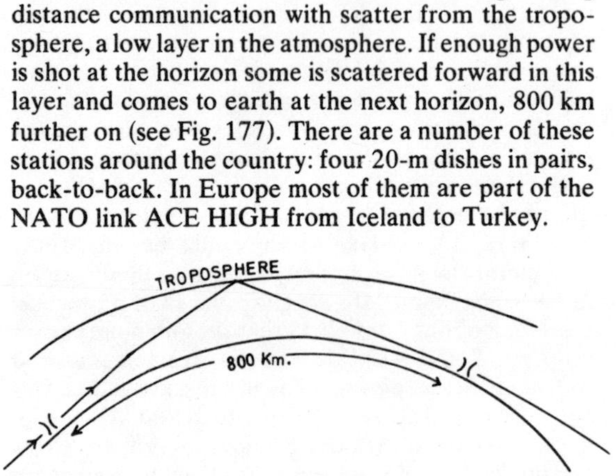

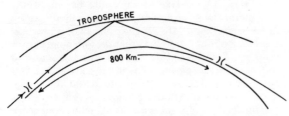

Fig. 177. Bouncing signals off the troposphere for long distance communication.

Above this band lie Super High Frequency: 3 GHz to 30 GHz, and Extra High, from 30 GHz to 300 GHz. Band planning is even more rational, and shared between satellites, microwave links on the ground and radars. 'Line-of-sight' at these frequencies means line-of-sight, and a screen of bushes is enough to blow things, so aerials are highly directional and there are no all-round transmitters as there are at VHF and UHF. Radars have their own bands, but satellites and microwave links have to share. This presents surprisingly difficult problems because although signals are highly directional, those used upwards to satellites are very powerful, and odd reflections getting into microwave receivers could cause much trouble. Goonhilly, the first UK satellite station, was sited at the far end of Cornwall not to be nearer America, but so it could not look down any microwave horns in the British chains—operated by the Post Office for the RAF and government, by the USAF, by civilian Air Traffic Control, and by the gas and electricity boards. But, as the aerials at Goonhilly swing in their arcs from east to west through south, they hose high power signals over the Netherlands, France and Ireland. Consequently such stations have to be laid out so they do not point to Goonhilly, and those that look near it have to work on different frequencies. Similarly, microwave stations should not look at satellites as they go down over the horizon.

There have been great advances in the numbers and sophistication of radars, mostly made by the military, though the advances in technique have not so much been in the radio department, which is relatively easy, as in signal processing and in manipulating the beams. One major development has been the replacement of aerials that scan slowly and mechanically, by multitudes of fixed dipoles whose drives are phase controlled by electronic circuits to produce a beam that can be steered extremely quickly.

The principle of phase shift steering is simple enough, see Fig. 178. Imagine two vertical dipoles

Fig. 178. Steering a radio beam from two aerials by altering the phase difference between them.

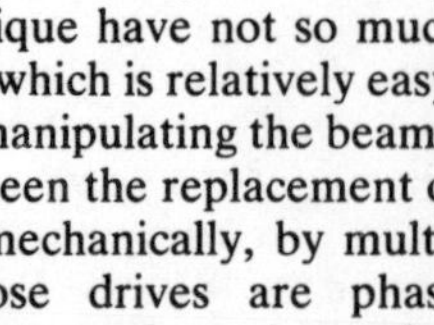

mounted d apart, side by side. If they are fed with carrier waves of length λ, Θ out of phase; then the signals will tend to cancel out in the ahead direction, and reinforce each other off to one side at an angle where the difference in path length from each dipole to a distant target is $(\Theta \times \lambda)/2\pi$.

From the geometry of the plan view (see Fig. 179):

$$d \times \cos \Phi = \frac{\Theta \times \lambda}{2\pi} \quad \text{and} \quad \Theta = \frac{2\pi d \times \cos \Phi}{\lambda}$$

This is the phase shift necessary to steer the beam at an angle Φ. Similarly, the beam can be steered vertically by phase shifts between the dipoles in columns. Since

* Peter Laurie, *Beneath the City Streets* (London, Granada, 1979).

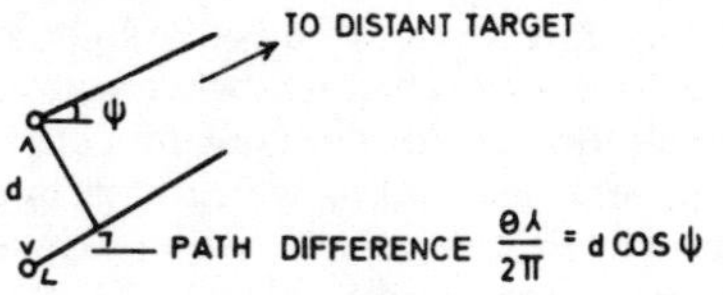

Fig. 179. A plan view of Fig. 178.

the phase shifting is done by electronic circuits, it can be very fast. The radar can be connected to a computer which can use the beam either to search large volumes of space, or to track individual targets with great accuracy.

Radars and their computers for modern aircraft cost as much or more than the airframe. A further advantage of phase scanning is that it does away with vulnerable rotating aerials: the USAF's AN/FPS85 (a second prototype, for the first was burnt out within a short time of start-up) which surveys Cuba from the Gulf Coast, is a solid concrete block that stands nearly 100 ft (30 m) high and has embedded in its face some 5000 transmit and 40 000 receive aerials.

Electronic warfare and intelligence gathering is a very big business. America's National Security Agency employs several thousand people on little else. The British Army has three regiments and a large civilian organization devoted entirely to the work. There are now many odd shaped planes in commission whose sole job is analysis and neutralization, if necessary, of energy transmitters. There are complicated airborne computers, like one recently announced by Loral in America, which weighs about 22 lbs (10 kg), can monitor 250 000 radar pulses a second, sorting them out by frequency, direction of arrival and repetition rate into the radars that generate them. It compares these characteristics with a memory store of the characteristics of enemy radars, and displays their positions and functions—friendly or enemy, early warning, anti-aircraft gun control, missile control, etc—evaluates the threat each one presents, identifies the most dangerous, and displays the frequency necessary to jam it. The new American B1 bomber exploits this by using banks of phase-steered transmitters to aim beams of jamming at enemy radars, timing and pointing them to interfere with each radar just at the moment it expects to get a pulse reflected from the bomber. At other times it deals with other radars. In this way far more radars can be jammed than if the aircraft just radiated continuous power on the frequency appropriate to a radar. Jamming, indeed, is another big business, and so too are methods for defeating it—broadband transmissions that have to be countered with power-consuming broadband jammers, frequency jittering radars, signals disguised as noise.

Even on the domestic front, governments are vitally interested in radio. The right to speak direct to almost every citizen is jealously guarded, disguised in quiet times by friendly disc jockeys, but in crisis, a basic tool of government. The official history of British Civil Defence attributes the collapse of the 1926 General Strike to the Government's ability to speak by radio straight to the voter. Hitler believed that his rise to power was made possible by better use of radio than the opposition. It is significant that every radio and television broadcast in the UK passes physically through the hands of the Post Office at some stage between the studio and the transmitter. Illegal transmissions are quickly tracked down with the help of a chain of Post Office DF stations round the country and suppressed. In case of nuclear war or revolution, the BBC has an elaborate system of diversified transmitters linked by protected landlines, with an underground emergency headquarters at Evesham, so that it can always keep control of the air. Unlike Prague, there need not be tanks outside the radio station.*

Looked at from one point of view, the radio spectrum is a natural resource like the wind, the sea, the heat of the sun, and there is no fundamental reason why it should remain the monopoly of governmments. Regulation is necessary to prevent chaos, but there are many who feel that more use could be allowed to the ordinary citizen.

There are amateur bands at 1.8 MHz, 3.8 MHz, 7.1 MHz, 14.35 MHz, 21 MHz, 29 MHz, 144 MHz and 440 MHz which can be used by those who pass quite a stiff examination in electronics and, in the lower frequencies, morse code.† But there could be more use yet, and in America there has for long been a citizens band at 29 MHz which anyone may use on payment of a nominal fee.

There are many good things about such a system—it provides a link between all those who can afford the reasonably priced set with a range of some 5 to 10 miles. Motorists use it to chat away the idle hours, pass on weather and report accidents. It is said to have eliminated multiple fog pile ups on American motorways. It warns of speed traps—which keeps speeds down and so achieves the objective of the police—and calls for assistance. People who use the wilds—the sea or the mountains—can call for help or (almost equally useful) report that help is not needed. Small businesses use it instead of the more expensive dedicated radiotelephone service. In Germany and America there are CB clubs with their own repeater stations that extend the coverage over 50 miles or more.

The bad things are that the American frequency is, at 29 MHz, just within the HF band and therefore can bounce off the ionosphere to disrupt communications thousands of miles away. This is aggravated by

* P. Laurie, op cit.
† For details contact Radio Society of Great Britain (RSGB) or in the US: Amateur Radio Relay League.

congestion in America, and the consequent use of huge strap-on amplifiers to give up to 1000 W of power so their owners can cut through other people's calls. This is now outlawed by the FCC, but it remains to be seen how a million users can be restrained. It is also bad that US CB is amplitude modulated, and its harmonics fall in the TV bands, so even modest nearby CB signals play havoc with TV.

RADIO: HOW IT WORKS

The whole mysterious and interesting business of radio depends on two simple physical effects.

The first explains how it is propagated over such large distances. Imagine an electron in a vertical wire. It radiates electrical lines of force, like a hedgehog; see Fig. 180. These lines of force extend to infinity—or the

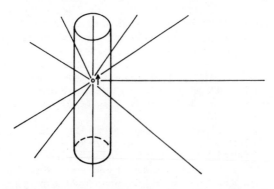

Fig. 180. A stationary electron radiates lines of force in all directions to infinity.

edge of the universe, whichever you think is closer—in all directions. Now, make the electron bounce up and down once. The *vertical* lines of force lengthen and shorten, which isn't very useful. But the *horizontal* ones have a kink put in them, and this kink runs outwards just as if the lines were ropes, and the electron your hand shaking the end; see Fig. 181. For the effect a little while later see Fig. 182. The kink runs

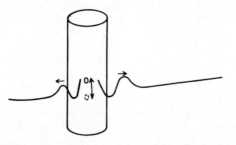

Fig. 181. Jerk the electron up and down: kinks fly out along the horizontal lines of force at the speed of light.

along the line of force at the speed of light, *c*, and is a radio wave. This is what happens when you, say, switch a light on: all the electrons in the wire get jerked into motion and send out kinks—which help to cause the static in broadcast receivers. When the kinks hit another wire, they encourage the electrons in it to bounce up and down in sympathy.

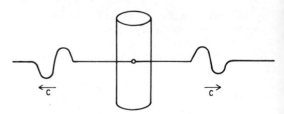

Fig. 182. Fig. 181 a little while later.

In radio we usually make the electrons bounce up and down continuously at a fixed, or nearly fixed frequency *f*. The length of the waves, λ, the period—the time *T* each wave takes to pass a fixed spot are related thus:

$$f = \frac{1}{T}$$

$$\lambda = cT = \frac{C}{f}$$

See Fig. 183. Another shorthand in calculations is $\omega = 2\pi f$, useful because the right hand side comes into so many formulae.

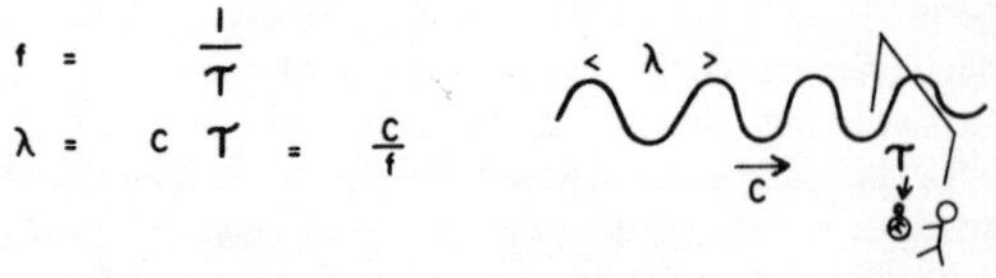

$$f = \frac{1}{T}$$
$$\lambda = cT = \frac{c}{f}$$

Fig. 183. The relationships between wavelength λ, velocity of light c, and wave period T.

The wire can be any bit of wire, but in radio we usually think of it as an aerial, and it is specially shaped to help this radiating process. We will say a little bit more later about aerials because they are one of the most interesting branches of the art, but for the moment all we need to know is that making the electrons bounce up and down causes them to radiate energy and this energy loss makes the aerial appear to have a 'radiation resistance' R_r, even though it is not connected to ground; see Fig. 184.

According to the design of the aerial this radiation resistance varies between fractions of an ohm—which means heavy currents have to flow to radiate any appreciable power, to thousands of ohms—which means high voltage ditto. The classical and simplest

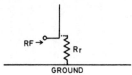

Fig. 184. Radiation
from an aerial is
equivalent to a
'radiation resistance',
R_r, from the input to
ground.

example is a quarter wave whip—like a police car's—which has an impedance of 50–70 Ω (see Fig. 185), which is why coaxial cable usually has these characteristic impedances. Medium wave radio is often transmitted through similar aerials—only several hundred metres high, resonated against the earth's surface.

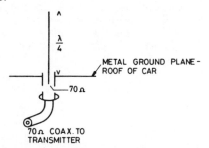

Fig. 185. A quarter wave whip aerial mounted on a metal ground plane—as on a car roof—has a radiation resistance of about 70 Ω.

Since a transmitting aerial is just a piece of wire with an oscillating current flowing in it, why, you may well ask, do electricity transmission lines not radiate all their power away? They would if they were single wires, but there is always a return wire running parallel, carrying the same oscillating current in the opposite direction. So, when one wire radiates an upward kink, the other wire radiates a downward one, and since the two wires are close together—if you travel at the speed of light—the two kinks cancel out and no energy is radiated at any distance from the pair; see Fig. 186. Just this principle is used to carry radio power from a transmitter out to its aerials, which may be some way away.

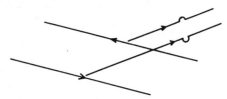

Fig. 186. Parallel wire RF-feeder radiates signals in opposite senses that cancel out.

Conversely, since the air is full of stray radio signals, all carrying power, why can we not light our homes by hanging an aerial up connected to a light bulb and then

to ground? In principle this is possible, in practice the sort of voltage one gets off an aerial is seldom more than milivolts, and more likely to be microvolts. The power that can be drawn out of it is the voltage squared divided by the impedance: $(10^{-3})^2/50 = 20$ nW at the most: a five thousand millionth of what is needed to power a 100 W bulb.

It is useful that an aerial behaves exactly the same when used to transmit or receive, as this means that in a two-way radio we don't have to alter the aerial for the two functions. If we make a transmitter which feeds a wave V peak to peak into a 70-Ω aerial, it will radiate $P_T = V^2/2R$ W (a VHF car mobile at 15 W needs 46 V of RF pp).

If we have another identical aerial L miles away, there will be a similar smaller current in it with power P_r—microwatts or picowatts. If we double the distance L, the received power falls to a quarter—for by the fundamental radiation law, power falls off as the square of the distance. So we can say:

$$P_r = \frac{k}{L^2} \times P_T$$

where k is some constant to do with the efficiency of the aerials, the terrain in between them, the state of the weather, politics—what have you. (It is a difficult one to calculate, but fortunately not often necessary.) Or to express it in voltages, which are more useful:

$$\frac{V_r^2}{2R} = \frac{k}{L^2} \times \frac{V_T^2}{2R}$$

The $2R$s cancel, and we can square root both sides:

$$\frac{V_r}{V_T} = \frac{\sqrt{k}}{L}$$

which means that the signal *voltage* falls off in *direct proportion to distance*, not to the square of distance, as one would perhaps expect. If the signal in the receiving aerial is 1 V at 1 mile (1.6 km), it will be 10 mV at 100 miles (160 km) and 10 μV at 100 000 miles (160 000 km), which is quite amazing. This is why NASA can control its robots on Mars and get information back from them using only milliwatts of power. It is why radio is possible at all, and not just a laboratory curiosity, limited to ranges of a mile or so.

The other basic fact is the resonance of an LC circuit which makes it possible to pick one transmitter out of all the thousands that are inducing currents in one's aerial. That then, is the whole art and mystery of radio.

Modulation

We have our electrons bouncing up and down in the aerial at the 'carrier frequency' f. This distinguishes our transmission from others, and makes it possible for a receiver to pick up ours and disregard all others. If you had a very fast acting voltmeter, and quick eyes, you could measure the voltage on the aerial transmitting a carrier f or on a parallel aerial some distance away—and you would get a reading which went up and down in a sinusoidal way. At any instant the voltage due to a steady carrier of frequency f_s where E_0 is the amplitude of oscillations

$$E = E_0 \times \sin 2\pi f_s \times t = E_0 \sin \omega_s \times t$$

At the moment our signal has only one frequency and takes up an infinitely small amount of bandwidth. As soon as we modulate it the situation changes: the signal spreads out each side of f_s.

There are several different basic types of modulation:

CARRIER WAVE (CW)

The oldest and simplest modulation is to switch the carrier on and off with a morse key—at about 50 Hz. One might think that since the carrier is unchanged the bandwidth is still infinitely small, but unfortunately this is not so. The 50 Hz switching causes side bands which, in effect, spread the signal either side of f_s. The arithmetic is a little complicated because of the abrupt switching, but the principle is the same as in amplitude modulation.

AMPLITUDE MODULATION (AM)

This is the method used for LW and MW broadcasts, and many communications channels. The amplitude of f_s is altered in sympathy with an audio frequency—usually voice or music. Assume for the moment that the modulating signal is another sine wave of frequency f_m. Mathematically, one signal is *multiplied* by the other, or as radio engineers say, they are *mixed* (audio engineers say 'mixed' when they mean 'added'). The upshot of mixing any two frequencies f_s and f_m is the two original frequencies plus their sum, $f_s + f_m$, plus their difference, $f_s - f_m$. If, for instance, a MW carrier at 1 MHz is mixed with an audio tone of 3 kHz, the upshot is the carrier at 1 MHz, an audio component at 3 kHz which we can ignore, and what is important for radio, the upper and lower sidebands at 1.003 MHz and 0.997 MHz. The signal is shown in Fig. 187. (We have already looked at mixing on p. 47, but for completeness, here it is again.)

Fig. 188 shows what you would see if you looked at the output on a scanning receiver (p. 84) (see p. 44 for the trigonometry). And since, in real life, the modulating frequency f_m alters all the time between

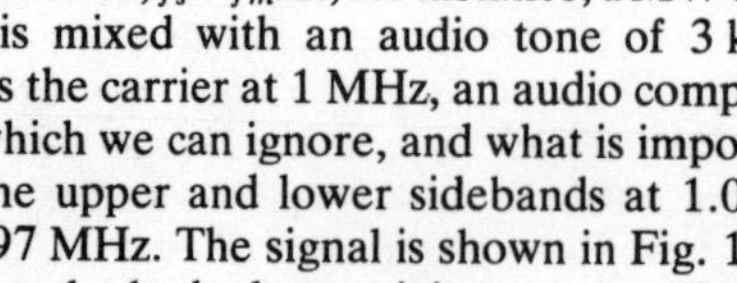

Fig. 187. Amplitude modulation: the size of the RF carrier wave is proportional to the audio signal.

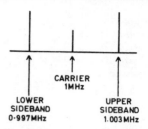

Fig. 188. A 3 kHz audio signal carried as AM on a 1 MHz carrier produces two sharp sidebands.

50 kHz and 5 kHz (for a music quality broadcast channel) or 300 kHz and 2.7 kHz (speech quality), the sidebands broaden out; see Fig. 189. Although this is simple to send, and relatively simple to receive, it isn't very economical,because one sideband simply duplicates the information in the other, and the central

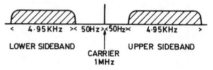

Fig. 189. A speech signal varying between 50 Hz and 5 kHz produces two spread out sidebands.

carrier just tells you that the transmitter is on, which one might have guessed anyway from the presence of sidebands. So the first step towards economy of spectrum is:

Double sideband (DSB) suppressed carrier By modulating f_s in a balanced mixer (p. 48) it is easy to remove the carrier; see Fig. 190. This saves a bit of

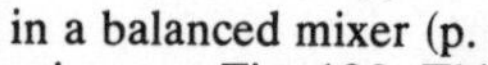

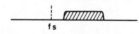

LOWER SIDEBAND   UPPER SIDEBAND

Fig. 190. Double sideband (DSB) or suppressed carrier: only the sidebands are transmitted.

transmitter power, but doesn't make any more useful space in the frequency band. The next step is:

Single sideband (SSB) By rather tiresome electronic signal processing in the transmitter (p. 44), the carrier and one of the sidebands are removed, making room for someone else's signal in their place; see Fig. 191.

Fig. 191. Single sideband (SSB), one only of the sidebands is transmitted; in this case, the upper.

Curiously, *reception* of SSB is in principle very easy: you just mix the RF with a frequency within 100 Hz or so of f_s and up comes the original audio. This is because the SSB signal consists of the carrier f_c plus (or minus, if we're thinking of the lower sideband) the audio frequency f_a. So, mixing this signal, $f_c + f_a$ with a locally generated frequency which differs from f_c by a small difference frequency f_d, we get two further sidebands:

$$(f_c + f_a) - (f_c + f_d) = f_a - f_d.$$

As long as f_d is less than 100 Hz the audio will be shifted down in frequency a small amount, but will still be intelligible. SSB makes the best possible use of space in the spectrum, and is therefore now used almost exclusively in the very crowded HF bands.

The other three methods rely on altering the frequency f_s while leaving its amplitude constant.

FREQUENCY MODULATION (FM)

This system shifts the signal frequency f_s by an amount proportional to the intensity of the audio signal. In VHF broadcasting the maximum frequency shift is 75 kHz. The mathematical analysis is lengthy, but the meat of the matter is this: a maximum frequency shift of f_s, which is large compared to the modulating audio frequency f_m, causes a large number of sidebands and uses a wide chunk of the radio spectrum; see Fig. 192.

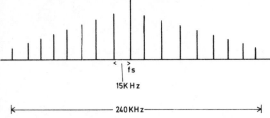

Fig. 192. *In frequency modulation, a single audio tone produces an infinite number of sidebands, though many of them are too small to notice.*

The BBC's VHF service transmits around 100 MHz, uses a maximum shift of 75 kHz and has a maximum signal frequency of 15 kHz. The *modulation index* is the ratio of these two: $75/15 = 5$ and it turns out there are sixteen significant sets of sidebands—eight upper and eight lower, spread out at 15 kHz intervals ('significant', for broadcasting, means more than 1% percent of the central sideband). This kind of bandwidth is only available at VHF and above, and explains why VHF gives so much better quality than AM: noise interference is unlikely to affect all the sidebands equally, so it gets cancelled out in the receiver.

Radio amateurs have not these lavish bandwidths, so they have to use narrow band FM (NBFM) where the ratio of deviation to signal frequency—the modulation index—is about $1:3$. In this case there are only two significant sidebands and the bandwidth is twice the modulating frequency—which, in a communications channel, is 3 kHz or a bit less. So the total bandwidth is

6 kHz. There is a price to pay: noise performance is worse due to the loss of sidebands. There is one important advantage to FM: if a receiver is exposed to two different signals at the same frequency, it will tend to lock onto the stronger and ignore the weaker. This 'capture effect' is very useful to planners of radio nets for mobile users, for it means they can assign the same frequency to closer transmitters, or in other words, use fewer frequencies to cover a given area. An AM receiver exposed to two signals on the same frequency reproduces them both. Unless one is less than 1 percent of the other, garbage tends to result. A disadvantage to FM is that when there is no signal the receiver produces white noise. This is very tiring for the listener, so it is necessary to provide communications receivers with a *squelch* circuit to turn off the audio amplifier in the absence of signal.

PHASE MODULATION (PM)

Phase modulation is a similar but less used system. Information is carried as a phase shift in the carrier. At first glance this would seem to have small bandwidth, but in the process of phase shifting longer or shorter waves have to be produced, and these are recognized by a receiver as being sidebands. The British colour TV system uses phase shifts to code the three primary colours.

FREQUENCY SHIFT KEYING (FSK)

The carrier is frequency shifted by a fixed amount to carry digital data—the higher frequency standing, say, for logic 1, the lower for logic 0. The effective bandwidth is made up by the actual shift deviation (which may be quite small), and the rate of keying (which may be high).

PHASE SHIFT KEYING

Digital information is carried by a phase shift on the carrier. As before, the bandwidth is still quite high. Some bandwidth economy can be made by:

Single sideband FM SSB FM is FM with all but one of the sidebands in Fig. 192 removed, and is, when you think about it, not much different from ordinary SSB with the amplitude modulation removed. This makes little difference to intelligibility. More properly, SSB FM codes amplitude variation in speech as frequency variations on the carrier. But amplitude variations include within them the frequency variations of speech, so the upshot is much the same.

Coding

Modulation is a form of coding, but in the usual language of electronics, *coding* means reducing the signal to some form of digital pulses; *modulation* means imposing this or audio on the carrier wave.

Much information today is carried in pulse form, using one of a variety of *Pulse Code Modulation* (PCM). The original form, which is still much used, divides the voice voltage into a number of amplitude levels—which are usually logarithmically related. Four is the minimum for comprehension, high quality circuits use up to 130. The levels are 1, 2, 4, 8 voltages units apart, and the separating could be done by four window comparators (p. 29); see Fig. 193. The state

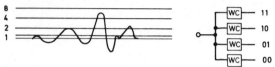

Fig. 193. Digitizing audio: window comparators determine the voltage level, which is signalled in binary code.

of the comparators is sampled at a rate of several kilohertz, and the level of the voice voltage signalled by sending '0', '1', '2', '3' in binary code: 00, 01, 10, 11. The sampling rate cannot theoretically be less than double the maximum signal frequency—in this case 3 kHz, and actually is more likely to be three times it, 9 kHz. So, every nine thousandth of a second we have to transmit two data bits, which makes a minimum bandwidth of 18 kHz, and since the bits have sharp edges, the real bandwidth will be more like 36 kHz.

Another system was described previously. This is a form of delta modulation—so called because the signal represents the difference between the voice level now and its value at the last sampling point. Sampling can be at a fixed rate, or, as in this system, when the level differs by a set amount from its last value.

A popular system first used in the last war samples the voice signal at a fixed rate, and then transmits a pulse of width proportional to the voice level: pulse width modulation (PWM); see Fig. 194. In effect this transmits the clock (the beginning of each pulse), and the marker (the end of the pulse).

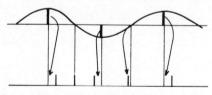

Fig. 194. In pulse width modulation (PWM) the width of the transmitted pulse signals the audio voltage at the time of the clock pulse. In pulse position modulation (PPM, shown here), a shorter pulse is transmitted to signal the varying end of the width pulse. The clock is reconstituted in the receiver.

PULSE POSITION MODULATION (PPM)

A more sophisticated system transmits only the marker, because the clock can be reconstructed in the

receiver with a form of phase-locked loop. The marker and the reconstructed clock then switch a bistable, which reconstructs the PWM, which is put through a low pass filter to recover the audio. However, PPM needs an even wider bandwidth since the single pulses have high frequency components in themselves.

THE BANDWIDTH OF A PULSE

If we generate a single pulse 1 μs long, and feed it to an aerial, what effect will it have on a receiver? From one point of view it looks like the positive half of a wave 2 μs long, at 500 kHz. It will set LC circuits tuned to that frequency twanging. If we generate the pulse with TTL, which has rise and fall times of about 3 ns, the *edges* will look like quarter waves at 83 MHz, and will affect receivers tuned to that frequency. If you pass a pulse through a high-pass filter with a time constant a tenth of the pulse length, you can see the high frequency components in the edges; see Fig. 195. If the pulse repeats every 1 ms, it will also look like a 1-kHz wave. But the evil doesn't end there: it generates harmonics starting at 1 kHz and repeating every 1-kHz period up to hundreds of megahertz; see Fig. 196. So, a

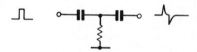

Fig. 195. A square pulse passing through a high pass filter reveals its high frequency components.

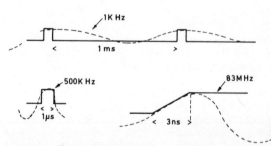

Fig. 196. Some frequency components of a 1 μs pulse repeated at 1 kHz with a rise time of 3 ns.

1 μs pulse is a damned antisocial thing, and we would do well to keep it well shut up, or we'll have the GPO's Radcontrol people banging on the door. Of course, harmonics like this are useful as well. A good way of calibrating radio receivers is to produce 100 kHz, 10 kHz and 1 kHz—say—square waves from a crystal source, in a divider chain. Fed loosely to the aerial, they will produce signals called 'marker pips' every 100 kHz, 10 kHz and 1 kHz throughout the set's range, and so can be used to adjust the tuning circuits.

A sine or a cosine is the only pure wave, the only waveform that has one single frequency. All others are complex waves consisting of more than one frequency, and will produce outputs in receivers tuned to other frequencies than the nominal one.

MW receiver

By way of getting to grips with the hardware of radio, let's think about a simple Medium Wave (MW) receiver. This band stretches from 0.525 MHz to 1.605 MHz (rather irritatingly, broadcasting authorities still talk about wavelengths in this band: 570 m to 186 m). MW receivers are so cheap it is hardly worth building one for real, but this exercise will serve to introduce some basic ideas.

Most radio receivers consist of the circuit blocks shown in Fig. 197. First comes the aerial, then some sort of circuit to select the frequency wanted, and to

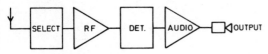

Fig. 197. Block diagram of a simple radio receiver.

reject all the others. There is an amplification stage to raise the radio signal from the minute voltage in the aerial above the noise generated in the receiver's own circuits and then there is a detector to demodulate the transmitted signal in order to get at the original audio. More amplification follows, and finally some sort of output device—a speaker, headphones, teleprinter, cathode ray screen, TV screen—what have you.

For an MW receiver the aerial can be very simple: a rod of ferrite induces an electronic signal in a coil wrapped round it; see Fig. 198. This coil is also a coil

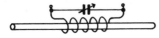

Fig. 198. Tuned coil wound on ferrite rod to act as aerial.

(p. 118) and a capacitor in series or parallel with it makes a resonant circuit. If the capacitor is variable, we have a tuned aerial, and we've made a start in selecting the signal we want and rejecting the ones we don't want. Making it needs a bit of inspired guesswork plus trial and error. We'll go through the process because something like it has to be done whenever coils are wound and resonated. The starting point is a variable capacitor. If we reckon that 200 pF is a likely figure for the maximum capacitance of an easily obtainable variable, then we need to choose an inductance that will resonate with it at the lowest frequency—525 kHz. Let's go back to first principles. On p. 114 we mention that a coil and capacitance resonated at the frequency which made their reactances equal and opposite.

i.e.:

$$X_c = \frac{1}{2\pi fC} = 2\pi fL = X_L$$

or:

$$L = \frac{1}{4\pi^2 f^2 C}$$

A bit of calculator work makes $L = 459\ \mu H$.

Since the graph on p. 114 wasn't drawn for designers of MW receivers, it won't tell us how many turns to wind. We can work back from what it does tell us, because the inductance of a coil is related to its length l, number of turns n, and cross sectional area A thus:

$$L = \frac{k \times An^2}{l}$$

But since we're going to be winding a coil whose turns touch, l is the diameter of the wire d multiplied by the number of turns n:

$$L = \frac{k \times An}{d}$$

So, if we wind our coil the same diameter as shown in the graph, we just need to wind more turns in proportion to the increase in inductance we want. The smaller d is, the smaller n is, so to save aggravation of winding hundreds of turns, we'll use the thinnest obtainable wire—40 swg, varnished to prevent short circuits. The graph on p. 125 gives 100 μH for 1 in. (25.4 mm) of winding. Since a ferrite core doubles the inductance, this is worth 200 pF at 525 kHz. So we need $459/200 = 2.29$ in. (58.2 mm) of winding—which is 466 turns. And, further, this graph shows that 459 μH resonates with about 20 pF at the other end of the frequency band we want—1.6 MHz. This is quite a reasonable figure.

The coil wire is hardly thicker than a human hair, so it needs leads of ordinary plastic covered wire. Scrape the varnish off before soldering, and wind the turns on a $\frac{1}{4}$ in. (6.35 mm) ferrite rod 6 in. (152.4 mm) long. It's probably easiest to wind it ten turns at a time—slide them down, pull them tight, and move on. Better to wind too much than too little, so put on, say, 490 turns. When the coil is finished, cover it in sticky tape.

In an MW receiver it probably is not necessary to test the resonance—it would be simpler just to turn on and see what comes out. But one often does have to test resonant frequencies (see Fig. 199), and here's how to do it. A signal simulating the radio station, but much stronger, is produced by an RF signal generator. Its output should be about 50 Ω—which will load the high Q aerial if connected straight to the hot end and so it will hardly resonate at all. To prevent this wind a secondary, which we'll need anyway, of 100 turns. Connect one end of each coil to ground. The other, hot end, of the aerial coil has an RF diode tacked onto it, a

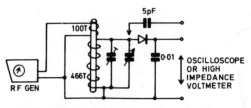

Fig. 199. Testing the aerial in Fig. 198.

smoothing capacitor to ground and then to the oscillo-scope or a high impedance voltmeter—like the circuit on p. 12. One can display the RF directly on the 'scope, but since the leads probably have a capacitance of 200 pF, direct connection would throw things out. Connection via, say, a 5 pF capacitor will leave the tuned circuit almost unaffected, but will also reduce the size of the display.

With the tuning capacitor in the right places, the circuit should tune up at the two ends of the MW band. It almost certainly won't, so recourse must be had to the trimmer capacitors which will probably be found on the variable. They will increase the capacitance and compensate for too much inductance. If they don't help it may be necessary to remove some turns—which is easier than joining up new wire and adding. Now we can assume that the aerial is resonating nicely and we can move on to the next stage.

Because signals in the MW band travel long dis-tances at night, and because there's so much frequency piracy and indiscipline, broadcasting authorities transmit much stronger signals then are ideally neces-sary (see *noise*, p. 76). An aerial like this will produce several milivolts from local station. All we need is a bit of amplification and a detector.

The RF amplifier

Amplifying radio frequency is actually quite simple. In essence, we replace the collector resistor in Fig. 6a with a tuned circuit. Result: a frequency selective amplifier; see Fig. 200. If the coil has the same value as the aerial coil, and the capacitors are ganged together (p. 113), they tune together or 'track', improving selectivity a lot more. In fact, life being what it is, they won't track perfectly, without help, so make the collector coil adjustable too. We could wind a second, identical coil on another piece of ferrite, but it would

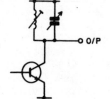

Fig. 200. Collector load in RF amplifier.

be cumbersome, and difficult to screen from the aerial, so wind this coil on a nice fat former with a ferrite tuning slug. The graph on p. 125 gives the turns for a standard 7/16 in. (11.11 mm) diameter former. This time we want to give the slug some play, so we need it half in and half out when the inductance is the wanted 459 μH. In other words, we need to wind a coil for $459/1.5 = 306$ μH. Once again, the chart runs out but we can work from the figure of 100 pF for 0.65 in. (16.51 mm) of 42 swg close-wound—we need 0.65 in. $\times 306/100 = 1.99$ in. (50.55 mm).

A neater solution would be to use a ferrite pot core (p. 117). Fig. 201 is a Siemens 'Siefferit' core type B65651.* Two cup-like pieces of ferrite enclose the coil which is wound on a plastic bobbin, and are held onto a plastic base with eight terminals by a spring clip.

Fig. 201. Siemens pot cores, used to wind and contain high inductance coils. Similar devices are available from other manufacturers.

Practically all the magnetic field is enclosed inside the ferrite, so only the number of turns affects the inductance value. (This feature makes a pot core use-less as an aerial because the magnetic component of the radio wave cannot affect the coil.) About a dozen different materials are available, suited to different frequencies. For this purpose we want 'high Q in resonant circuits and filters' in the frequency range 0.2 MHz to 1.6 MHz—type M33. The inductance of the finished coil in nanohenries is given by the 'A_L' value of the core times the number of turns squared. M33 material is available in two versions—one with A_L 63, and the other 100. Since we want a large inductance, the 100 type is better.

How many turns? Adjustment in a pot-core is by a small slug that more or less connects the centres of the top and bottom halves. This particular core has an adjustment range of 12 per cent—which isn't worth bothering about when calculating the number of turns. Best, again, to overdo the inductance and add capaci-tance. So let's aim for the same final inductance as the aerial—482 μH, or 482 000 nH. So:

$$n^2 = \frac{482\,000}{1000} = 482, \quad \text{and} \quad n = \sqrt{482} = 22$$

This time the size of wire is immaterial, so long as it all gets in. Just as we didn't want to load the aerial and

---

* Information about this pot-core is taken from the *Electrovalue Catalogue.*

spoil its Q, so we don't want to load this circuit too much. So we'll wind a lower impedance secondary to drive the next stage. How low? The Q of a circuit like this can be quite high—say 100. The normal reactance of 480 μH at, say 1 MHz, the middle of the band, will be 3.5 kΩ, and magnified by $Q = 100$ (p. 000), will be 350 kΩ. The more turns on the secondary, the greater the voltage ratio, but the more the next stage will load the tuned circuit so the worse the selectivity will be. If we aimed for 5 kΩ we ought to be all right. The ratio of impedances is the *square* of the ratio of the turns (p. 115) so we need

$$\sqrt{22 \times \frac{5}{350}} = 2.6 \text{ turns}$$

This can be wound between a second pair of terminals, lying on top of the primary.

To drive this amplifier we need some sort of connection with the aerial coil. Connecting the base of the transistor direct to the hot end would overload the tuned circuit and spoil the aerial Q (p. 118). So we drive the transistor with the smaller coil of 100 turns. The cold end of this secondary is biased at $V_{cc}/5$ just like the audio transistor on p. 4. It's also kept free of RF by the decoupling capacitor C. The hot end applies the RF signal plus the DC bias to the base of the transistor. However, there remains one further snag. If we have one transistor with base and collector tuned to the same frequency it will without doubt oscillate. An oscillator is simply an amplifier with positive AC feedback—and the feedback will be through stray capacitances, power line ripple, magnetic coupling between the two coils.

There are several ways of neutralizing an RF amplifier: the easiest in my experience is simply to use a second transistor in *cascode* (p. 13); see Fig. 202.

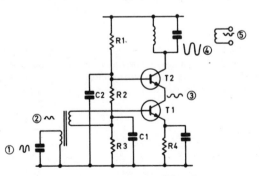

Fig. 202. Cascode input amplifier. See text.

Amplification goes like this: Waveform 1 is quite big because of the high Q of the tuned aerial. Waveform 2 is smaller because the drive coil has 1/4 the turns and therefore gives 1/4 the voltage. Waveform 3 is the same size but inverted because T_1 has no collector load. Waveform 4 is the payoff, and should be 10× to

50× the size of waveform 1. It is reduced to waveform 5 in the interests of keeping Q high.

Biasing is simple too: T_2 base should be about $V_{cc}/2$ and T_1 base $V_{cc}/5$. Because the gain of a transistor amplifier depends on the collector current (p. 5), we can easily control the RF gain by adjusting the bias levels with the 10-kΩ variable resistor in Fig. 203. One further refinement is an RF choke (p. 117) and its decoupling capacitor to keep the positive rail pure.

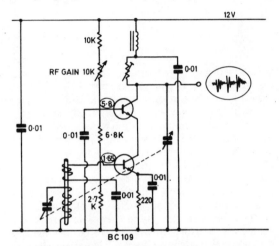

Fig. 203. Practical version of cascode amplifier, with tuned input and output stages and RF gain control.

Fig. 203 shows what the RF amplifier now looks like. The dotted line between the variable capacitors means they're ganged together; the collector capacitor goes to ground because it shares the same chassis as the aerial tuner—but it is in effect connected to the top of the collector coil through the right hand 0.01 μF. The bias voltages (with the 10 kΩ RF gain control wound down) are shown ringed.

What sort of voltage will we get at the output? We might start off with, say, 10 μV on the aerial. This will produce $100/466 \times 1 = 2$ μV on the secondary. The maximum emitter current is $12/5.220 = 11$ mA. The formula on p. 5 tells us that the gain is $20 \times 11 \times 350 = 77\,000$ times, or an output at the collector $2.10^{-6} \times 0.77000 = 0.154$ V. In the output secondary this will be $0.154 \times 2.6/22 = 0.018$ V. In practice, a strong local station will more likely produce 1 mV on the aerial, so we might have an output of nearly 2 V—providing the amplifier doesn't oscillate—which it almost certainly will, forcing us to reduce the voltage on the upper base and so the emitter current and gain.

The output should be rocking away with Radio Rubbish at about 1 MHz. All we have to do is detect it and amplify the audio. Detecting an amplitude modulated signal is usually extremely simple: you just rectify (p. 18), discarding the negative half waves of the carrier, and filter off the RF. The easiest way to do this

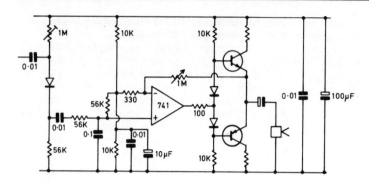

Fig. 204. Detector, audio amplifier and output stage.

is to use a diode (p. 18); see Fig. 204. The snag is that, just like the base-emitter junction of a transistor (which is itself a sort of diode), there is a 0.6-V drop across it. This means that it will only pass positive half waves greater than 0.6 V. Since we're starting with a signal of perhaps 10 mV and amplifying it perhaps 10 or 20 times, we've only got 200 mV to play with. The answer is to help the diode by turning it on slightly to start with, using the 1 MΩ pre-set (p. 109). The resistors above and below the diode let a little current through it while keeping a high impedance to ground so that the amplifier output resonant circuit isn't loaded too heavily. The diode can be any RF type (probably germanium with a 0.2 V forward voltage drop, but this makes no difference to the argument).

Next we need something to get rid of the RF while leaving the audio. Obviously we need an RC low pass filter, but there has to be a compromise. If its cut-off frequency is low, it gets rid of the RF beautifully but also reduces and distorts the audio. If it is too high, the audio is fine, but we're left with RF which will mess up the audio amplifier. So we choose an RC low pass network with a time constant midway between the RF with a period of 1 μS, and audio with a period of 33 ms; 16 ms is near enough. R had better be 56 kΩ to keep up the impedance, so C has to be 0.3 μF. In practice 0.1 μF would be fine and easier to get. All we need now is a high impedance audio amplifier: the + input of a 741 will do nicely.

The amplifier is basically the one on p. 29, with gain controlled by altering the feedback resistor. Biasing is a bit boring because we have only one supply rail—a pseudo ground for the op-amp is provided by the first pair of 10 kΩ with the middle decoupled with a 0.01 μF and 10 μF in parallel. The supply rails need good decoupling too.

LINING UP

Make sure you've connected everything correctly. Connect the 12 V supply (9 V or 15 V would do just as well), through an ammeter. The whole circuit should draw about 20–30 mA with no signal. With the RF gain wide open, check the bias voltages. Check that the inputs and output of the op-amp are at mid rail.

Tune the capacitor to a strong local station. Adjust the 1 MΩ variable for the loudest output. Twiddle the slug in the collector coil to increase loudness again (it may be necessary to ease back on the RF gain to get room to manoeuvre). Remember how many turns you moved it and in what direction to get maximum output—*then go back half way to where it was*. Tune to a station at the other end of the range, repeat the process. Carry on until the two tuned circuits track satisfactorily.

Et Voilà! A rather low quality receiver. But, one, nevertheless, that demonstrates some of the principles of the trade. Next time we will do something rather better.

A not very good SSB receiver

Since radio traffic in the HF band—which stretches in effect from the top end of the MW broadcast band up to 30 MHz—is now almost completely CW for morse, FSK for teleprinters, and SSB for voice, we can take advantage of the homodyne method of reception (p. 46) which will handle them all (except for AM propaganda broadcasts). It has one serious snag, but is still instructive.

In its simplest form (see Fig. 205), all we need for such a receiver is an aerial, a mixer, oscillator working at *signal* frequency, an audio pass filter and a lot of audio gain. The whole thing could be put together, using the appropriate ICs, on a couple of μDecs (p. 121).

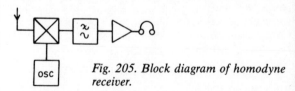

Fig. 205. Block diagram of homodyne receiver.

The good joke about this method is that we can build quite a good receiver without any tuned circuits at all. The last set was typical, in a crude way, of the vast majority of receivers: their selectivity depends on tuned circuits which have to be numerous and of high

Q if they are to be effective in picking out one channel from the crowded radio spectrum. Here the whole RF spectrum is, as it were, folded about the wanted carrier, so that the channel we're interested in comes out as audio, and all the rest—both above and below it in the spectrum—are *higher* in frequency and can be filtered out.

At first sight it seems too good to be true. There are, of course, snags. The first is that the channel *below* is superimposed on the channel above. As it stands, the set will only work if the channel immediately to the other side of the mixing frequency is vacant. We can easily see how this happens: suppose we mix the signals from the aerial with a frequency C corresponding to the carrier we are interested in. C might be anywhere between 1 MHz and 30 MHz. Imagine that the channel we want is an audio frequency A carried as an upper sideband on C, so that the actual RF signal is $C + A$. When we mix this with C we get A, and $2C + A$ which can be filtered out. But the same thing happens if there's also a signal $C - A'$ in the lower sideband channel. Mixing with C produces $C - A' - C = -A'$, and $2C - A'$. The audio output is $A - A'$, compared to which Donald Duck is a master of elocution. (There is a cure for the unwanted channel problem: it consists in passing the radio signals $C + A$, $C - A$, through a single sideband generator so that the unwanted sideband $C - A$, cancels out. But that puts us back with the complexities of p. 46.

The other snag is the audio filter. This has to be very very sharp to give results as good as a communications quality heterodyne receiver (p. 78). The Post Office says that a communications receiver output can be 6 dB down at 2400 Hz—the top edge of the speech band, but must be 35 dB down or 1/58th at 3100 Hz—the lower edge of the next channel. This needs six or eight stages of active filters, like those on p. 26, which interact on each other and are generally not the pleasantest things to design. Even so, there are enough SSB transmissions without neighbours at any particular moment to make exploring with such a simple set quite amusing. The last time I tried it, there was a French fisherman explaining to his wife (surely not his girlfriend) why he couldn't get back for the weekend, never mind what sort of party Gaston and Jeanne were getting up, and an oil rig off the Hebrides ordering amazing quantities of food and drink for another party. Of course we would not dream of listening to any but broadcast transmissions, and we would be careful to take out a licence for a receiver before doing that.

CW morse is sent simply by activating a transmitter while the key is down. If the local oscillator (LO) of the receiver is, say, 1 kHz away in frequency from the carrier, and 'dahs' and 'dits' will be heard as a 1 kHz tone.

RADIO TELEPRINTER

Communication receivers often have a beat frequency oscillator (BFO) which runs 1 kHz or so away from the LO (p. 67) to make morse audible. FSK transmissions switch the carrier frequency by 850 Hz in a form of SSB to make up the teleprinter code. These two carrier frequencies can be translated into any two audio frequencies 850 Hz apart in the receiver, but it is conventional to use 1650 Hz as 'space', and 2500 Hz as 'mark'. The code usually used is called after a Mr Murray, and renders the alphabet, numerals, and punctuation marks in five bits (p. 18). Lower case 'a', for instance, is M–M–S–S–S. Again, an offset LO will produce these two tones, and it is not hard to build an array of audio filters feeding rectifiers and Schmitt triggers (pp. 25, 30 and 28) to separate them and drive the teleprinter. For information on teleprinters, see the RSGB's *Teleprinter Manual*, though the discriminator circuits given there are unnecessarily clumsy and can easily be improved using op-amps. Teleprinters can be bought from Teleprinter Equipment Ltd, 70 Akeman Street, Tring, Herts.

The point about FSK and morse is that, because they transmit information at a slow rate, they take up less bandwidth than voice and therefore make better headway against noise—or alternatively go further for the same power (p. 57). To take advantage of this, one can filter the mixer output even more sharply with bandpass filters (p. 26). For FSK a bandwidth of 850 Hz centred on 2075 Hz, a Q of 2.4 is necessary, and for morse 100 Hz centred at 1 kHz, a Q of 10. These filters will also help to some extent with co-channel inteference.

Antennae are matters for endless ingenuity and the functioning of any receiver, but particularly those working in the HF band, depends critically on them. Something like Fig. 206 would serve for our purpose.

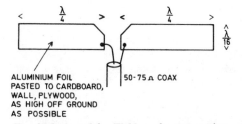

Fig. 206. Aerial for FM broadcast reception.

The aerial elements are made of aluminium kitchen foil pasted to cardboard, plywood, walls etc. They should be as high above ground as possible, and if mounted at right angles will give reasonably, even all round coverage. The width makes them suitable for a wide band of frequencies centred about $f = c/\lambda$* (c is the speed of light $= 3 \times 10^8$ m/s).

* For further material on this subject see L. Blake, *Antennas* (New York, Wiley, 1966) and *The ARRL Antenna Book* (New York, American Radio Relay League, 1974).

Super-regenerative receiver

An oscillator is just an amplifier with enough positive feedback at one particular frequency (usually depending on a tuned ciruit) to drive itself. If we reduce the feedback so it just isn't oscillating, we have a very high gain amplifier at that particular frequency. Connect the thing to an antenna and you have a radio receiver in one. The snag is that it will not sit at just the right point. Either the gain rises and it oscillates, or it falls and it won't receive. The solution is to sweep it through the right point, into oscillation and out again, at some low frequency which is still too high to hear. Hence 'super' in the name, standing for 'supersonic'. In the days when the radio spectrum was less crowded than it is today, the super-regenerative circuit made a simple and effective receiver. Nowadays, since its selectivity depends on one tuned circuit, and that rather heavily loaded, it isn't nearly good enough for use in crowded wave bands. But for interest's sake, Fig. 207 shows a

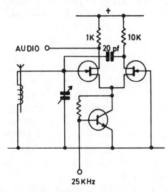

Fig. 207. Super-regenerative receiver: apply about 0.6 V of 25 kHz to the transistor input to switch the amplifier through its maximum gain condition.

version based on the FET oscillator of p. 73. The tuning coil is also an MW or LW ferrite aerial (p. 61) and the common sources are swept by a transistor driven by an audio oscillator (not shown) at about 25 kHz. In some cunning designs one transistor is made to work as both RF and audio oscillator, but that's much too clever for me. As well as being crude, it is an antisocial device since the receiver becomes a transmitter when it is in the oscillating phase of its cycle.

Superheterodyne receiver

We come now to the superheterodyne receiver; see Fig. 208. This is now the almost universal system for getting selectivity, tunability and gain. We amplify RF from the aerial to get it out of the level of device noise (p. 76). We mix it with a slightly different frequency generated by the local oscillator (LO) and amplify the difference frequency in the intermediate frequency

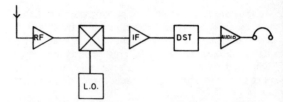

Fig. 208. Block diagram of superheterodyne receiver.

(IF) amplifier—often called the 'IF strip' because it has a lot of gain, and is laid out long and thin to keep the output away from the input. The output of the IF amplifier is essentially the same as the original transmission, but at a lower frequency and much higher amplitude. The modulation remains the same: if the original transmission was AM, so will the IF output be; if FM, or PCM—no different. If the signal is AM, we can just rectify the IF, and amplify the resulting audio.

This seems a long way round, but this 'superheterodyne' system (super = supersonic, i.e. the IF is too high to hear; hetero = different; dyne = frequency) has several advantages. The first is that the main gain producing element, the IF strip, is always tuned to a *fixed frequency*. To tune the whole receiver from one station to another, we alter the local oscillator in such a way that the difference product is always at the IF. For instance, you're listening to Radio Rubbish on 195 m, or 1.538 MHz, and you want to change to Radio Nausea on 1.214 MHz. The usual IF for medium wave receivers is 450 kHz, so for Rubbish the local oscillator was running ast 1.538 MHz − 450 kHz = 1.088 MHz; now you retune it to 1.214 MHz–450 kHz = 0.764 MHz, simply by turning a variable capacitor in the tank circuit of the oscillator, or by altering the voltage on a varicap diode. In a sophisticated set there might be an RF amplifier as well to be retuned the same way, but since MW signals are usually above device noise, most receivers just feed the aerial straight into the mixer.

This is much easier than trying to retune five stages, say, in a set that relied on direct amplification. However, there is another advantage too, as because the IF amplifier normally runs at a much lower frequency than the tuning stages for the aerial and RF amplifier (if there are any), it can have a much higher Q, and therefore be more selective. This selectivity is enhanced by the mixing down, because the frequency *difference* between two stations stays the same.

Suppose there is a boring Zendian propaganda station 10 kHz away from Rubbish, at 1.48 MHz. If we relied on the Q of the aerial to reject it, we'd need a Q of 1.5/0.02 = 75 just to reduce it by 3 dB—which you can hardly notice. To get it 30 dB down so that it didn't interfere at all, would need an astronomical Q—so high, in fact, that it would also distort the very programme we wanted to listen to. However, after mixing down to the IF, the situation is much easier. *Rubbish* is at 450 kHz, the interloper is at 440 kHz. The Q

needed is one third as much, and because we are dealing with stages that are set once and for all, we can: (i) make them of very high Q; and (ii) stagger tune them so that the overall response of the IF strip is something like Fig. 209. The light lines suggest the response curves of the three stages which combine to give a flat topped band-pass amplifier.

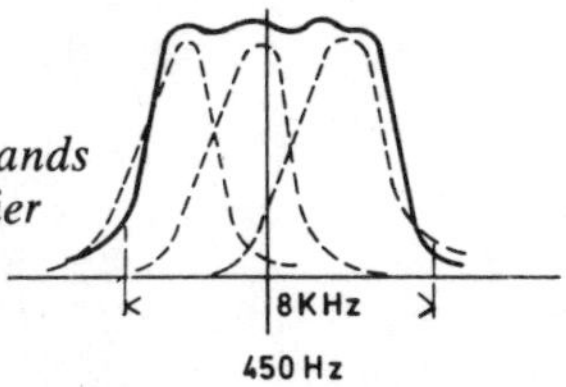

Fig. 209. Staggered passbands of a three stage IF amplifier combine to give a squarer response.

Even so, although the IF amplifier makes the rejection of adjacent stations much easier, high quality sets still rely on extra filtering: using a crystal or a mechanical resonant filter to pass only the IF frequency. Sometimes they have two mixers and IF stages in series for good measure.

Of course, there is a snag to the superheterodyne principle. It is this: the mixer produces the sum and difference frequencies between the wanted station and the LO: in this case 1.538 MHz − 1.088 MHz = 0.450 MHz, and 1.538 MHz + 1.088 MHz = 2.626 MHz. It isn't hard to get rid of this last-mentioned, but suppose there is another station yet at 0.638 MHz. The difference frequency is now 0.638 MHz − 1.088 MHz = −0.450 MHz. The minus sign just means a change of phase, so that the IF strip is presented with another signal just at the right frequency, and naturally, will amplify it. This 'mirror frequency' is ineradicable one it has entered the receiver chain, and can only be dealt with by selective circuits at the aerial and RF stages. (Actually this example is not too difficult because the RF and LO are relatively close to each other: this makes the mirror frequency—which is RF − 2 × IF—quite different and easy to eliminate. But in a VHF set, which we shall look at in a moment, the RF is around 100 MHz, the IF is 10 MHz, and so the mirror frequency is proportionately closer at 80 MHz. To prevent trouble, VHF sets need much more selective RF stages than MW ones do.

On the other hand, a high IF, which reduces mirror problems, also makes amplifications and stability more difficult. As so often in electronics, the answer must be a compromise.

Detection

This technique of taking the signal on the aerial—which may be only microvolts—altering its frequency to something lower and more manageable and amplifying that, is almost universal in modern receivers. The IFs used vary according to signal bandwidth, and range

from 450 kHz in a MW broadcast receiver to 10.7 MHz in VHF sets, to 30 MHz for TV, and 400 MHz or so in radars and microwave communications systems.

The problem still remains of detection, which is to say the demodulation of the carrier wave to restore the original programme material. An amplitude modulated carrier can be demodulated simply by rectifying it with a diode, as we have seen (p. 18). If we had an oscillator which ran exactly in time with the carrier—or rather the carrier reduced to the IF—we could compare its output with the signal, and so detect the modulation with greater sensitivity than is possible with the diode. The reason is easy enough to see: suppose we have a 3 kHz signal amplitude-modulating a 1 MHz carrier. One audio peak will last 1/6000 s (i.e. 160 µs). In that time there will be 160 carrier waves. Because we are dealing with a weak signal, some of these will be missing, some bigger than they should be, some smaller, owing to the effects of atmospheric and device noise. But because we compare them with the 'original', unmodulated carrier which we get from our oscillator, we can average out these imperfections, and recover an almost perfect version of the original 3 kHz audio wave.

How do we come by this pristine carrier? What we do is run a tunable oscillator in the receiver which is locked electronically to the incoming carrier. Because the transmitter uses a carrier which is frequency stable—at least over periods of seconds—we can average our synthetic oscillator over equally long periods, if we want, and so get it to run in harmony with the transmitter with great accuracy. Like the superheterodyne principle, it sounds a long way round, but again, it is well worth the trouble. The circuit for the job is the Phase Locked Loop, the PLL.

Phase locked loops

This type of circuit is a basic tool of today's communication technology. Although it was first described in the 1930's, it has only recently come into use—as with so many other good old ideas—because ICs make their realization so much easier than with valves. A PLL has three essential units: a voltage controlled oscillator (i.e. one whose frequency is proportional to a control voltage), a mixer where it is multiplied by (p. 43) the incoming signal, and a low pass filter where the result is smoothed and applied back to the VCO as control voltage; see Fig. 210.

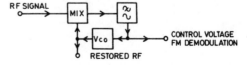

Fig. 210. Block diagram of phase locked loop.

The PLL will have a capture range of frequencies around a centre frequency f_o—the free running VCO frequency signal. If we imagine a signal well below that in frequency gradually being raised, it will get to a point at which the control voltage will dip, and the PLL will lock. The VCO will then run exactly in frequency with the signal.

The mixer output will consist of two main frequencies: $f_s + f_o$ (i.e. the signal frequency plus the oscillator frequency), and $f_s - f_o$. Because f_s and f_o are the same if the PLL is in lock, the first output is twice the signal, and the second zero. The low pass filter does not have to be very complicated to eliminate the sum term. If either the signal or oscillator frequencies change slightly, the first effect will be a phase shift. This will produce a positive or negative DC shift in the mixer output which will make the VCO run either faster or slower to bring the two back into synchrony.

As the signal frequency rises, so will the VCO's until lock is lost at $f_o + f_c$.* The control voltage looks like Fig. 211 if one scans the signal frequency from below $f_o - f_c$

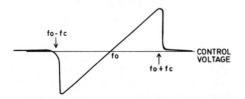

Fig. 211. *Control voltage (at demodulation output) of PLL as input signal rises from below the free-running frequency f_0 to above it.*

to above $f_o - f_c$. The width of the lock range, $2f_c$, depends on several things:

1 The size of the incoming signal.
2 Heaviness of filtering.
3 Attenuation in the feedback loop.

Point 1 is a needless confusion, so most practical PLLs are fed with signal from a limiter (see p. 24) which keeps the input at a constant level—usually 0.3 V peak-to-peak. Points 2 and 3 can then control the lock width, and what use one makes of them depends on the use to which one wants to put the PLL.

The simplest application is to use the PLL to demodulate frequency-modulated transmissions. Since this method of modulation codes audio amplitude by shifting the carrier frequency slightly above and below a certain value, it is clear that as long as the carrier is within the lock range, the control voltage reproduces the audio signal. In this application frequency is a problem, since the limit of IC versions of the device is about 30 MHz, while FM is commonly used at much higher frequencies. But a PLL to run at

10 MHz or so is no problem, and it can be used to demodulate the intermediate frequency (IF) (see below pp. 82–83 for a simple method). Used as an FM demodulator, one wants to keep the lock range fairly small since this excludes neighbouring channels and reduces the amount of noise bandwidth which the PLL can reproduce—for it will tend to lock to the strongest signal available. If there is a noise pulse in its lock range stronger than the signal, it will be reproduced.

The first PLLs were used to solve a particularly difficult problem: to receive early satellite signals. Because power available in the satellite was limited, transmissions often used only 10 mW. On the ground their signals were buried in noise. To make the problem of recovering them more difficult, the signal was wildly doppler-shifted in frequency as the satellite shot from horizon to horizon. The PLL, which is in effect a narrow band tracking filter, was just the answer. Often it is necessary to demodulate telemetry sent as frequency shift keying (FSK). In this system, 'mark' and 'space' are sent by slight high and low shifts of the carrier frequency. Accurate tracking needs a shorter time constant in the PLL's low pass filter.

The cheapest and easiest way of building a PLL is to use (rather surprisingly) a 7401 TTL logic gate—a quad two input NAND; see Fig. 212. This circuit was

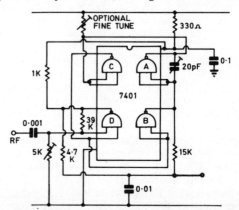

Fig. 212. *7401 Quad NAND gate wired as phase locked loop.*

designed by Rodney King, and published in *Wireless World*, in July 1973. Gates A, B and C are arranged as a multivibrator; see Fig. 213. When A output goes high, it charges the capacitor up through the gate's output impedance. When the capacitor is charged up, it sends C input high, C output goes low, B output goes high which switches A output low, and the cycle repeats in reverse. Current from the low pass filter, speeds the oscillation rate up, or slows it down.

---

* This is a slight simplification, since a PLL will go on locking to a slightly lower or higher frequency than it will capture. But it makes no fundamental difference to the argument.

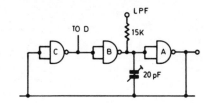

Fig. 213. Gates A, B, C are wired as an oscillator.

Gate *D* is wired as a mixer; see Figs. 214 and 215. One input is switched high and low by the output of *C*; the other is biased so that when the gate is enabled by a high on the first input, it acts as an amplifier and gives a voltage gain of 100. This looks an odd way of biasing the gate, but is equivalent to the transistor system

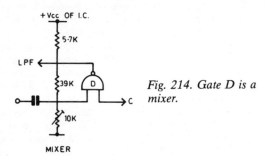

Fig. 214. Gate D is a mixer.

Fig. 215. Its output is filtered, and the DC component changes the rate of oscillation by injecting current into B input.

LOW PASS FILTER (LPF)

shown in Fig. 216. The output of gate *D*, then, is the sum and difference of the signal frequency and the multivibrator's.

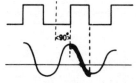

Fig. 216. Replace the NAND gate in Fig. 214 by a transistor to get this familiar bias scheme.

The first step in building this PLL is to get the bias for gate *D* right. It is worth starting on a breadboard, and playing with the values so that one gets an intuitive idea of how the thing works. Bias one input of gate *D* high, and then adjust the bias on the other input until it amplifies. The output will be at 2.4 V. This will not be quite the final bias position, because the low pass filter and input to *B* slightly alter the load. Try the effect of different resistors in the 15 kΩ position—it also

changes the free-running frequency of the multivibrator. For operation around 10 MHz the capacitor can be a 6–30 pF variable. For lower frequency operation, the capacitor is larger and fine tuning is best carried out with a variable resistor between the output of gate A and the positive rail.

With FM signals, the control voltage reproduces audio. If it is passed through another low pass filter with $f_c = 300$ Hz to remove the audio, it will yield a direct voltage which can be used to give an off-tune indication; see Fig. 217. If it is amplified, inverted and

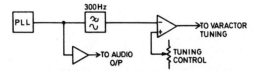

Fig. 217. If the PLL output is filtered to remove audio, it can also produce a tuning correction voltage.

added to the tuning voltage of an elecronically tuned front end, this becomes a simple automatic frequency control (AFC) system. In theory, amplitude modulated signals produce no effect on the control voltage of a PLL because during the positive sectors of the multivibrator waveform, the mixer has equally high and low segments of RF to amplify; see Fig. 218. The AM

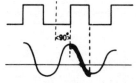

Fig. 218. When the PLL's oscillator and the signal are 90° out of phase the mixer amplifies equal positive and negative components of the signal, and so produces no output. If the phase shifts, + or −DC is produced.

element cancels out. (As with so much of electronics, this is truer in theory than in practice; but still, a PLL is a poor AM demodulator.)

Although a PLL is a good way of demodulating FM, it is only just coming into use in expensive sets. Most broadcast sets demodulate the carrier by passing it through an LC circuit tuned to the centre frequency. As the FM signal falls below or above the centre frequency, so the LC circuit looks to it like a coil or a capacitor instead of pure resistance, and so it leads or lags in phase (p. 113). This leading and lagging is detected in a pair of diodes and amplified to give audio. There are many detailed variations, but the original Foster–Seeley circuit is shown in Fig. 219. The response is very like that of a PLL, but the noise performance is worse at low signal levels.

To cope with AM and DSB signals, it is necessary to shift the RF signal by another 90° in a simple RC

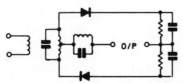

Fig. 219. Foster–Seeley type FM demodulator. As the input frequency deviates from the resonant frequency of the (vertical) tuned circuit, so the circuit looks like either inductance or capacitance. The diodes detect the resulting lead or lag. The (horizontal) tuned circuit keeps RF out of the audio output.

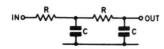

Fig. 220. A cascaded low pass filter.

network (Fig. 220). This is not critical (see p. 43 for calculation of values). Once the RF signal is shifted, it comes back into phase with the oscillator, and the second mixer amplifies only the positive peaks. This gives the original AM signal; see Fig. 221.

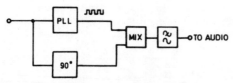

Fig. 221. If the RF input to a PLL is shifted by 90° and mixed with the PLL's restored RF, the circuit will detect AM. Refer to Fig. 218: RF in the second mixer is now passed or amplified only during positive or negative peaks so amplitude variations are reproduced.

Frequency synthesis

Phase locked loops are often used for frequency synthesis. The idea is to insert a frequency divider between the VCO and mixer, and to feed into the other port of the mixer the output from a stable reference oscillator. Suppose we want a series of frequencies 5 kHz apart from 5 MHz up; see Fig. 222. When the 'Divide-by-n' counter is set to divide by 1000, the

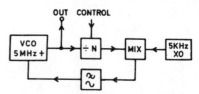

Fig. 222. Frequency synthesizer using PLL and digital divide-by-n circuit. The divided down VCO output is locked to a 5 kHz frequency, so as n is changed, the VCO's frequency alters in 5 kHz steps.

action of the mixer and low pass filter will pull the VCO to 5 MHz. When n is 1001, the VCO will run at 5.005 MHz, when n is 1002, the VCO runs at 5.010 MHz, and so on, up in 5 kHz channels. The divide-by-n counter is a logic circuit which can be bought complete either in TTL or COS/MOS (see data books). 'n' is set into it by switches.

In practice this sort of channel spacing is more likely to be needed at VHF and UHF, and it is usually necessary to derive the reference frequency from a crystal controlled oscillator running at about 2–3 MHz for the best stability. Since it is impracticable at the moment to make a PLL which will run at hundreds of MHz, it is necessary to shift the VCO's output into the PLL's range by dividing (prescaling) it or mixing it with a crystal oscillator offset in frequency.

OFFSET SYSTEM

See Fig. 223. Here the output of the voltage controlled oscillator VCO is reduced to a frequency that the 'Divide-by-n' counter can handle by mixing it with an offset crystal oscillator. For 'Receive' a second offset oscillator is used, differing from the first by the IF—in this example, 8 MHz. 'n' is set into the counter by switches—here Channel 1 selects $n = 1000$, Channel 2 selects $n = 1001$ etc. The output of the PLL mixer, or phase comparator, is put through a low pass audio filter so that the FM signal (between 300 Hz and 2.7 kHz) is not cancelled out.

PRESCALER SYSTEM

See Fig. 224. The VCO output is divided by 24, say, in a high speed divider, to bring it down to a frequency suitable for the 'Divide-by-n' counter. The channel

Fig. 223. Offset synthesizer for use in transceiver. See text.

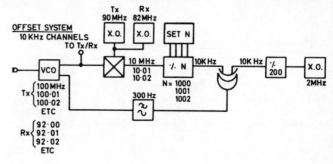

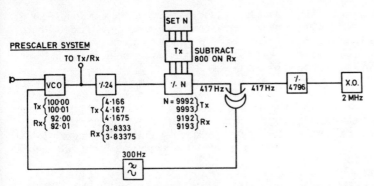

Fig. 224. Prescaler system. See text.

spacing reference frequency also has to be divided by 24, so is now 415 Hz. For transmit on Channel 1, n is 9992; on Channel 2, n is 9993 etc. To receive on Channel 1, n has to be 9192, and on Channel 2, n has to be 9193, so we need a circuit to subtract 800 from n when the set is to receive. This is not all that difficult.

The alert reader who checks these figures will find that since decimals have been dropped to round n to whole numbers, the VCO frequencies are not just what they should be. In a practical system a certain amount of juggling is necessary to reconcile whole number n's with the wanted frequencies. Naturally the Prescaler system is easiest and cheapest, since it does away with two crystal oscillators and a mixer stage. But it can only be used up to the frequency limit of prescaling dividers, which is about 2 GHz. For SHF synthesis, the offset technique is the only practical one.

So far we have been considering analogue PLLs, albeit with some digital techniques. One can build phase locked loops which deal with digital signals equally well.

A common problem arises when a signal consists of a pulse train in which information is coded by advancing or delaying pulse position. This is known as pulse position (or phase) modulation (p. 60). Signal pulses lag or lead the clock pulses accordingly as the audio signal is more or less positive or negative at the time of the clock pulses. Only the signal pulses are transmitted.

To decode this pulse train it is first necessary to reconstitute the clock pulses in the receiver. This information is contained in the signal train as a whole, but not in any particular pair of pulses, for the time between them varies with the audio signal. One way of doing this is to switch a bistable alternately with the signal pulse and a variable oscillator pulse. The bistable output is smoothed, amplified, inverted and used to control the oscillator; see Fig. 225. The capacitor feedback across the op-amp averages the output. The pnp transistor acts as an emitter follower and the zener diode shifts the output upwards so that the unijunction emitter charging voltage starts from a high enough level. The circuit will set itself so the uni-junction pulses occur half way between the average positions of the signal pulses. The output of the bistable is a square wave with a variable mark-to-space ratio: if this is put through a low pass filter the audio can be recovered. This circuit works well with communication frequency audio (300 Hz to 3.3 kHz) and clock rates of 8 kHz to 10 kHz.

This circuit was designed for use with signal pulses of about 1 μs—so short that it was irrelevant whether the bistable switched on the rising edge or the DC level. But the diodes in the bistable inputs make it possible to use much wider pulses. In this case we used a bistable as a phase comparator: one could just as well use an IC flip-flop, like a CD4013. Another possibility is to

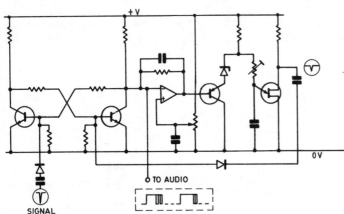

Fig. 225. Phase locked loop for reconstituting clock pulses in a PPM system (see Fig. 194) using discrete components.

connect two NAND gates together to make a flip-flop, or to use an exclusive OR gate. This latter has the advantage that if signal is lost, the output returns to the mid-position, where it is mostly likely to make a quick capture once it returns. The snag about mixing ICs and discrete components is always supply levels. Here the flip-flop would have to be COSMOS since the average value of its output (i.e. half its supply rail), has to be the same as half the op-amp's rail voltage. If we used TTL, with its 5-V supply, the op-amp couldn't work properly.

It is also possible to get complete phase lock loops ready packaged in an IC. At the time of writing only RCA and Signetics supplied them. The RCA device CD4046 is COSMOS (see Fig. 226) and therefore relatively slow: 1.2 MHz with a 10-V rail. But it uses little power, and has the useful option of two different phase comparators: 'I' is an ordinary exclusive OR gate, 'II' is an edge controlled logic network (i.e. directly applicable to the problem above) with a secondary output that yields a phase-pulse output only when the PLL is locked—this can be used for an 'in-tune' indication.

R_1 and C_1 determine the tuning range of the VCO, R_2 offsets the free running frequency from the centre if necessary. Pin 10 is the output of an emitter follower on the control voltage to reduce loading from later audio stages. It need not be used. If it is, a resistor greater than 10 kΩ goes to ground. Pin 15 is a 5.2-V zener to pin 8 and ground for supply regulation if needed.

I haven't described the 4046 in greater detail because it is better to get the data sheet and application note ICAN 6101 from RCA. The Signetics application note is extremely informative on the general history of PLLs, and is well worth getting. Signetics offer a range of ICs: the 560B, 562B and 656 are for general purposes, 561B has a built-in extra mixer for AM demodulation and 567 is specially designed for tone

decoding as, for example, in FSK signalling. Again, it would be silly to try to go into greater detail here. I haven't used Signetics PLLs because they're somewhat expensive. The RCA one is quite cheap and works well, if slowly.

A reasonable radio receiver for MW in strong signal areas can be made simply by driving the PLL with a secondary winding on a ferrite aerial primary tuned by a fixed capacitor, and phase shifting the PLL waveform by 90°, mixing it with the RF in another NAND gate, smoothing and amplifying the result; see Fig. 227.

RF oscillators

We now have to consider the slightly tedious subject of RF oscillators, the circuits which generate the wide range of frequencies that are necessary in all branches of the art. An oscillator is simply an amplifier with positive AC feedback—the output starts going positive, the positive feedback encourages it to go more positive, and it carries on until it hits the positive rail. If it had DC feedback it would stay there, 'latch up' as it's called—a malady early op-amps were prone to—but since the feedback is AC (usually via coil or capacitor), the input stops and the output starts to go negative. As soon as it moves, feedback starts again, encouraging it to go more negative. And so on. Most amplifiers will oscillate if they are allowed, at a frequency which depends on some oddity of their internals; a properly designed oscillator has its frequency determined by an accessible timing circuit.

Oscillators divide into two families according to whether the timing is done by a resistor–capacitor combination, or coil–capacitor. Until recently audio oscillators used the former and radio the latter, but in recent years accurate and stable IC oscillators using a resistor–capacitor timing mechanism have become available. They have the great advantage that the

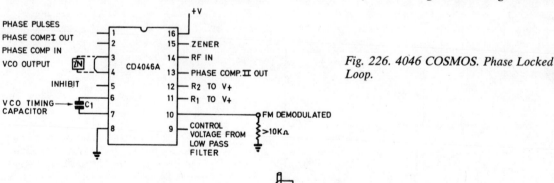

Fig. 226. 4046 COSMOS. *Phase Locked Loop.*

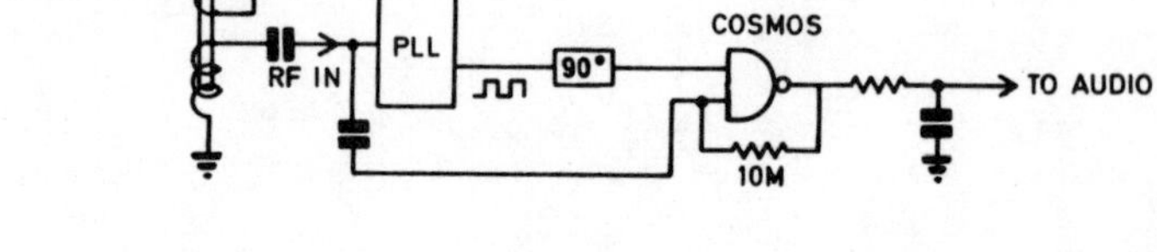

Fig. 227. Simple AM receiver based on PLL for use in high signal strength areas.

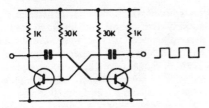

Fig. 228. Two-transistor multivibrator.

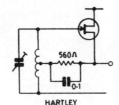

Fig. 230. Hartley oscillator.

frequency can be altered over a very wide range with a single control voltage. The original name for this class of circuit was multivibrator, and the original valve circuit, translated into transistors, is shown in Fig. 228. The most desirable quality in an oscillator is stability— that is, its frequency should vary as little as possible. The main cause of change is, again, heat: it causes coils and capacitors to expand and contract, thus changing their characteristics, and worse, it alters the gain and internal capacitance of bipolar transistors. For this reason they are to be despised in oscillators and the lower-power FETs which do not do these things, used in preference.

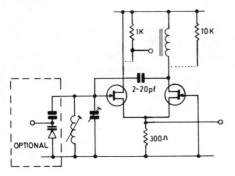

Fig. 229. Two-FET oscillator with alternative loads for high and low frequency, and high and low impedance outputs.

My favourite RF oscillator is shown in Fig. 229. At low frequencies the left hand FET can have a 1 kΩ drain load, the right hand one a 10 kΩ—and in this case a higher impedance output is available from the left hand drain. At high frequencies, when you need all the gain you can get, the left hand drain should go directly to rail, and the right hand drain through an RF choke. In both forms, a low impedance output is available from the common source. It is not necessary to match the devices for I$_{dss}$. The feedback capacitor, marked '2–20 pF', needs to be adjusted to the *smallest* value that will give oscillation, otherwise the right hand drain loads the tuned circuit and spoils Q. It has the great advantage that the frequency determining LC circuit is well separated from the outputs, so loading them doesn't change the tune.

There is a set of classical oscillator circuits which get positive feedback by tapping down the LC resonant

circuit and feeding the result back to the source of an FET; see Fig. 230. There should be about twice as many turns above the tap as there are below it—the total number, of course, determines the inductance and therefore the resonant frequency. The 1 nF capacitor just has to present a low reactance at the oscillation frequency.

The equivalent circuit using a capacitive tap is the Colpitts; see Fig. 231. The top capacitor should be a half to one third of the value of the bottom one; their combined value (p. 118) again determines the frequency.

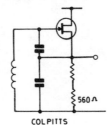

Fig. 231. Colpitts oscillator.

Both—or indeed any—oscillators should be very well decoupled from the supply. This can be done with a choke, but since they draw very little current, a 100-Ω resistor would be better since there is no possibility of joke oscillations caused by the choke resonating with some odd capacitance. The Hartley–Colpitts circuit will produce a voltage swing of 1 V or so across a 500-Ω resistor, which means a power output of 1 mW. A very good thing about this is that the outputs are well isolated from the frequency determining LC circuit, so loads will not pull the frequency. I muss confess that I've never had a lot of success with one transistor oscillators. They tend to be unwilling to start, temperamental, and low powered.

If you want a radio transmitter in a small space, and aren't too worried about frequency stability—as it might be because you are in missile telemetry in some remote spot, or surveillance bugging, or you're just irresponsible—then you can use a power oscillator. The simple circuit shown in Fig. 232 is said by RCA to produce 4 W at 420 MHz, which could otherwise be quite a performance.

The transistor is wired in common base, with a slight forward bias on the base and a little bit of bias on the emitter through the 3.9-Ω resistor. The output is matched to 50-Ω coax by tapered strip line (p. 122).

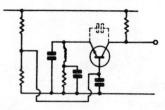

Fig. 232. UHF oscillator using transistor in common base.

Positive feedback is through the internal collector–emitter capacitance C_f, which in this device is 3 pF. A BFY90 would be a good transistor to use for a lower powered version, and it might be necessary to provide an external feedback capacitor.

Crystal oscillators

A crystal is simply a thin wafer of quartz cut in a special way with an electrode on each side. When a voltage is applied to one electrode, the crystal changes shape, owing to the piezo-electric effect—and a pressure wave is set going to the other side. When it arrives there, it is partly reconverted into voltage on the electrode, and partly reflected back; see Fig. 233. If the reflected wave

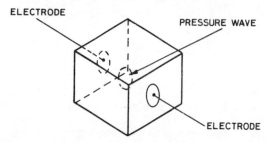

Fig. 233. A voltage on an electrode attached to quartz causes the crystal to contract, and launches a pressure wave through it which is reconverted to a voltage on the opposite electrode.

arrives at the first electrode at the same time as a new electric impulse, we have resonance, and a very accurate frequency determining device. When digital watch manufacturers advertise 'computer quartz accuracy' this is all they mean—a device used in radio for the last 40 years. In many ways a crystal works like a very high Q LC circuit. It is equivalent to the circuit shown in Fig. 234. L, C_s and R are the equivalents of a

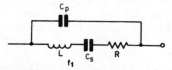

Fig. 234. Equivalent circuit of crystal: an inductance with parallel Cp and series Cs capacitance to pass or resist similar frequencies.

series tuned circuit which has some resistance. C_p is the capacitance of the crystal and its electrodes viewed simply as a capacitor. If this last were absent the crystal would *pass* a frequency f_1 depending on L, C_s, and resist all others. Because of C_p, it also acts as a *parallel* LC circuit which *resists* a slightly higher frequency f_2. Consequently a crystal's frequency-impedance curve looks like Fig. 235. When a crystal vibrates at its

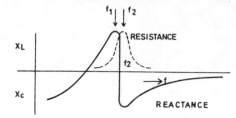

Fig. 235. Resistance and reactance curves for crystal.

Fig. 236. A crystal operating in its fundamental mode: the centre is still, while the sides move in and out.

resonant frequency, each side goes in and out like a jelly, while the centre, the 'static node', stays still. This mode of operation is called the 'fundamental'; see Fig. 236. Fundamental resonance works up to 20 or 30 MHz. Then the crystal gets too thin for comfort, and the manufacturer makes it thicker, while encouraging it in subtle ways to resonate at the third overtone—which is not quite three times the fundamental, see Fig. 237.

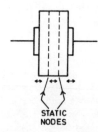

Fig. 237. Second harmonic: there are two static zones.

This time there are two static nodes inside, while the middle and outsides shake to and fro. This covers 20 MHz to 60 MHz. From 60 MHz up to 120 MHz, fifth and seventh overtones are used. There is no particular magic which tells a crystal it is to work on the fundamental, or fifth, overtone or whatever. To make sure that it goes off at the right frequency a tuned circuit is necessary somewhere in the oscillator.

At f_1 reactance is zero and resistance is low—the crystal passes a chosen frequency. At f_2 the reactance is also zero, but the resistance is high, so it resists that frequency. The separation between f_1 and f_2 is typically 0.2 per cent of either (i.e. a crystal which resists 27 MHz will pass 26.946 MHz). For practical purposes the two frequencies can be taken to be the same. Generally a crystal working in series can replace a capacitor in an oscillator. For professional equipment crystals are specially made either for series or parallel operation, but the amateur tends to use whatever he can pick up from the surplus and supply houses and it doesn't matter very much which way round they are used. It is also important to note that a crystal likes to drive a small capacitance—something around 30 pF—and if the circuit does not provide it, we should. This improves stability. Finally one must remember that the enemy of all oscillators is temperature change. Most modern crystals are cut in such a way that their temperature coefficient—the change of frequency per °C—is a minimum at 25 °C.

The frequency at which a crystal resonates can be slightly changed by shunting it with more or less external capacitance—not too much or the thing will stop altogether. This is called 'pulling' a crystal, and frequency modulation is often achieved by connecting a variable capacitance diode across a crystal and biasing it with the amplified voice voltage; see Fig. 238. (C is 10× or more of the diode capacitance.)

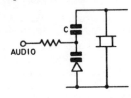

Fig. 238. The natural frequency of a crystal can be 'pulled' slightly by external capacitance in parallel—here, a varactor.

A very useful crystal oscillator for use below 10 MHz is that shown in Fig. 239, on a COSMOS inverter or NAND gate.

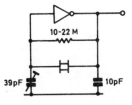

Fig. 239. Crystal oscillator using COSMOS buffer or NAND gate.

Fig. 240 is a one transistor crystal oscillator, using a IGFET (the diode is for bias, not tuning).

There are a number of crystal oscillators for digital circuits which have more or less attractive features, like complementary outputs (Plessey SP705B), two independent outputs (TI74S/LS124) and so on, but since their amplifiers usually have huge bandwidth, there is no real guarantee that they will go off at the frequency you think you want. The oscillator in Fig. 229 can be crystal controlled (a) by replacing the feedback capacitor with a crystal; (b) by putting the crystal in parallel with the tuned circuit. The ideal

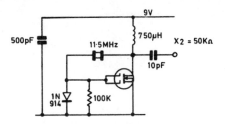

Fig. 240. Crystal oscillator with IGFET.

oscillator would have the stability of crystal and the tunability of a VCO. It doesn't exist. The nearest we can get to it is a crystal-stabilized frequency synthesizer (p. 70). Of course, by making the reference frequency low enough, and n large enough, one can approach the ideal.

A new development in crystal technology is the Surface Acoustic Wave Device; see Fig. 241. This is a

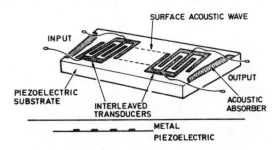

Fig. 241. Surface Acoustic Wave Device: this version passes a frequency determined by the distance between the teeth of the combs.

slab of piezo-electric crystal along whose surface waves are set going. They can be used for delay lines, filters, oscillators. At the moment they are not available on the amateur market, but no doubt will be within a few years (see *Wireless World*, August 1976, p. 39).

FREQUENCY MULTIPLICATION

The best frequencies for crystal oscillators are between 2 MHz and 27 MHz. Rather than try to generate frequencies directly above this range, it is often better to multiply up. This process relies on the presence of harmonics in the oscillator outputs—second and third are usually strong enough to be useful. A 'doubler' or 'tripler' consists of an RF amplifier biased in Class C (p. 8) to encourage harmonics, with the input tuned to the oscillator frequency, and the output to twice or three times that; see Fig. 242. Because the tuned input has a low impedance at the output frequency, it usually isn't necessary to neutralize the amplifier to prevent oscillation (p. 12). UHF receivers and transmitters may have three or four successive multipliers to get up to the high frequencies needed from a starting point in the tens or twenties of MHz.

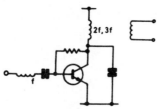

Fig. 242. Frequency doubler or trebler—depending on resonant frequency of load. The transistor is in Class C, to increase output harmonics. Input must therefore exceed 0.6 V pp.

NOISE

Much of electronics is to do with making the very small large enough to be appreciated by our senses. Since the amount of gain we can create is, in principle, unlimited, there seems no end to the sensitivity of the devices we can build. However, nature steps in and sets a very effective limit through noise: that is the true music of the spheres.

Noise is the hissing in between stations in a radio: you are listening to the remains of the big bang still ricocheting about the cosmos—you are listening to thunderstorms in Africa, car ignitions in the next block, you are listening to the clashing together of atoms in the input circuits of that same set. As one delves deeper into the tiny, noise appears everywhere, and a lot of real electronics—and many other studies—is concerned with how to reduce it, and how to dig deeper into it for what you want. It is a business full of difficulties; many a frightening tome has been written on the subject. But, happily, we can salvage enough for our purpose without too much trouble.

First things first: imagine a resistor lying on a bench, not connected to anything. One imagines that the two ends should be at the same voltage. In fact, because of the random thermal movements of electrons in it, at any moment more are likely to appear at one end than the other. It is as if there were a tiny generator inside the resistor whizzing away, delivering an infinite range of frequencies, keeping the ends a few millionths of a volt different from each other. If you had a very sensitive voltmeter, you could measure this fluctuating potential. You would find that the *power* developed by this atomic generator is

$$k \times T \times B \times R \text{ Watts}$$

where k is Boltzmann's constant (1.37×10^{-23}); B is the bandwidth of the voltmeter in Hertz; T is the absolute temperature (°C + 273) and R is the resistance in ohms.

We are normally interested in voltage, and since power is proportional to voltage *squared* (p. 110) divided by resistance, it is not surprising to learn that the voltmeter reading (actually the root mean square of

the random noise fluctuations) will be:

$$V_n = R \sqrt{(2 \times k \times T \times B)}$$

If we have a 50 Ω resistance—say a dummy aerial for a VHF radio under test, which has a 25 kHz bandwidth: at room temperature, $V_n = 0.72$ μV which is quite a lot.

From this equation several useful conclusions flow:

1 Since noise *powers* are additive, if we have several sources giving voltages v_1, v_2, v_3 etc. the total noise voltage V_t

$$V_t = \sqrt{(v_1^2 + v_2^2 + v_3^2 + \ldots)}$$

If one of these voltages is a third or less than the biggest, it can be neglected because its contribution to the quantity under the root is only one ninth.

2 The noise voltage in any system is proportional to the square root of the bandwidth. This means that if you can reduce the bandwidth by 4, you halve the noise level, which is often worth doing since it doubles the range. It might help to think of the frequency spectrum as one of those long, spotted-dog puddings one used to get at school. The dough is noise and the raisins are signals: the object is to cut the thinnest slice of dough that still encloses the raisin you want.

3 One way of looking at the communications game is as a gamble: betting that the signal you think you have detected is a real signal and not a chance product of noise. When the sums are done, it turns out that if your amplifier output jumps to twice the rms noise voltage there is a 20 : 1 chance that you have signal. If it jumps to 4 times the rms value, it's better than 10 000 : 1 against chance. And if an amplifier is designed to handle ·10 times the expected rms voltage it will get overloaded by noise for a pico-second per century. Which you can forget.

4 The name of the game is maximizing signal while minimizing noise. At any particular point in the frequency spectrum, each source of noise contributes a uniform amount of power per unit bandwidth—or per unit width of spotted-dog pudding. Hence the noise voltage from each source is proportional to the square root of bandwidth multiplied by source impedance, and minimizing this product is our powerful weapon in the fight against this manifestation of nature.

5 The effective bandwidth of a radio receiver with a radio bandwidth of Δf_1 followed by a detector and amplifier with bandwidth Δf_2, is $\sqrt{(2\Delta f_1 \times \Delta f_2)}$. Imagine a set with a radio bandwidth of 20 kHz and an audio bandwidth of 3 kHz—just enough for voice communication. The effective bandwidth is $\sqrt{(2 \times 20 \times 10^3 \times 3.10^3)} = 11$ kHz. If we changed to morse instead of voice, which needs a bandwidth of, say, 100 Hz, and reduced the radio bandwidth to 10 kHz, the noise bandwidth would be 1 kHz—an improvement by a

factor of 11, which means that the signal could be heard eleven times as far away, or the transmitter could use about one hundredth the power. It is evident that if you use very slow signalling rates to get very narrow bandwidths, you can transmit with minute amounts of power and produce a signal that may be invisible to normal wideband receivers.

So far we have been talking about noise in an idealized sort of way, without taking into account the imperfections of the real amplifiers and detectors we have to use. Any piece of equipment produces noise to add to that which comes in along with the signal. Just how much it adds is expressed by its *noise figure* (NF) which is defined as the ratio, in dB, of noise volts produced by the device to that produced by a resistor equal in value to its input impedance, at the same temperature. So, a receiver with an input impedance of 50 Ω and a NF of 6 dB will produce $1.995 \times 0.13 \ \mu V = 0.26 \ \mu V$ of noise. A rough rule of thumb is that a signal must produce at least that voltage on the aerial to be any use. Obviously each stage of an amplifier produces noise, but since the first one amplifies the signal way above the tenths of microvolts at which noise is found, only the first stage makes any important contribution. (Don't confuse this with the effect of the *bandwidth* of later stages on both input and device noise at the output.) The main thing that can be done to minimize noise is to choose the right input device for the frequency involved, and to make sure it is driven by the right impedance.

A bipolar transistor has a mid-range of frequencies over which its internal noise is least. The lower bound is $f_T/\sqrt{(2 \times \beta)}$ and the upper is $f_T/2$. A 2N2926 with $f_T = 200$ MHz, $\beta = 300$, is suitable for the range 8 MHz to 100 MHz (which is odd, since it's sold as a low noise audio device!). A BFY90 with f_T 1300 MHz, $\beta = 80$ suits the range 102 MHz to 650 MHz. The practical upper bound is less than this, since one reckons that in a common emitter form, a transistor's gain falls off after $f_T/5$. For a bipolar transistor in its low noise range, the best input impedance is given by.[*]

$$F_{s0} = \frac{f_T}{f \times g_m} \sqrt{[\tfrac{1}{2} + (R_b \times g_m)]}$$

A minor snag here is R_b, the base resistance, which has to be found by doing a little experiment because it is in series with the *b–e* diode junction; see Fig. 243. We measure the current through the base as the voltage between base and emitter alters. If a sufficiently sensitive ammeter is lacking, one can measure the collector current and divide it by the β of the device in question to get base current. The 10-kΩ fixed resistor is to protect the base junction in case things get out of hand. The voltmeter must have a high input impedance. I got these results with a 2N2926, which plots as a nice straight line (see Table 3). In the 0.3 V change from the

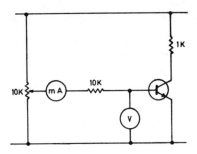

Fig. 243. Set-up to measure transistor base resistance.

TABLE 3

V_{be} (arbitrary 0):	0.2	0.3	0.4	0.5
I_b, mA	0.05	0.13	0.21	0.29

first reading to the last, the base current altered 0.24 mA. The base resistance is then $0.3/(0.24 \times 10^{-3}) = 1.2$ kΩ. From p. 5 g_m is $20 \times I_e$. So, let us contrive an input stage to work at 1 MHz using this transistor, whose f_T is 200 MHz. We can choose g_m by altering I_e which let us set, for the moment, at 5 mA; $R_{s0} = 10\ 950$ Ω.

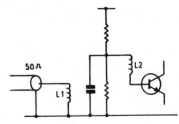

Fig. 244. Broad band—untuned—coupling to input transistor.

Supposing we have an input as shown in Fig. 244; and that L_1 has 10 turns to match 50 Ω: then remembering that the ratio of impedances is the square of the ratio of turns, L_2 needs to have 10 turns, $\sqrt{10950/50} = 148$. Not very difficult (but remember: neither coil is resonated, see p. 122). If for some reason R_{s0} were fixed, one could alter I_e to suit. The best input impedance for an FET is (either junction or insulated gate):

$$R_{s0} = \frac{1}{\sqrt{(30 \times I_g \times g_m)}}$$

For a BF244 I_g, the gate current, is 5.10^{-9} A, $g_m = 5$ mA/V, so R_{s0} is 36.514 Ω. The FET input would need $\sqrt{36\ 514/50} = 270$ turns. Very similar results apply to cascode amplifiers, either bipolar or FET.

[*] F. N. H. Robinson, *Noise and Fluctuations in Electronic Devices and Circuits* (Oxford, OUP, 1974), pp. 136–145.

F. N. H. Robinson, the writer from whose book these useful results are drawn, says that in critical applications up to 1–10 MHz the FET is better for noise, *if* it can be driven by a suitably high impedance. Although an FET can give high gain, it needs a high drain impedance to do so, which may make driving later stages difficult. Generally, a bipolar transistor gives much better gain, but where the signal is small and surrounded by unwanted and possibly much larger signals at slightly different frequencies—as is the case with high quality communication receiver front ends—then the FET is better since it resists the temptation to cross modulate the wanted signal with unwanted ones. For this reason one might well use an FET in a 1 MHz broadcast receiver. Its own noise would be negligible compared to signal noise in this band.

Insulated-gate devices have comparable gate leakage currents and therefore need similar driving impedances for minimum noise to junction FETs. At low frequencies they suffer from high flicker noise and are not suitable for use in audio amplifiers. However, when used as a variable resistor, the gate is grounded to AC and therefore this disadvantage would not apply.

Although transistors are the main source of noise, all components contribute. Generally, it is best to keep front ends simple.

A VHF BROADCAST RECEIVER

We can now start to think about hardware for a receiver to work in the VHF broadcast band.

The first weapon in our battle against noise and unwanted signals is the aerial. This can be resonant at the frequency of the wanted signals—between 88 and 95 MHz—and the simplest shape is a dipole with quarter-wave arms. The Q of this arrangement isn't high, so the signal amplification is not great. But there is some, and signal appears across the inner ends with an impedance of about 70 Ω. The obvious thing to do next is to connect the inner ends to some 75-Ω coaxial cable to convey the signal to the receiver; see Fig. 245. The centre frequency of the broadcast band is 91.5 MHz, and a quarter wavelength at this frequency is 81.6 cm.

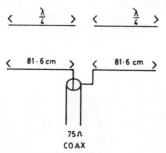

Fig. 245. *Aerial dimensions for FM broadcast reception.*

Strictly speaking we should not connect one arm of the aerial to the outer braid of the cable, since that unbalances it (the right hand arm of the aerial is now as long as the coax, rather than the correct 81.6 cm). In practice it makes little difference for reception of strong broadcast signals, but in a higher quality aerial one would have to use a device called a 'balun' to transform the balanced signal on the aerial to an unbalanced signal in the coax (balun = '*bal*ance to *un*balance'). There are many possible circuits for baluns described in standard texts. A particularly neat one is the quarter wave trap; see Fig. 246. The upper limb of the aerial is a wire or rod, the lower limb a tube, both

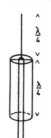

Fig. 246. *Lower, tubular element of dipole encloses and isolates coax feeder to match balanced aerial to unbalanced line.*

are λ/4 long. The coaxial feed runs up the centre of the tube. The outer braid is connected to the top of the tube. Any signal which tries to sneak up the inside of the tube and down the coax has to traverse a cavity a quarter of a wavelength deep. Consequently a positive voltage, say, takes half a cycle to run up and down again so it cancels out the following negative voltage.

Siting the aerial

Having constructed an aerial, there are two more problems: should it point up and down, or from side to side or what? And where should it be—on the chimney, in the cellar—where? The first problem is easily solved. Your friendly local VHF station(s) transmit either vertically or horizontally polarized signals (i.e. their aerials—which are very much like yours—will either be vertical or horizontal). Yours should be the same. A vertical aerial is a vertical aerial, but a horizontal one can point towards any point of the compass. Which is the right one? It should be at right angles to the line joining you to the transmitter, that is, parallel to the aerial responsible for broadcasting into your sector; see Fig. 247. Transmitter sites and polarizations are published by broadcasting authorities—any local radio or TV dealer will know. Or you can just wave the aerial about and listen to the results from the finished set. Having settled the aerial orientation, we'll now settle its position—after a short digression about propagation. Radio waves spread in three main ways:

1 By surface wave along the ground, which acts as a conductor—up to 3 MHz.

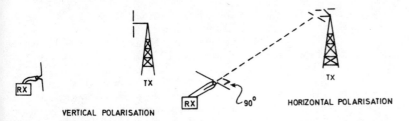

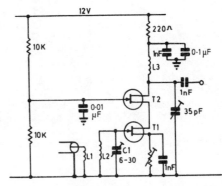

Fig. 247. Vertical and horizontal transmissions: receiver aerial orientations.

2 By reflection from the ionosphere—3 MHz to 30 MHz.
3 By direct propagation along line of sight between aerials—any frequency in principle, but in practice VHF and up.

Setting alternative 2 aside, because it is rather special, the operation of the other two modes depends very much on the effect of the ground. Because the ground conducts below 3 MHz, a vertically polarized wave is reflected in phase, which means that a receiver at ground level gets twice the signal strength—the direct wave plus a reflected wave—it would in free space. This is why long and medium wave broadcasting works so well into receivers with built in aerials which may be physically on the ground, as at a picnic, or in a small boat.

Just the reverse happens at VHF. The ground hardly conducts, so the reflected wave is out of phase and cancels the direct signal at ground level. Thus, although in free space, milliwatts of power will carry a signal thousands of miles (hence TV pictures from lunar and martian probes), on the surface of the earth things are very different. The range of a link for a given power is determined mainly by the height of the transmitting and receiving aerials. Why? Because the higher they are above ground, the greater the difference between the direct and reflected path lengths, so the less the effect of cancellation. This formula is used for estimating VHF signal strength. E at range r is:

$$E_r = E_1 \times \frac{4\pi h_1 h_2}{\lambda r^2}$$

where h_1, h_2 are the heights of the receiving and transmitting aerials, and E_1 is the field strength at 1 km and everything is measured in metres. In other words, the higher the transmitting and receiving aerials are, the better.

So much for the aerial. It is connected to the receiver by 75-Ω coax, not too long because of the loss figure. The first thing in the receiver is the preamplifier which has two functions:

1 To select the signal we want and to reject others.
2 To lift the wanted signal out of the level of device noise.

The input amplifier is an FET cascode—using either BF244s or a double MOSFET; see Fig. 248. The first

Fig. 248. Fixed tune FET cascode input amplifier. See text.

problem to resolve is whether the tuned circuits in this amplifier should track the wanted station, using varicaps (p. 20), or should stay put. To decide, we must think about the Q of the input. The broadcast band stretches 3.5 MHz either side of 91.5 MHz. This means that a circuit tuned to 91.5 MHz and with a Q of $91.5/7 = 13$ will give acceptable amplification over the whole band. In practice, at this frequency, it's unlikely that we could build a circuit with a better Q using discrete components (it is possible to do better with resonant cavities, but that's going beyond both our abilities and the exigencies of the problem), so there's no point in the elaborations of making the input and outputs track.

So, we will settle for a fixed frequency amplifier whose input and outputs have a Q of 10. (If they both had a Q of 13, signals at the ends of the band would be 6 dB down, which is a bit much.)

The next question is: how many turns for L_2? It depends on the size of C_1, which is going to be a smaller trimmer. 6–30 pF is a reasonable sort of value, so let's take C_1 to be the mean at 18 pF. That makes $L_2 = 16\ \mu H$, and it can be six turns close-wound of 22 swg, 5 mm internal diameter (p. 128). The reactance is 85 Ω. To produce a Q of 10, the circuit must have a load of 850 Ω. There are two contributors to this load: the 75-Ω input coax—equivalent to the 75 Ω impedance of the dipole aerial—and the gate of T_1. Well, the gate has such high impedance we can ignore it, so we're left with the transformed up impedance of the coax. The impedance ratio is $850/75 = 11.333$ and the square root of that, 3.4, is the turns ratio. So,

L_1 should have $6/3.4 = 18$ turns—which can either be on the same axis as L_2 at one end, or wound over the top.

As usual, T_1 source resistor has to be adjusted for gain. T_2 gate is held at mid rail by two 10 kΩs K. The supply for the amplifier is via a 220-Ω resistor, well decoupled. The remaining problem is L_3, the drain load for T_2. Before we can decide on it, we need to know what load it has to drive. It's the author's job to know what's going to happen next, and I can reveal that as a result of an upcoming decision, the input impedance of the next stage is 500 Ω shunted by 5 pF. The 5 pF will tune out. The 500-Ω load with a Q of 10 implies a reactance of 50-Ω, which makes $L_3 = 1$ μH. And that can be realised with a coil like L_2 but with only four turns.

There are two different ways of tackling the rest of the receiver. The old fashioned way uses discrete components to build mixer and IF amplifier. Bandwidth limiting, which is necessary to reduce noise (p. 76) is mainly achieved by sharply tuned circuits in the IF strip. A much easier method is to use broadband IC amplifiers, like the Plessey SL series, and to limit bandwidth with a ceramic filter. Not being masochists, we'll take this second route.

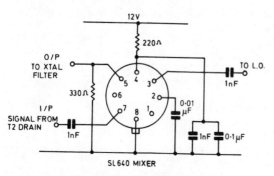

Fig. 249. Plessey SL640 mixer.

The Plessey SL640 mixer (see Fig. 249) is a double balanced type (p. 48) with an input impedance of 500 Ω, so it can be driven directly from T_2 drain through a 1 nF capacitor. It draws 14 mA at 9 V, so if our positive supply is 12 V, we can use a 3 kΩ/14 = 220 Ω resistor to decouple it. Pin 2 must also be well decoupled. The output is available at two pins—pin 6 is connected to the collectors of the mixer transistors, pin 5 is an emitter follower. We'll use pin 6 for a reason which will become apparent. The mixer drives the IF amplifier through a filter which strips off unwanted signals. A suitable one, the CFS10.7, is made by Toko. This is a three pin device whose centre pin goes to ground, and the other two are input or output according to choice. It passes a centre frequency of 10.7 MHz. Bandwidth 3 dB down is 280 kHz, and 20 dB down it's 650 kHz. Both input and output have an impedance of

330 Ω, so if we connect pin 5 of the SL640 to ground by a resistor of this value we're set.

The next thing we need is a local oscillator producing a variable frequency 10.7 MHz higher or lower than the broadcast frequency. We'll run it higher; see Fig. 250. The mixer needs 100 mV of local oscillator into kΩ, which corresponds to 5 μW of power, and can easily be supplied by this circuit. The only difficulty is with the frequency range. A BB103 varicap gives a capacitance curve as shown in Fig. 251. At 12 V it gives

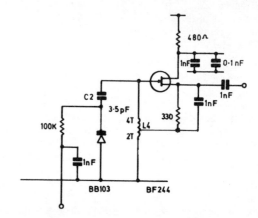

Fig. 250. Tunable Colpitts oscillator.

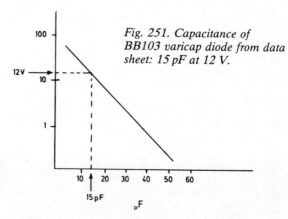

Fig. 251. Capacitance of BB103 varicap diode from data sheet: 15 pF at 12 V.

about 15 pF, at 0.5 V, 48 pF. By choosing a correct value for C_2 we can make it resonate L_4 with these values at the top and bottom ends of the frequency range (which is 98.7 + 105.7 kHz). The effective value of C_v and C_2 in series is (p. 113):

$$\frac{C_v \times C_2}{C_2 + C_v}$$

Remembering that in a tuned circuit:

$$C = \frac{1}{(2\pi f)^2 L}$$

we can write two equations:

$$\frac{C_2 \times 48}{C_2 + 48} = \frac{1}{(2\pi f \times 98.7)^2 \times L_4}$$

$$\frac{C_2 \times 15}{C_2 + 15} = \frac{1}{(2\pi \times 105.7)^2 \times L_4}$$

Dividing these to get rid of L, we have:

$$\frac{(C_2 + 15) \times 48}{(C_2 + 48) \times 15} = \left(\frac{105.7}{98.7}\right)^2$$

$$C_2 + 15 = 0.358(C_2 + 48)$$

$$C_2 = 3.4 \text{ pF}$$

Putting this value for C_2 in the first equation (or the second), we have

$$L_4 = 8 \text{ }\mu\text{H}$$

L_4 needs a reasonable number of turns so we can tap down it. A solution would be nine turns close wound (tapped three turns from the cold end) of 22 swg 10 mm internal diameter (Appendix 2). So much for the oscillator.

Now we can go back to the signal path, which leaves the mixer via pin 5 at an impedance of 330 Ω, due to the emitter–follower resistor. It then goes through the ceramic filter and has to find another 330-Ω input impedance into the next device, an SL612C IF amplifier; see Fig. 252. This useful object gives a voltage gain of 50. Input is direct to the base of a transistor through pin 5. The correct bias voltage for this transistor is available at pin 6 which has to be decoupled. So if we connect these two together with another 330-Ω resistor, we set up the right impedance for the filter. The 612 draws 15 mA at 9 V, so it too can be decoupled with a 220-Ω resistor to a 12 V rail. Pin 7 is the AGC input: the 612's gain is maximum when the voltage on pin 7 is 0.2 V, and is 70 dB down when the

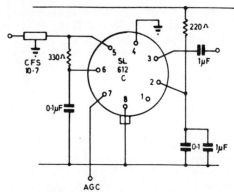

Fig. 252. Plessey SL612 IF amplifier fed through Toko 10.7 MHz, 330 Ω filter.

voltage is 5 V. We will see later about this. Output appears at pin 3, and if it's to drive a capacitative load, a 47-Ω resistor should be put in series with it to prevent oscillation. Also, since gain is quite high, it is important to mount the device on an earth plane with the leads as short as possible.

Fine. Now, will one IF amplifier be enough? Or will we need more? Since the noise figure of the input stage isn't likely to be less than 6 dB, we can start with a noise voltage of 1 μV (p. 76). If we end up with a SL624C FM limiter and detector, we need a minimum output from the IF chain of 100 μV. The RF amplifier will give a gain of 50 and an output of 50 μV. The mixer gives no gain. The ceramic filter attenuates the signal by 6 dB to 25 μV. The 612 amplifier we've already got gives a gain of 50, raising the noise signal to 1.25 mV, which is ample.

The SL624 (identical with the TBA 750) is a versatile IC which can be used, with different peripheral passive components, to demodulate FM, AM, SSB and CW; see Fig. 253. Wired as an FM detector, the SL624

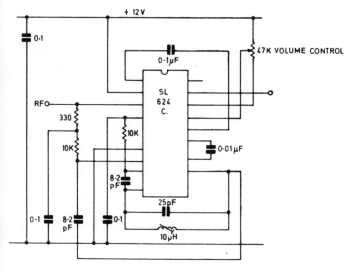

Fig. 253. SL624C limiter amplifier and FM detector.

needs one tuned circuit at the intermediate frequency. In this case 10 µH—100 turns of 42 swg on a 3 mm slugged former—would do, in parallel with 25 pF. Audio output is available on an emitter follower at pin 15. If current doesn't matter, it can drive the base of an audio power transistor directly to operate it in class A. Alternatively, a crystal at the intermediate frequency, shunted by a high value resistor (10 kΩ or so) could replace the tuned circuit.

All that is needed now is an IF gain control. If the set is to be used for listening where signal strength is high—for instance in a city—then there is no real need for automatic gain control. The gate of T_2 in the RF amplifier can be held at mid rail, and IF gain reduced by connecting pin 7 of the 612 to a potentiometer whose maximum voltage is 6 V; see Fig. 254. When everything is set up, reduce IF gain until hiss is just inaudible when the set is tuned between stations.

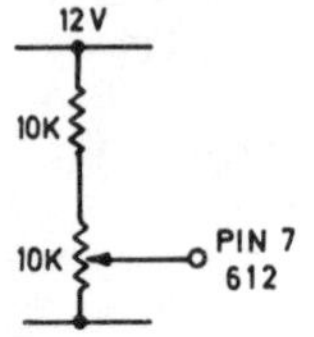

Fig. 254. Manual IF gain control for SL612.

If AGC is necessary, because the set is to be used in weak signal areas where a certain amount of noise might be tolerable in order to hear a faint station, then it would be best to include something like an SL613 C limiting amplifier/AGC generator. This device gives an RF gain of 4 and limits on an input of 120 mV. Since the first 612 has a minimum output of 1.25 mV, a second will raise the noise level to 62 mV. This doesn't look quite enough to make the 613 limit, but these figures are all rather vague, and anyway ignore man-made and atmospheric noise which may well be more than 1 µV.

So, we have two 612s, each with its own supply decoupling resistor, the first driving the second through a 47-Ω resistor and the second driving the 613

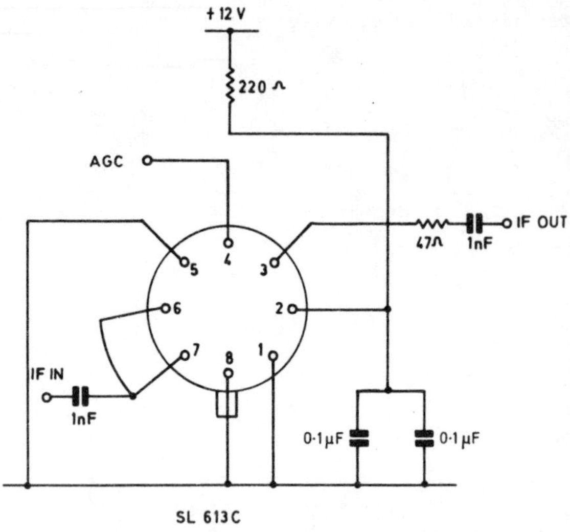

Fig. 255. SL613 limiter and AGC generator.

in the same way; see Fig. 255. On the 613, pin 7 provides input bias and is strapped to pin 6. The AGC voltage comes out at pin 4 and should be connected to pin 7 on both the 612s. The output of the 613 is high enough to drive the TTL phase locked loop (see below).

The phase locked loop is built on the same board using a 7401 NAND gate; see Fig. 256. The hatched lines represent connections underneath the board; thin lines connections and components on top. This circuit has already been described (p. 68). To line it up, apply power to the PLL, but not to the IF amplifier, and connect the signal generator to the PLL input, with an audio amplifier or a voltmeter on the output. An audio amplifier will give a very characteristic fizz–click–fizz as the frequency is swept through the locking range. A voltmeter will kick down something like 100 mV as the oscillator approached the locking range from below and swing up as much before it unlocks. Make sure that

Fig. 256. 7401 phase lock loop, view from above. Hatched lines are connections beneath the circuit board. See Fig. 212.

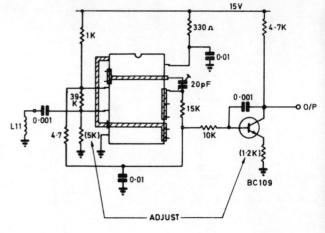

the range covered by the tuning capacitor is centred on 10 MHz.

The transistor output is necessary to raise the DC output level for automatic frequency control. The emitter–collector resistor should be adjusted until the output is at mid-rail. This transistor is exposed to IF, which we don't want to amplify, so it is discouraged by capacitative feedback and lack of a decoupling capacitor.

The automatic frequency control (AFC) circuit is simple but works satisfyingly well. The output from the PLL goes up and down in voltage as the signal frequency changes. That's the idea of FM. But it will also alter if the local oscillator frequency changes—the most likely cause of detuning. Since our LO runs *faster* than the signal, the IF is $F_o - F_s$. A too-high IF is cured by reducing the LO frequency and that is done by reducing the tuning control voltage. We need a low pass filter to remove audio signals, otherwise the AFC will cancel out the broadcast programme, and an inverting DC amplifier to produce an error voltage.

Tuning is done by using the second op-amp to subtract the tuning voltage from the error voltage. This set-up will lock on to stations and stay in tune as long as the set is turned on. If and when the LO drifts, the AFC circuit will put it back. The drawback is that tuning goes in swoops; it will try to stay locked to a station, and then get pulled away and rush to the next strong one. In the process it can leap over weak stations in between. The strength of lock is determined by the gain of the second amplifier, and that is set, in the usual way by the value of the feedback resistor (shown in Fig. 257 as 1 mΩ)—which must be a matter of individual choice.

Lining up

Although this process is described all at once, it should be done bit by bit as the various sections are built.

First let's deal with the RF amplifier. Disable the oscillator and solder one end of an RF diode to the hot end of L_3, attaching the other end to the oscilloscope or sensitive high impedance voltmeter. Disconnect the AGC, using a 10-kΩ pot to control the tuning voltage. Put power on the RF amp, and feed in 93 MHz from the signal generator. The amplifier should peak at about 90 MHz.

Now, make the oscillator work and monitor the output of the mixer. With the signal generator at 93 MHz, twiddling the tuning control should produce two very sharp outputs as the oscillator frequency is above and below the generator frequency by 10 MHz (roughly the resonant frequency of L_4). Choose the output when the tuning voltage is higher—that is, the LO is running *faster* than the generator.

Connect the audio output to an amplifier, and modulate the signal generator. Cheap ones produce a mixture of amplitude and frequency modulation. The PLL will produce a low level audio output from the amplitude modulation even when it's not in tune. The limiter should eliminate the amplitude modulation, but may not do this completely. However, when the PLL is locked, the signal generator tone comes through much more strongly. Simply twiddle the PLL variable capacitor until it locks to the IF strip output.

Now is the moment when everything is bolted down in the chassis for a last tune up: and the moment when the whole thing should be fun to play with. Check that the tuning control will bring in the signal generator with its little wire aerial right through the broadcast range. Turn off the modulation, so that the signal generator is producing RF. Notice how when you increase the signal strength, by altering the generator attenuator, noise in the receiver reduces. This is because the PLL locks more reliably to the stronger signal, and spends less time locked to noise trains that happen to be within the locking range. Try the AFC now. If it shoots off tune, that means you have the local oscillator running below signal: retune the front end.

When it all works right, drop hot wax into the RF coil formers to lock the slugs, connect up to an aerial, and happy listening.

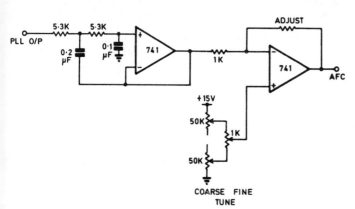

Fig. 257. Automatic Frequency Control.

Let's play Elint (electronic intelligence)

One of the main amusements of the military is the gathering of electronic intelligence. The first question that has to be answered in this field is 'Who is transmitting in the band of interest'? The tool for the job is a panoramic receiver, and with the addition of an oscilloscope, this receiver is just that. The gimmick is to use the oscilloscope's X-ramp voltage to scan the receiver instead of the normal tuning voltage, and to display the audio output on the screen; see Fig. 258. As the ramp

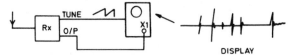

Fig. 258. Using an oscilloscope's X-axis ramp voltage to scan the receiver across a frequency band.

voltage increases from 0 to its highest value, it tunes the receiver across the band. Whenever it crosses a signal—whatever kind of signal that may be—it produces a vertical pip on the screen. The local FM broadcast stations will show up strongly, of course, but there will also be other signals that may be quite interesting. If the signal generator is loosely coupled to the receiver, it too will produce a pip that can be used to calibrate the display (or you can use an FM station to calibrate the generator). If the 'scope has two beams, the second can be used as a cursor to line up the ordinary voltage; see Fig. 259. When the tuning

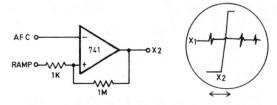

Fig. 259. A Schmitt trigger, whose output is displayed on the 'scope's second beam, compares the manual tuning voltage ('AFC') with the ramp voltage, showing which station will be recieved when manual tune is switched in.

voltage and the ramp are equal, the Schmitt trigger will switch and produce a step on the screen. This is the point on the band at which the manual tuning control is set: a changeover switch will then bring in that station.

Noise source

The simple circuit* shown in Fig. 260 is useful for testing radio receivers for sensitivity; and for noise factor

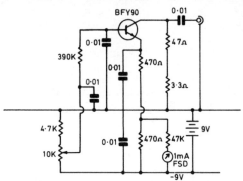

Fig. 260. Noise source, for testing receiver sensitivity and noise figure.

(NF). This looks a little complicated, but the essence is simple. A current, which is varied by the 10-kΩ pot, is passed through the collector–emitter junction of a high frequency silicon transistor—which might as well be a BFY90. The collector load is 50 Ω to match the usual receiver input. In order to use an npn transistor and still have a + earth, the emitter and bias circuits are referred to − rail. The circuit is made up in a small diecast box and powered by a 9 V battery. The current through the transistor is measured by a meter—here 1 mA full scale deflection (FSD), so it shunts one of the emitter resistors. A 10 mA meter could go in directly.

The instrument is connected to the receiver and the pot by a 50-Ω coax, and adjusted until no current flows. An AC voltmeter is connected across the loudspeaker of the receiver, and the gain turned up until the noise voltage is, say, 1 V. If you can't measure the noise voltage, the receiver isn't sensitive enough. You then increase current through the noise source until the AC voltmeter reads 2 V—which means you have doubled the noise. The noise factor is then the source current in mA. As simple as that. It should be between 2 and 8. If not, you have a rather noisy receiver, a fault that is due, if not to bad design (p. 76), then to some faulty component. Check all the soldered joints in the RF amplifier, and if it stays noisy, start replacing components. If that fails, give up.

* From Robinson *op. cit.*

Part III: Electronic logic

FIRST PRINCIPLES

This branch of electronics is certainly the one with the most potential: its limits are set largely by the imagination of the person who uses it, for every day advances in computing hardware put greater power in his hands at ludicrously low prices.

The principles are simple. Instead of using signals whose amplitude or frequency or phase convey information, electronic logic uses the voltages of the two supply rails alone. Either an output is high, or it is low—no other state has meaning. Although there are, theoretically, several ways of using these two voltage states, the chips one can actually buy all use 'positive' logic, where the supply voltage is operative, '1', and ground is its inverse '0'.* (This may sound obscure, but all will be made plain.) With the two voltage states, go three basic logical operations OR, AND and NOT. These words have special meanings which sometimes seems quite contrary to their natural meaning.

Logical text books like to talk about 'true' and 'false'. To avoid emotive context, and make it all simpler, 'true' means + voltage or high or 1; 'false' means zero volts or low or 0. Having settled that, we can look at the workings of the simple gates. Fig. 261 shows an AND with two inputs. The internals of this gate—which we will look at in turn in a moment—are arranged so that if input A is high, and B is high, then so is C, if either or both are low, then C is also. This is simply expressed in a 'truth table':

TRUTH TABLE 1.1

A	B	C
1	1	1
0	1	0
1	0	0
0	0	0

AND

AND is something like multiplication: $1 \times 1 = 1$, $0 \times 1 = 0$, $0 \times 0 = 0$. Hence the symbol '.' in logical equations.

If we were dealing in *negative* logic it would go:

TRUTH TABLE 1.2

A	B	C
0	0	0
0	1	1
1	0	1
1	1	1

AND ($-$logic)

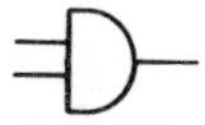

Fig. 261. Two-input AND gate.

2 I/P AND

In practice, because the wiring is simpler, and it makes little logical difference, we usually use a NAND gate, which is shorthand for NOT AND and means the 'inverse of AND'; see Fig. 262. The little circle means

2 I/P NAND

Fig. 262. Two-input NAND gate.

TRUTH TABLE 2

A	B	C
1	1	0
0	1	1
1	0	1
0	0	1

NAND

* With the usual lack of consistency, you will find the supply voltage marked as 'V_{cc}' or 'V_{DD}', and ground as 'V_{ss}' or *Gnd*. On some complex chips a negative voltage can be necessary, marked 'V_{BB}'.

'inverse'. An AND or NAND gate can have as many inputs as one likes: eight is the most one gets on an IC, but they can be cascaded together to give the same effect; see Fig. 263. The diligent reader may like to

Fig. 263. Four two-input AND's with an inverter, or NOT, are equivalent to a five-input NAND.

TRUTH TABLE 3

A	B	C	D	E	F
1	1	1	1	1	0
0	1	1	1	1	1
1	0	1	1	1	1
—	—	—	—	—	—
—	—	—	—	—	—
0	0	0	0	0	1

5-input NAND

make sure that this is the same as Fig. 264.

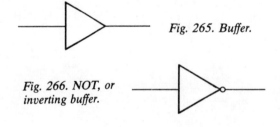

Fig. 264. Five-input NAND.

Fig. 265 shows a non-inverting buffer.

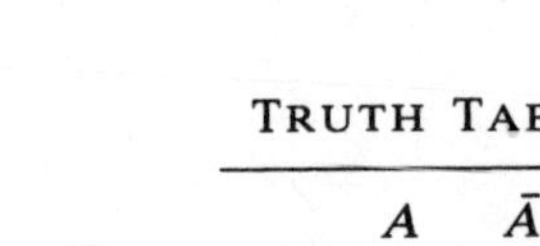

Fig. 265. Buffer.

Fig. 266. NOT, or inverting buffer.

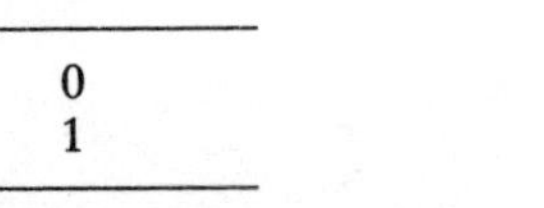

TRUTH TABLE 4

A	$\bar{A}$
1	0
0	1

NOT

The symbol for NOT A is $\bar{A}$, produced by an inverting buffer; see Fig. 266. The other logical function, OR, is thus as shown in Fig. 267. In words: if either A OR B is

Fig. 267. Two-input OR.

TRUTH TABLE 5

A	B	C
1	1	1
0	1	1
1	0	1
0	0	0

OR

high, then so is C. This is a bit like *adding*: $1+1=1$, $1+0=1$, $0+0=0$. Hence the symbol in logical equations '+'. And NOR is shown in Fig. 268. These three

Fig. 268. Two-input NOR.

TRUTH TABLE 6

A	B	C
1	1	0
1	0	0
0	1	0
0	0	1

NOR

logical functions AND, OR and NOT make possible every operation on words, mathematical symbols and figures that can be written down in accordance with unambiguous rules. They look too simple to do the work of language or mathematics, but you just need an awful lot of them—or you need to use the same ones an awful lot of times.

Let's combine these gates to make a more sophisticated one: an Exclusive OR; see Fig. 269. The output of C is to be high when either A or B is, but not both:

TRUTH TABLE 7

A	B	C
1	1	0
1	0	1
0	1	1
0	0	0

EXCLUSIVE OR

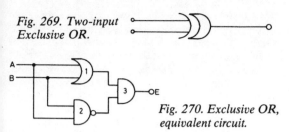

Fig. 269. Two-input Exclusive OR.

Fig. 270. Exclusive OR, equivalent circuit.

The symbol in equations is '$\oplus$'.

For the moment we have no other way of arriving at the circuit but by trial and error. Fig. 270 looks promising. Starting with the four possible combinations of A and B, and looking back to Truth tables 5 and 7, we can fill in columns C and D; using them as inputs and referring to I, we can do column E:

TRUTH TABLE 8

A	B	C	D	E
1	1	1	0	0
0	1	1	1	1
1	0	1	1	1
0	0	0	1	0

TRUTH TABLE 9

E	F	$\bar{E}$	$\bar{F}$	G	H	J
1	1	0	0	0	0	0
0	1	1	0	1	0	1
1	0	0	1	0	1	1
0	0	0	0	0	0	0

Fig. 271 is another way of doing the same thing. Either way, it's what we wanted. And, of course, there is an exclusive NOR; see Fig. 272.

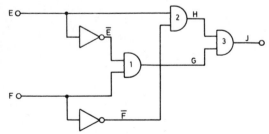

Fig. 271. Exclusive OR, another equivalent circuit.

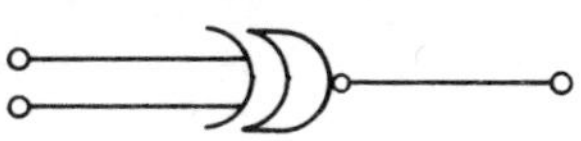

Fig. 272. Exclusive NOR.

TRUTH TABLE 10

K	L	M
1	1	1
0	1	0
1	0	0
0	0	1

EXCLUSIVE NOR

Having established the basic gates and what they do, we can now look at the hardware which embodies them. There are, at the time of writing, two main families of logic devices readily available: TTL—transistor–transistor logic—and CMOS.

TTL

This family's gates are made from fast acting bipolar transistors with an ingenious technique that gives each transistor several emitters. A two-input NAND is shown in Figs. 273 and 274. Notice the two forms: one has an integral collector load, so it works without any other components; the other, for the sake of speed, has no load, and relies on the input to the next gate for its + supply. All TTL gates are designed to work

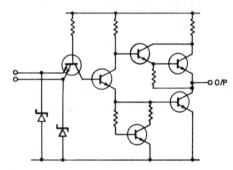

Fig. 273. TTL: internal wiring of AND gate, totem-pole output.

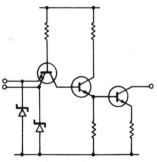

Fig. 274. TTL AND gate with open collector (O/C) output.

together in either form: if there isn't a subsequent gate, the open collector type needs a 1-kΩ resistor to V_{cc}. A TTL output acts as a current sink; when it is off, the voltage 1 state is supplied by the next input, or by the collector load. Usually one output will drive—or sink the current from—ten standard inputs. This is called the 'fan-out' figure, and can vary with some gates. The zener diodes protect against over-voltage on the input.

The *open collector* gates can be connected in parallel to give the effect of an OR gate: this is called WIRED OR. Looked at as an amplifier, a TTL gate has a lot of gain—which explains its high speed and heavy current consumption. It is a rule with logic technology that speed is proportional to power consumption. TTL is the fastest, and the greediest.

Texas Instruments, the leading manufacturer, offer their logic gates in five different families: high power, normal, low power, Schottky and low power Schottky. They are identified by initials in the middle of the type number. For instance an ordinary flip-flop is 7473. The high power version is numbered 74H73, the low power 74L73, the Schottky 74S73 and the low power Schottky 74LS73. All that matters to the user is the power/speed trade-off (see Table 4).

(It is slightly confusing that there is a second completely parallel dynasty of logical gates which start

two signals that have to work together don't arrive out of step. The maximum frequency a gate will work at is roughly 1/propagation time. 'Power dissipation' is useful, remembering that the supply is 5 V, so 19 mW, for example, corresponds to 3.8 mA. 'Maximum frequency' gives an idea of how fast a complex gate will work—though these figures are optimistic. In case of doubt consult the *TTL Data Book*. In fact, it is always necessary to have the data book at your elbow. Electronic engineers like to give people the impression that *everybody* knows the pin assignments, propagation delays and truth tables of the thousand or so available logic gates off by heart, but that is certainly not essential. The road to success is paved with constant consultation of these useful works.

So, back to TTL. A 5 V nominal (7.5 max) power supply is needed, delivering quite a lot of current. This low voltage supply is the biggest drawback to TTL because one almost always needs analogue circuits at input and output which demand a higher voltage, and that means that two separate supplies are needed.

Complementary MOS

This family uses insulated gate FET—in complementary n and p forms; see Fig. 275. Early versions were

TABLE 4

| Series | Gates | | | Flip-flops |
	Speed–power product	Propagation times	Power dissipation	Clock: maximum frequency
74LS73	19 pJ	9.5 ns	2 mW	45 MHz
74L73	33 pJ	33 ns	1 mW	3 MHz
74S73	57 pJ	3 ns	19 mW	125 MHz
7473	100 pJ	10 ns	10 mW	35 MHz
74H73	132 pJ	6 ns	22 mW	50 MHz

(Source: *TTL Data Book*, p. 59.)

with '54' numbers. These, however, are military and not available through ordinary retail suppliers. Many other manufacturers offer pin-for-pin, or 'chinese' copies of Texas' '74' family ICs. Some have their own numbers; most use TI's without the TI prefix 'SM'.)

What does the Table 4 mean? 'Speed–power product' is of academic interest. 'Propagation time' is of great importance in designing logic circuits: it is the time the signal takes to get through the gate, and is quoted in the data sheet. During this time the gate cannot accept a new signal, so, in complicated systems it is very important to work the signals through the gates, adding the propagation times, to make sure that

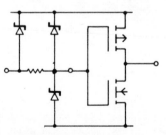

Fig. 275. COSMOS inverter, showing protective zeners. The p- and n-channel output is typical of most COSMOS devices.

hard to handle because static electricity built up on the very high impedance inputs to high voltages and burst the devices. Modern circuits have 11-V zeners to ground from the gates and are supposed to be static-proof. However, I find they die rather more readily than TTL, or than one would wish.

RCA recommend these precautions to prevent damage:

1 Except during use, all the leads of COSMOS devices should be connected together. The easiest way to do this is to stick the pins through a piece of kitchen foil into a small block of polystyrene foam. Devices sometimes come in lengths of aluminium channel which fit round them and short the pins together, or stuck into black rubbery foam that conducts electricity.

2 Make sure that your soldering iron tip is grounded. Check this frequently: the earth lead came undone on mine within the plug, and I broke several expensive ICs before I realized what had happened.

3 Turn power off before inserting devices into, or removing them from, circuits.

4 Do not apply signals to device inputs while power is off.

5 Connect unused input leads to ground or device supply—whichever is appropriate to the logic in question.

The action of COSMOS is to switch the output either to the + or − rail by opening either the n or the p device—which then becomes a low value resistor (p. 11)—and closing the other. As a result, current flows from rail to rail only during the small period of time that both gates are open, and this family is very economical on power. In many applications, such as a car clock, it is not worth switching off the logic from the car's battery; it can safely be left permanently switched on.

COSMOS is relatively slow—with maximum data rates of about 1 MHz, but it uses any supply from 3 V to 15 V, which makes it much easier to work in with other circuitry, particularly op-amps. The early RCA *COSMOS Data Book* was an excellent source of information about design philosophies as well as devices because it incorporated several 'Application notes'.

Ripple counting

An obvious application of simple logic gates is counting things—or rather pulses. The operation of counting is also the operation of division, as we shall see.

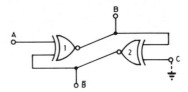

Fig. 276. Flip-flop using two exclusive ORs.

The simplest counting circuit is the divide-by-2 flip-flop, bistable or electronic memory; see Fig. 276. Two EXCLUSIVE NOR gates are cross connected. The truth table of each is:

TRUTH TABLE 11

IN		OUT
A	B	C
1	1	1
1	0	0
0	1	0
0	0	1

FLIP–FLOP

Assume that A in Fig. 276 is 0 and B is 1. The inputs to gate 2 are therefore 0 and 1, so its output is 0—which makes the gate 2 inputs 0 and 0—which is why its output is 1. So far so good. Let a 1 arrive at A: for an instant the inputs to gate 1 are 0 and 1 and its output B goes to 0. The inputs to gate 2 in the same instant are 0 and 0 so $\bar{B}$ becomes 1. When the next 1 arrives at A, the situation will reverse: B will go to 1 again and $\bar{B}$ to 0.

Two consequences follow: the outputs are always each other's inverse—which is why they are labelled B and $\bar{B}$; and, if we look at say B, a pulse appears there for every two pulses on A; and if we look at $\bar{B}$ a 0 appears there for every two 0s on A. Two NANDS will also do the trick; see Fig. 277. A secondary use for a

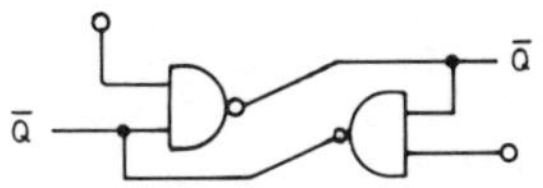

divide-by-2 circuit is to produce accurate *square* waves (i.e. in which the + and − durations are equal). We've held the second input, C, at ground to get divide by two. But if we had another chain of pulses arriving at C, the output would 'toggle', see Fig. 278.

Now back to Fig. 276. We are counting in binary,* or dividing by two, whichever way you care to look at it.

Fig. 277. Flip-flop with two inputs, using NANDS.

---

* In decimal counting we write a number in powers of 10 increasing to the left. Thus, '526' means 5×10^2 (500) plus 2×10^1 (20) plus 6×10^0 (6). In binary counting we do the same, only with powers of 2. Thus 10111 means 1×2^4 (16) plus 0×2^3 (0) plus 1×2^2 (4) plus $1 + 2^1$ (2) plus 1×2^0 (1) = 23. Binary coded decimal (BCD) is sometimes used, particularly when transferring from the binary used in calculations to decimal displays (p. 91). In BCD the digits of decimal numbers are coded separately into binary. Thus '23' is '10, 11'.

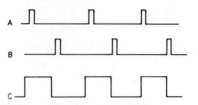

Fig. 278. Timing diagram of Fig. 277 as circuit toggles between two inputs.

And it's called a memory because the state of the outputs remembers what the last input was. If we cascade five of these circuits and run in, say, twenty-three pulses, we would get 111101 backwards at the outputs, which is the decimal number 23 in binary. This kind of circuit is called a 'ripple counter' because the data ripples along it; see Fig. 279.

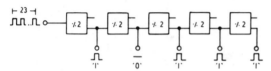

Fig. 279. Divide-by-two counter chain showing '23' in binary.

Practical flip-flops come in several slightly different forms. Fig. 280, for example, is a COSMOS 4013. It contains two identical circuits each with a 'clock' and a 'data' input, a 'set' and 'reset' input and two outputs Q

and $\bar{Q}$. This looks rather formidable, but the nub of the thing is that on a *positive going* clock pulse the state of the data input—the D terminal—is transferred to the Q output. When the clock goes negative nothing further happens. Set and reset—S and R—are provided for applications where the counter has to be zeroed for the beginning of a run. When they are 0 they have no effect. This, as it stands, is more of a memory, or a latch, than a flip-flop. But it can easily be made into one; see Fig. 281. Often we want to count in tens. A

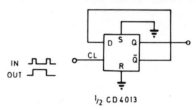

Fig. 281. One half of 4013.

useful TTL device is the 7490 which produces a binary output corresponding to the number of pulses in.[*] After nine pulses it produces a carry out and sets the binary outputs to zero again.

Suppose we feed in seven pulses to such a circuit,[*] and then stop with the input still high. The outputs would read as shown in Fig. 282. A 'divide-by-10' counter like this produces BCD—binary coded decimal. Since 4 bits are needed to code the number 10, such a counter must have four outputs. It is a—perhaps

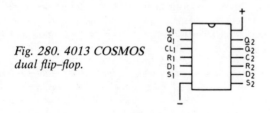

Fig. 280. 4013 COSMOS dual flip-flop.

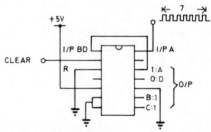

Fig. 282. 7490 decimal counter, showing 0111 = 7.

TRUTH TABLE 12

CL	D	R	S	Q	$\bar{Q}$	
↑	0	0	0	0	1	
↑	1	0	0	1	0	
↓	X	0	0	(Q)	$\bar{Q}$	(No change)
X	X	1	0	0	1	
X	X	0	1	1	0	
X	X	1	1	1	1	

4013 FLIP-FLOP
'X' means 'state immaterial'.

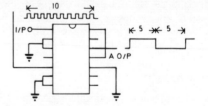

Fig. 283. 7490 decimal counter, wired to produce divide-by-five square wave.

[*] Actually the 7490 is more versatile than this. It contains a ÷2 counter: 'A' input and 'A' output; and a ÷5 counter: 'BD' input with 'B', 'C', 'D' outputs. When 'BD' output is connected externally to 'A' input (as in Fig. 282), the device counts 10's and gives a binary coded decimal (BCD) output. When 'D' output is connected to 'A' input and 'BD' used as the device input, output 'A' gives a symmetrical ÷10 square wave.

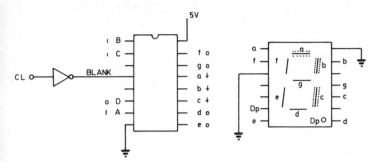

Fig. 284. 7447 BCD-to-seven segment converter, with typical seven-segment display.

confusing—convention of electronic logic that they are labelled from 'A' to 'D', starting with the least significant bit (LSB). So the decimal number '7', whose BCD equivalent is 0111, appears as '0' on output D, and '1's on outputs C, B and A. One might want to display this fact, so a special logic chip 7447 is made to convert this binary coded decimal (BCD) number to the seven segment code needed to drive a standard numerical display; see Fig. 284.

Often though, the pulses keep on coming, and we want to count how many there are in a fixed time. To do this a third logic chip called a 'Quad latch' SM 7475, is inserted between the other two. It is a sort of quadruple flip-flop. It has four data inputs (labelled A to D, as above) to each of its four latches, four outputs and a latching pulse input; see Fig. 285. As long as the latch

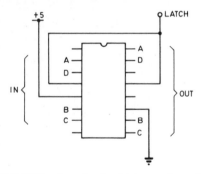

Fig. 285. 7475 latch, a circuit which samples a changing BCD number and remembers it.

input is high, the outputs follow the inputs. When it goes low, the outputs freeze at their last value. To get a true count, we have to clear the counter at the beginning of each high—otherwise it would add the count of the second period to that of the first. To do this the counter has a 'clear' input which returns the four outputs to zero during the clock low. One last problem: during clock high, the latches are open so the displays will be counting furiously, giving an unpleasant fuzzy appearance to the digits illuminated during clock low. To avoid this, the BCD seven-segment decoder 7447 has a blanking input which shuts of the display when inverted clock high is applied.

What is the meaning of the number we see? Suppose the clock is a 50 Hz square wave. The counter was open for 0.01 s during which time it was counting up to 9, going back to 0 and starting once more, over and over again. Suppose the oscillator whose output we are counting is running at 1 823 724 Hz. In 0.01 s 18 237 pulses will have been fed in. The final 4 Hz will not have had time to appear. Neither will the 20 Hz but the 700 Hz will. The 3000 Hz will have run through, and so will the higher numbers. So the counter will display 7, the number of hundreds of Hertz in the frequency. As well as counting and displaying '7' this counter is also dividing by 10. One pulse appears on the 'carry' output of the 7490 for every ten pulses in. So it passes on 1823 cycles in 0.01 s. To take advantage of this, we put an exactly similar circuit of counter, latch, decoder and display to the left of the first. This one, if clocked at 0.01 s will display '3', the number of the kilohertz in the frequency. Similarly the next to the left will show '2' (tens of kilohertz), the next '8' (hundreds of kilohertz), and the last '1', the number of megahertz.

The next problem is to come by accurate 0.001 s high and low pulses. A rather crude method would be to use the 240-V (50-Hz) mains via a 5-V transformer driving a NAND gate to get a square wave. The drawback is the variability of the 50 Hz (60 Hz) standard, which can alter by 2 per cent or so according to the load on the national electricity grid. However, a better—in fact the best—source of accurate time pulses is to receive one of the standard frequency service radio transmissions which are radiated for the use of scientific laboratories. There are several which broadcast intermittently: for this purpose one wants a transmission with continuous carrier. Suitable stations are: GBR from Rugby (UK) on 16 kHz with an accuracy of ±2 in 10^{12}; BBC Droitwich on 200 kHz with an accuracy of ±2 in 10^{11}; IAM, Rome, on 5 MHz; OMA, Prague, on 2.5 MHz; WWV, Fort Collins, Colorado, USA on 2.5 MHz, 5 MHz, 10 MHz, 15 MHz, 20 MHz and 25 MHz; and WWVH, Kauai, Hawaii on 2.5 MHz, 5 MHz, 10 MHz, 15 MHz and 20 MHz (see Wireless World annual Diary for up to date data). A receiver like that on p. 63, but with two tuned RF stages driving COSMOS or TTL dividers, could easily produce an extremely accurate clock pulse. Many of these stations not only transmit an

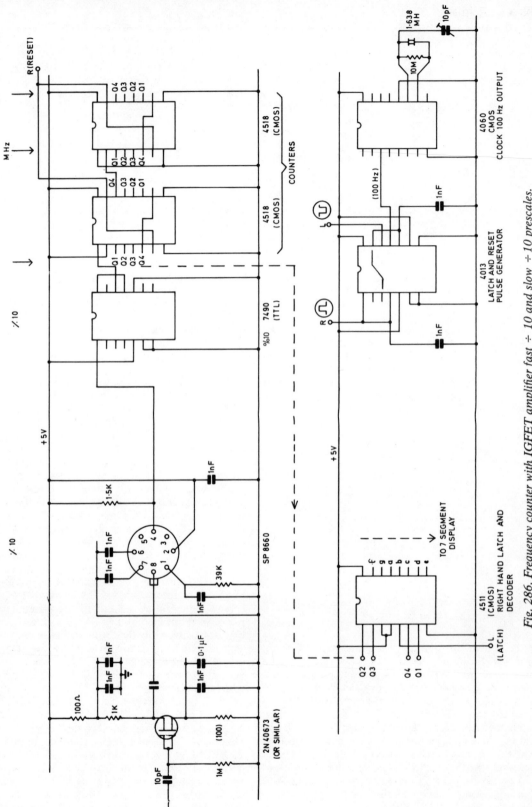

Fig. 286. Frequency counter with IGFET amplifier fast ÷ 10 and slow ÷ 10 prescales.

extremely accurate carrier, but also code it with standard time. Such a receiver, with some not too difficult logic, can drive an hours, minutes, seconds display with great accuracy.

A third, and more convenient timing method, is to use a crystal oscillator (see Fig. 286). Since these are at their best when running at a few megahertz, dividers will be necessary. My bench version (see Fig. 286) uses a 5 MHz crystal driving CMOS 4060 oscillator and divide-by-2^{14} IC. The output is a 100 Hz square wave. So we need the counters to count for the whole of its 0.01 s cycle. That means we have to generate a very short low pulse at the end of each cycle to freeze the latches. An easy way to do this is to use one half of a 4013 flip-flop, wired so that Q is connected to reset. As soon as a plus-going voltage on clock transfers the high data voltage to Q, the circuit resets itself so that Q goes to low. With a 1 nF capacitor to ground from Q to slow things up a little, this apparently self defeating arrangement produces a 1 μs positive pulse, also available as a negative pulse at $\bar{Q}$, to operate the 4511 latches. Immediately after we have transferred the count into the latches, we need to return the counters with a second pulse to 0 to begin a new cycle. If these pulses are simultaneous nothing will happen: they must follow one another. So we also use the positive pulse on Q, to trigger an identical circuit in the other half of the 4013 to produce a second 1 μs pulse. These two follow each other as shown in Fig. 287. Since it is

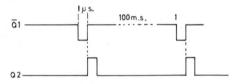

Fig. 287. Timing pulses for latch and counter reset.

useful to measure frequencies up to 99 MHz, and a 7490 TTL decade counter runs out of speed at 32 MHz, the input is prescaled by a fast divide-by-ten IC—in this case a Plessey SP8660, which works up to 180 MHz (others in the range will divide at up to 1.3 GHz). In fact, it is easiest to make the display sections of the frequency counter using CMOS devices, so a second prescaler is necessary to divide the input down to CMOS speed. The SP8660 is an expensive device, so it drives a cheaper 7490 wired to give a divide-by-10 square wave output. This produces a maximum frequency of 99 MHz ÷ 100 = 0.99 MHz, which is within the capabilities of CMOS, even on the 5-V supply which the fast counters need.

A fast counter like the 8660 has a tremendous amount of voltage gain inside it and will oscillate if its input is held too long around mid-rail. As far as this device is concerned, this happens if the input slews at less than 100 V/μs. At the minimum input voltage of 400–800 mV, this means a minimum input frequency

of 40 MHz as a sine wave. We can improve the slew rate and so lower the minimum frequency by amplifying the input—which also helps sensitivity. So the 8660 is preceded by a resistance loaded IGFET amplifier. The circuit in Fig. 286 will count reliably down to 1 MHz or so. To count slower than that, it would be good to provide a second input, with the amplifier driving a TTL Schmitt trigger. This could bypass the 8660, thus making the display read down to 1 kHz.

The 4518 counters are double, so we need two to get the four BCD outputs. The first will show the least significant digit. What will it signify? We count for a period of 0.01 s, having divided the input by 100, so it shows $100 \times 100 = 10$ kHz. The left hand side of the first 4518 produces a carry-out pulse on pin 6, which goes across to drive the right hand side counter at pin 10. The carry pulse from the second counter comes out on pin 14, which is connected to the third counter at pin 2 of the second 4518 (note that the input this time is *not* on pin 1: this corrects a phase inversion in the first two counters). Resets for the counters are on pins 7 and 15: these are connected together and to the output of the second half on the pulse producing 4013.

We now need latches and BCD-seven-segment decoders. These are available in one IC: the 4511, of which we need one per counter. This IC has CMOS logic for the latch and decoder, driving bipolar transistors to deliver a relatively high current—up to 25 mA—per segment to the displays.

Pin 3 on the 4511 is lamp test—all segments light up when it is put low. For operation it should be held high, and since segment failure will be quite obvious, it might just as well be wired high. Pin 4 blanks the display when low—since the latches follow the counters only during the 1 μs of the high pulse on the latch line, this facility is unnecessary, and it too can be wired high. Each 4511 is connected to its counter as shown. The segment outputs—which are high when operative—are on the right hand side of each IC. No display is shown because there are a number of suitable types, both filament and LED. The standard segment lettering is shown in Fig. 284.

We could build this meter into a direct conversion radio receiver like that on p. 64, to show the received frequency directly. (A superheterodyne receiver would need some arithmetic logic to add or subtract—as necessary—the intermediate frequency to or from the local oscillator frequency, see p. 67). But we can make better use still of all this circuitry. As we saw on p. 75, the problem with radio reception—or transmission, for the matter—is to generate a frequency which is infinitely variable, and yet stable to at least one part in 500 000. In practice, an HF receiver has a bandwidth of 2.5 kHz, and must stay tuned to within 100 Hz. One way of dealing with the problem is to make a frequency synthesizer (p. 70) with 100 Hz-steps. Readers with a taste for tiresome problems are invited to try designing one to work from 1.5 MHz to

30 MHz. Another is to use a frequency counter of the sort we've discussed to generate a voltage proportional to frequency error, and then to use that as negative feedback to correct the tuning voltage.

As it stands this circuit won't do. Firstly, it reads so far only to tens of kilohertz. If we add another stage and divide the clock again by 10, to 0.1 s, we can read kilohertz on the least significant digit. But to hold the tune to 100 Hz, we need to read at least to 25 Hz, and 10 Hz would be better. To achieve this in the same way means adding two stages more and increasing the clock to $10 \times 10 \times 0.1$ s. And that means the local oscillator gets corrected every 10 s. Which is much too long. The root of the trouble is in the two divide-by-ten stages at the front end of the clock. Since we only want to read to 30 MHz, we can use an ordinary 7490 which is guaranteed to count at 32 MHz. It might be an idea to precede it with a 74S132 two-input positive NAND Schmitt trigger which fires on 0.55 V and has a propagation delay time of 8 ns, corresponding to a toggle rate of 125 MHz, so the first two stages can be TTL at least. This is fine because in TTL the latches are separate and we can get at the BCD voltages directly. We want the least significant digit to show tens of hertz, so the clock must run at 0.1 s. We already have the circuit for that.

How many stages do we need to feed into the digital to analogue converter? The question we really have to ask is: how far is our oscillator likely to wander in 0.1 s? If we include too many stages we reduce the corrective effect of the 10 Hz errors, if we include too few, it could jump say 100 Hz and lock in the wrong place. One would need to do some work to find out, but I should

imagine that if the kHz were included, that would be enough. So we have to get at the BCD voltages representing the number of kilohertz as well. The last three stages could be CMOS for simplicity and power economy. How many of the first three stages do we need to display? Certainly not the tens of hertz, because they'll be jigging about as the oscillator wanders. One hopes that the hundreds won't, because the object of the exercise is to keep them stable. But in practice it wouldn't actually be very useful to display the hundreds because HF channels are spaced at 2.5 Hz or 3 kHz, and you find the one you want by the kilohertz and a bit of fiddling to get the tune right (the transmitter may have altered tune by a few hundred hertz to avoid another station). Still, if one could be bothered, there would be no harm in a hundreds display, and it would certainly make one confident that things were working right.

We now have four terminals on each of three latches which carry BCD numbers corresponding to the tens, hundreds and thousands digits of our frequency, but how do we turn these digital voltages into an analogue form, suitable for feeding back into the tuning control?

Digital to analogue converter (DAC)

To start with, let's just consider four digital outputs representing a single BCD digit. Reading from the top, high voltages (if present) represent 8, 4, 2 and 1. If we connect these four terminals to a voltage adder (p. 32) through, say, 1 kΩ, 2 kΩ, 4 kΩ and 8 kΩ resistors the total voltage will be in proportion to the BCD number. In practice, these resistor values, or indeed any in those

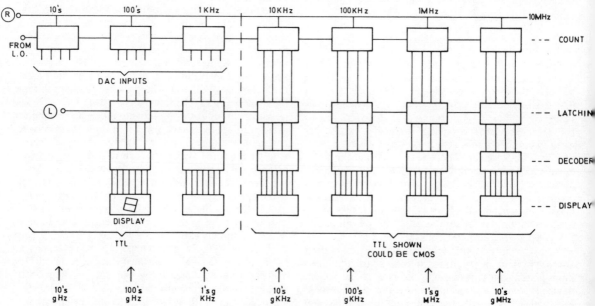

Fig. 288. Frequency counter with external latches to provide inputs for DAC and frequency synthesis. See text.

proportions are hard to come by. A simpler method is to start with, say, 10 kΩ for the 1 terminal, two 10 kΩ in parallel for the 2 terminal, making an effective resistance of 5 kΩ, four in parallel for the 4 terminal and eight for the 8 terminal; see Fig. 289. This needs fifteen

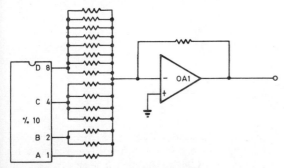

Fig. 289. Digital to analogue (DAC) converter. DAC output to be added to tuning voltage for automatic frequency control.

identical resistors. Some ingenious person has worked out a more economical method: the $R/2R$ ladder; see Fig. 290. All the vertical resistors are $2R$, and all the horizontal ones R. This produces an analogue voltage at the plus input of the op-amp proportional to the total BCD number. The op-amp needs to have a high input impedance to work accurately—it had better be one of the newer types with a IGFET input stage.

The upshot is that if the oscillator frequency rises, so does the output of the DAC. If we add it to the tuning voltage, the rise in frequency produces a correcting voltage. Just how much depends on the value of R^* which controls gain in Fig. 290. The value of R^* is rather critical, because if the circuit over-corrects, it will be constantly jigging about; if it under-corrects it will steadily drift away from its nominal value. What one wants is a slight oscillation of, say, 20 Hz about the nominal value, and R^* would have to be adjusted until results were satisfactory. The capacitor shunting R^* is to smooth the output to get rid of the 10 Hz ripple from the clock. The voltage swing at the top of the $R/2R$ ladder will be a couple of volts. We need a correction of a few mV, so R^* will have to be less than R. If we take R to be 10 kΩ, then a value for R^* of 1 kΩ might be sensible as a starting point.

I haven't built this circuit so it may well be that a reasonable oscillator will keep stable within, say, 500 Hz over 0.1 s, so that the kilohertz stage is an unnecessary refinement. It might be best to build the first two stages and be prepared to add the third if necessary.

Analogue to digital conversion

The reverse of this process, turning an analogue voltage into digital form, is often used nowadays because of the need to connect computers to devices that sense their environment. These devices—which might measure temperature, pressure, windspeed, partial pressure of oxygen, for example, usually produce an analogue voltage output. Before electronic logic can make any sense of it, it must be converted into a digital form.

First we'll look at the basic principles, and then discuss some difficulties. The essence of the scheme is to compare the analogue voltage with an increasing step voltage. In Fig. 291 there are ten reference steps

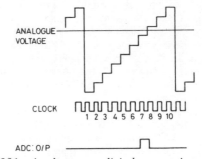

Fig. 291. Analogue to digital conversion (ADC): comparing an analogue voltage with a digitally generated ramp.

before the ramp recycles, and the two voltages coincide at the seventh. Compared in a window comparator (p. 29) a voltage pulse is produced which tells the computer that the two came equal on the seventh clock pulse. Since it is programmed with the voltage increase per step, and knows how many steps there are before the ramp recycles, it knows the analogue voltage. That is, it knows the voltage to within 10 per cent. The circuitry to do this job might look like Fig. 292. The

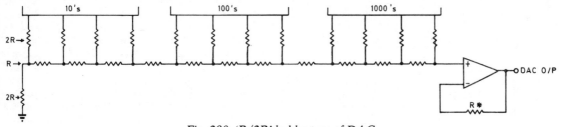

Fig. 290. 'R/2R' ladder type of DAC.

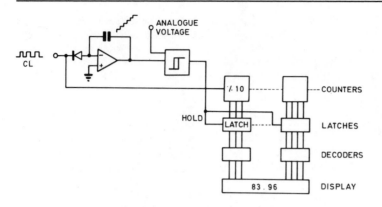

Fig. 292. Block diagram of a circuit to realize Fig. 291.

clock is fed into a 4518 BCD counter, whose outputs are buffered by the 4041 to reduce their impedance. As before, an analogue voltage is formed by the $R/2R$ ladder which is compared with the step voltage in the window comparator. We could add some simple arithmetic logic which would, instead of sending a pulse to coincide with the seventh clock pulse, actually translate '7' into binary and send the number '0111' as a reading of the analogue voltage level.

This circuit produces a rather inaccurate reading from a static input voltage. In real life much greater accuracy than 10 per cent is often needed and the input voltage may be varying very fast. Accuracy is affected by the gain stability of the amplifiers which raise the analogue voltage up to the range of several volts needed for ADC. It is affected by the accuracy of the $R/2R$ ladder and the hysteresis of the Schmitt triggers in the window comparator. Obviously, the hysteresis (p. 29) must be a good deal less than the step voltage in the ramp, otherwise we will get ambiguous indications. Accuracy is also affected by the way in which the analogue voltage is sampled. Consider an analogue voltage with a frequency of 1 MHz fed into the window comparator with a ramp voltage based on a clock running at 10 MHz. The ramp repeats at 1 MHz, effectively in step with the analogue voltage, so that, depending on their relative phases, the ADC circuit will report a constant value—in this case, '3'—for an analogue voltage which is actually varying over the maximum possible range; see Fig. 293.

A proper analogue-to-digital conversion has to do four things: first, it must sample the incoming wave-

form quicker than twice the highest frequency present (according to the Nyquist criterion—and it may be necessary to put the input through a low pass filter to assure this); secondly it must store the sample long enough for the logic circuitry to decide what output code to produce (see the discussion of choppers on p. 16); thirdly, it must compare the stored voltage with a number of preset reference voltages (there must be $2^n - 1$ of these to produce an 'n' bit output); finally the output needs to be coded in some useful form and, as in the example above, it may be coded as binary number.

Digital coding of speech at good enough quality for communications can be achieved with two bit discrimination (four levels) on a 2.5 kHz bandwidth, which means sampling at 5 kHz, with an information rate of 20 kbit/s (p. 60). On the other hand acceptable coding of PAL colour television needs an 8 bit output (256 levels) sampled at 13 MHz, corresponding to a data rate of 3.3 Gbit/s. For a review of high speed ADC work, see O. J. Downing and P. T. Johnson, *Wireless World* December 1977, pp. 65–70.

BOOLEAN ALGEBRA

Back on p. 87 we designed an EXCLUSIVE OR gate by guess, and it is only due to the infallability which we book-writers enjoy that it came out right first time—the two first times, indeed. But this is a simple gate; anything more complicated might never come out at all using this method. Happily, mathematics comes to the rescue, and provides a system for building logical gates of any complexity. The name of the game is boolean algebra.

Casting back to the three logical functions and the gates which embody them, we remember OR, AND and NOT. If you want to say A OR B, which are either 0 or 1, you write—thanks to the ingenious Boole, aided and abetted by Lewis Carroll—$A + B$. It is unfortunate that this looks like A plus B *but it is not*! If you want to write A AND B you put $A \cdot B$. This might look like A times B *but it is not*! Sorry about that. However, compensations for this confusion will appear. If you

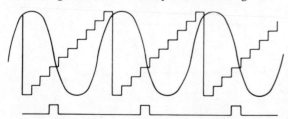

Fig. 293. Gross error due to sampling an analogue voltage at a rate equal to its own oscillation.

want to say NOT A you write $\bar{A}$.* No problem about that.

Let's look again at the EXCLUSIVE OR circuit (Fig. 270). We can write it down in equation form like this:

$$(A+B) \qquad (\bar{A}.\bar{B})=E \qquad (3.1)$$
OR gate 1   AND gate 3   NAND gate 2

We can expand this by using the first of de Morgan's laws.† Which are:

$$\overline{A.B}=\bar{A}+\bar{B} \tag{3.2}$$

$$\overline{A+B}=\bar{A}.\bar{B} \tag{3.3}$$

The easy way to prove equation (3.2) is by writing a truth table for the different possible values of A and B. The left hand side is simply NAND (see Truth table 2). The right hand side is OR (see Truth table 5), with inverted inputs:

TRUTH TABLE 13

A	B	$\bar{A}.\bar{B}$	$\bar{A}$	$\bar{B}$	$\bar{A}+\bar{B}$
0	0	1	1	1	1
0	1	1	1	0	1
1	0	1	0	1	1
1	1	0	0	0	0

De Morgan's First Law   QED

The faint hearted and incredulous may care to do the same for equation (3.3).

Now, going back to equation (3.1) we can say:

$$(A+B).(\overline{A.B})=(A+B).(\bar{A}+\bar{B})$$

We can multiply like ordinary algebra:

$$=A.\bar{A}+\bar{A}.B+A.\bar{B}+B.\bar{B}$$

$A.\bar{A}$ means, in plain language, A AND NOT A. Looking at Truth table 1 we see that the result of this is 0 in both cases. So we can forget it, and also $B.\bar{B}$. We're left with $\bar{A}.B+A.\bar{B}$. This is the end of the road, and to prove it, here's the Truth table:

TRUTH TABLE 14

A	B	$\bar{A}.B$	$A.\bar{B}$	$\bar{A}.B+A.\bar{B}$	EXC OR
0	0	0	0	0	0
0	1	1	0	1	1
1	0	0	1	1	1
1	1	0	0	0	0

Will you believe that boolean algebra works?

The circuit of Fig. 271 goes straight into the equation we want:

$$\bar{E}.F+E.\bar{F}$$
gates   1   3   2

Now for something more ambitious: a two-bit parallel adder ('parallel' because it adds both bits at the same time; as will become apparent, there are easier ways of doing the job). Guesswork is out of the question, so we'll write the equations, simplify them and then turn them into hardware. We have four inputs to this circuit, A and B, C and D, two for each number. A represents 2's, B, 1's in the first two-bit number; the second number has its 2 on C and its 1 on D. The output can obviously have three bits, so we have three outputs: X for the 4, Y for the 2 and Z for the 1. To make sure we have this quite clear: a 1 on A and a 0 on B is the binary number 10, or 2 in decimal. Let's add it to 1 on C and 1 on D, the binary number 11, or 3 in decimal.

$$\begin{array}{r} 10 \\ \underline{11} \\ \underline{101} \end{array}$$ (note the carry in second place)

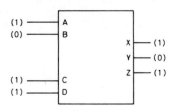

Fig. 294. Two-bit parallel adder.

This will appear on the outputs thus: X: 1; Y: 0; Z: 1. The truth table for all the possibilities is:

TRUTH TABLE 15

CB	$A,0$ $B,0$	$A,0$ $B,1$	$A,1$ $B,0$	$A,1$ $B,1$
00	000	001	010	011
01	001	010	011	100
10	010	111	100	101
11	011	100	101	110

Each three-bit number is the sum of the appropriate AB and CD, and is XYZ in order. What we want is a circuit that will produce it automatically.

---

* Mathematicians might prefer A', but since $\bar{A}$ is what engineers use, we're stuck with it.

† De Morgan's Laws imply that you only need NAND gates to do all logical operations. But that would make life more complicated than is necessary, so we note it here only for interest.

Z depends only on B and D. No carries influence it, so it, at least, is likely to be simple. A familiar table, which we instantly recognize as EXCLUSIVE OR. So much for Z.

TRUTH TABLE 16

B	D	Z
0	0	0
0	1	1
1	0	1
1	1	0

This translates straight away into the equation:

$$Z=\bar{B}\,.\,D+\bar{D}\,.\,B$$

And is realized as gate 1, Fig. 294.

Y is more complicated. We look through the boxes for outputs where Y is 1, and write down the necessary inputs:

TRUTH TABLE 17

A	B	C	D	Y
1	0	0	0	1
1	1	0	0	1
0	1	0	1	1
1	0	0	1	1
0	0	1	0	1
0	1	1	0	1
0	0	1	1	1
1	1	1	1	1

We could build a circuit for each line and combine them in an 8-output OR to get an output for Y. This would need eight 4-input ANDs and sixteen NOTs, which is expensive and tiresome. So, de Morgan comes to the rescue. We can write down this circuit as a boolean equation and simplify it. Line 1 is 1 0 0 0, $A\,\bar{B}\,\bar{C}\,\bar{D}$. Taking the lines in order, and writing '$A\,.\,B$' as 'AB' etc:

$$\begin{aligned}Y=&A\bar{B}\bar{C}\bar{D}+AB\bar{C}\bar{D}+\bar{A}B\bar{C}D\\&+A\bar{B}\bar{C}D+\bar{A}B\bar{C}\bar{D}+\bar{A}BC\bar{D}\\&+\bar{A}\bar{B}CD+ABCD\end{aligned}$$

Factorizing:

$$\begin{aligned}Y=&(D+\bar{D})(A\bar{B}\bar{C}+\bar{A}\bar{B}C)\\&+AB\bar{C}\bar{D}+\bar{A}BC\bar{D}+\bar{A}B\bar{C}D+ABCD\end{aligned}$$

Since $D+\bar{D}=1$, this reduces to:

$$\begin{aligned}Y=&A\bar{B}\bar{C}+\bar{A}\bar{B}C+AB\bar{C}\bar{D}\\&+\bar{A}BC\bar{D}+\bar{A}B\bar{C}D+ABCD\end{aligned}$$

This can be simplified again by using two new theorems called *redundancy* and *optional products*. A simple example to show redundancy:

$$F=KL+L$$

This factorizes:

$$F=L(K+1)$$

But $K+1$ must be 1 (see Truth table 15) So

$$F=L$$

Since any logical function, however complicated in its make-up, can only be either 0 or 1, this applies to anything that can be written in the form $KL+L$. However, the problem is to write things in that form and the trick is the optional product:

$$G=P\,.\,Q+\bar{P}\,.\,R$$

The rule says we can take the 'multiplier' of P and the multiplier of $\bar{P}$, 'multiply' them together and 'add' them to the original expression without penalty:

$$G=P\,.\,Q+\bar{P}\,.\,R+Q\,.\,R$$

A Truth table to prove it:

TRUTH TABLE 18

P	Q	R	$\bar{P}$	$P.Q.$	$\bar{P}.R.$	QR	$PQ+\bar{P}R$	$PQ+\bar{P}R+QR$
0	0	0	1	0	0	0	0	
0	0	1	1	0	1	0	1	1
0	1	0	1	0	0	0	0	0
0	1	1	1	0	1	1	1	1
1	0	0	0	0	0	0	0	0
1	0	1	0	0	0	0	0	0
1	1	0	0	1	0	0	1	1
1	1	1	0	1	0	1	1	1

These work together thus:

$$H=\bar{S}+ST$$

Give it an optional product:

$$H=\bar{S}+ST+T\,.\,1$$

Using redundancy:

$$H=\bar{S}+T$$

'So far so good', we hear the patient reader groan, 'but how does this help with Y?'

Like this:

$$Y = \bar{A}\bar{B}C + \bar{A}BC\bar{D} + ABCD + A\bar{B}\bar{C}$$
$$+ ABC\bar{D} + \bar{A}B\bar{C}D$$

Factorizing:

$$Y = \bar{A}C(\bar{B} + B\bar{D}) + A\bar{C}(\bar{B} + B\bar{D})$$
$$+ BD(AC + \bar{A}\bar{C})$$
$$= (\bar{B} + B\bar{D})(\bar{A}C + A\bar{C})$$
$$+ BD(AC + \bar{A}\bar{C})$$

Using both new theorems to simplify the first bracket:

$$Y = (\bar{B} + \bar{D})(\bar{A}C + A\bar{C})$$
$$+ BD(AC + \bar{A}\bar{C})$$

By de Morgan's second rule this is:

$$Y = \overline{BD}(\bar{A}C + A\bar{C})$$
$$+ BD(AC + \bar{A}\bar{C})$$

Although this won't simplify any more, we notice that we need only to form BD and its inverse; saving a gate and that $\bar{A}\bar{C}$ is $(\overline{A + C}) = $ NOR

$$Y = \overline{BD}(\bar{A}C + A\bar{C}) + BD(AC + \overline{A + C})$$
$$\quad 3 \quad 7 \quad 4 \quad\quad 10\, 2 \ 9 \ 5 \ 8 \ 6$$

X should be easier. The Truth table is:

TRUTH TABLE 19

A	B	C	D	X
1	1	0	1	1
1	0	1	0	1
1	1	1	0	1
0	1	1	1	1
1	0	1	1	1
1	1	1	1	1

And as before with Y, the equation is:

$$X = AB\bar{C}D + A\bar{B}C\bar{D} + ABC\bar{D}$$
$$+ \bar{A}BCD + A\bar{B}CD + ABCD$$

Factorizing:

$$X = AB\bar{C}D + AC\bar{D}(B + \bar{B})$$
$$+ \bar{A}BCD + ACD(B + \bar{B})$$
$$= AB\bar{C}D + AC\bar{D} + \bar{A}BCD + ACD$$

Factorizing again:

$$= BC(A\bar{C} + \bar{A}C) + AC(D + \bar{D})$$
$$= BD \,.\, (A\bar{C} + \bar{A}C) + A\,.\,C$$
$$\quad 2 \quad 11 \quad\quad 4 \quad\quad 12\ 5$$

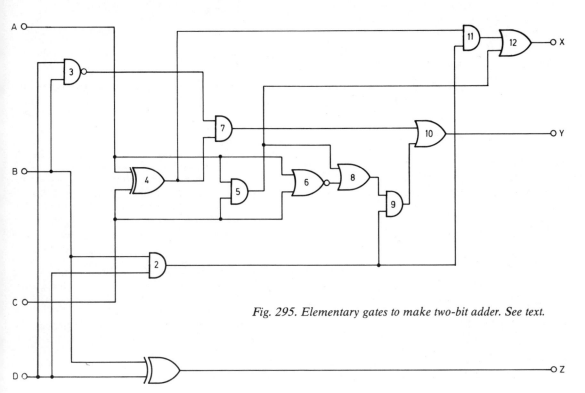

Fig. 295. Elementary gates to make two-bit adder. See text.

All we have to do now is turn this into hardware; see Fig. 295. It is surprising that such an apparently simple operation should require so many gates. It is not surprising that in general, computer engineers should have given up the idea of large scale parallel data processing, and use instead, serial systems.

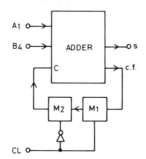

Fig. 296. Serial adder.

Consider a two-bit serial adder; see Fig. 296. In this scheme the two numbers to be added are fed in bit by bit to the adder, and the result fed out. It requires the extra complication of a clock, but the result is so much simpler that it's worth it, especially since it will handle unlimited numbers of bits. The bit pulses are the same width as and synchronous with the clock pulses. They're fed into A and B and added. The sum appears at S, and the carry forward digit, Cf, is stored in a memory, M_1. On the negative clock pulse the carry digit is transferred from M_1 to M_2 and on the next high added in at C with the next two bits. When the clock is + the truth table reads:

TRUTH TABLE 20

A	B	C	S	C_f
0	0	0	0	0
0	0	1	1	0
0	1	0	1	0
0	1	1	0	1
1	0	0	1	0
1	0	1	0	1
1	1	0	0	1
1	1	1	1	1

2-BIT Serial Adder

The equations are:

$$S = \bar{A}\bar{B}C + \bar{A}B\bar{C} + A\bar{B}\bar{C} + ABC$$

gates　　　　　1　　　　　3　2

$$C_f = \bar{A}BC + A\bar{B}C + AB\bar{C} + ABC$$

gates　　　　　4　　　　　5　2

The first three terms of S are the output of a 3-input exclusive OR, and the same is true of the first three terms of C_f with the output inverted. There are master-slave flip-flops like the 4095 specially for the memory function. In real life, you wouldn't build either adder from separate gates. The CD4008 is a four bit full adder with fast carry out—which means that several can be used in parallel to deal with multi-bit numbers. The CD4032 has three serial adders in one IC.

TV display and read only memory

My first job after leaving school, twenty years ago, was a lab boy at Mullard's Research Laboratories. A handsome bonus was advertised there for anyone who could design a circuit to write alphanumeric characters on a TV screen. At that time no-one could; today it's easy, and this is how it's done.

Let's write the character '2', quite small, in any position that may be wanted on the screen. A TV display is generated by scanning an electron beam successively along 625 (525 in USA) horizontal lines: where a bright spot is wanted, the electron intensity is increased, and vice versa. An enlargement of the bit of screen where we've written 2 would look like Fig. 297.

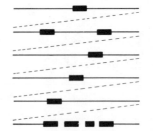

Fig. 297. The numeral '2' displayed on TV screen.

The light lines represent the forward movement of the beam, the dotted lines the fly-back path. The light lines would not be written—only the heavy ones would show. What we have to do is brighten up the beam at those points. To do it we use a read only memory (ROM), which looks like Fig. 298. The scan logic is a counter that makes one horizontal conductor + at a time, as the appropriate line on the screen is scanned. Where we want a spot, there is a diode, and this lets current onto the appropriate vertical conductor. The potential dividers, R, R_1; R, R_2 etc., put each vertical line at a slightly higher voltage than the one to its left. The ramp voltage which scans the electron beam across the screen is compared with each of these voltages in the window comparators (p. 29): as they come equal, a pulse is generated by a monostable (MS) which goes to the brightness control, thus writing a short line on the screen. The length of this line can be set by the hysteresis of the WCs; or can be increased by the monostable. The horizontal position of the 2 on the screen is controlled here by a potentiometer, but in a real application would depend on another variable voltage. In another application, the ROM might be

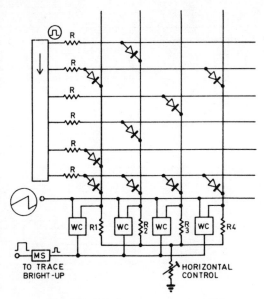

Fig. 298. Diode memory to store '2'.

		In binary:					
Clock count		32 A	16 B	8 C	4 D	2 E	1 F
2		0	0	0	0	1	0
8		0	0	1	0	0	0
10		0	0	1	0	1	0
17		0	1	0	0	0	1
22		0	1	0	1	1	0
26		0	1	1	0	1	0
29		0	1	1	1	0	1
43		1	0	1	0	1	1
48		1	1	0	0	0	0
49		1	1	0	0	0	1
50		1	1	0	0	1	0
52		1	1	0	1	0	0
53		1	1	0	1	0	1
54		1	1	0	1	1	0
56		1	1	1	1	0	0
58		1	1	1	0	1	0

TRUTH TABLE 21

required to produce a one dimensional output—say to send a standard morse message.

Suppose that, wishing to advertise to a captive—and probably irritated—audience I want to program a radio transmitter to send this message in morse: READ LAURIES BOOKS. We have three characters to send to the transmitter, via appropriate logic to form them: dot '.', dash '—', and blank, 'B'. The signal is:

$$. \underset{2}{\_} . B . B . \underset{8}{\_} B \underset{10}{\_} . . BBB . \underset{17}{\_} . .$$

$$B . \underset{22}{\_} B . . \underset{26}{\_} B . \underset{29}{\_} . B . . B . B . . .$$

$$\overset{------?}{}$$

$$BBB \underset{45}{\_} . . . B \underset{48}{\_} \underset{49}{\_} \_ B \underset{52}{\_} \underset{53}{\_} \_ B \underset{56}{\_} . \underset{58}{\_} B . . . B$$
$$\underset{49}{} \underset{53}{}$$
$$\underset{50}{} \underset{54}{}$$

There are sixty-three characters, so we need a binary counter with 6 divide-by-2 s ($64 = 2^6$). The first thing to do is to write a Truth table for each character and the divide-by-2 flip-flops. Truth table 21 is 'dash's'.

It would be possible to simplify this by the methods already described, made easier for so many variables by a tabular method explained in *Switching Circuits for Engineers* by Mitchell P. Marcus. But since one can buy diode matrices already packaged in ICs the necessary brain wrenching is hardly worth the 30 per cent saving in hardware that would be gained. These ICs have diodes at each intersection, and the unwanted ones, corresponding to 0s, are blown by passing a heavy current through them.

The Texas Instruments 74186 is one of these, a Programmable Read Only Memory (PROM) with 64 words of 8 bits each, so there's plenty of space for what we want. The memory has six inputs: F to A, and as the binary numbers from 1 to 63 are fed into them (the bits in parallel), so the pre-programmed pattern of 0s and 1s appears on the eight outputs. In this circuit we only need three of the outputs; say, V_1 for dashes, V_2 for dots and V_3 for blanks. They are connected permanently to the logic necessary for producing these morse symbols, and that in turn to the transmitter. The memory input is controlled by a six-stage ripple counter like the CMOS 4024. A clock fed in at the input is divided by two at each stage. There are six outputs, Q_1 to Q_6, which will show the binary number corresponding to the clock count. They can be connected direct to the six memory inputs A to F. The seventh stage of the 4024 is connected to its own reset, so that the count, and the message, starts again on clock pulse 64. See Fig. 299. The routine for programming the 74186 is described in the handbook and can be performed by the user. However you must be very careful to get it right as you can't go back and start again.

This application is obviously very wasteful, but it illustrates how PROMs can be used. What they can do depends again on the ingenuity of the user. For instance, a similar set up could be used to programme a washing machine, issuing sixty-four different orders in turn to eight different controls. One might be cold water fill, another wash, and another spin. A PROM could be loaded with morse-to-teleprinter conversion or with a code to encrypt and decrypt teleprinter signals (but don't expect your government to be baffled for long). It could be programmed to write complicated symbols on a TV screen, to draw sine curves, to set up the logic to control a fast arithmetical processor in a small computer, to draw a static background for a TV game—or to store the data of Truth table 15.

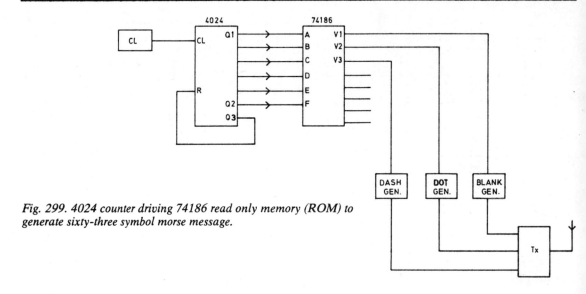

Fig. 299. 4024 counter driving 74186 read only memory (ROM) to generate sixty-three symbol morse message.

Shift registers

A useful kind of IC is a shift register which is halfway between a latch and a memory. This consists of a string of latches connected so the output of one drives the input of the next. If we ran a serial stream of binary data into the input, say 011011100011, then on the first clock pulse—which must obviously coincide with the first data bit—0 will be loaded into the first latch. On the next clock pulse, that 0 will be passed to the second latch, and the 1 that follows will be loaded into the first. On the third, 0 will appear at the third latch, 1 at the second and 1 at the first, and so on. In this example, we'd need a twelve-bit shift register to accommodate this particular chunk of data, and on the twelfth clock pulse it would be present on the twelve output pins as parallel data; see Fig. 300.

So, conversion of data in serial form to parallel is one very useful application. The need for this arises in many places: suppose we have a computer running a chemical works. It has half a dozen sensors which measure—say—acidity in various places and convert the measure to a twelve-bit binary number. To save having twelve wires to join each sensor to the computer, we'd have one and read the data down it in serial form. A shift register would then convert it to parallel for fast action. Another use for a shift register is to multiply. Each time the binary number is shifted to the right, each bit is multiplied by two and divided by two each time it's shifted to the left.

A third application is as a memory. In the example above, it took twelve clock pulses before the first 0 appeared at the last shift register. This can be useful as a memory, without the complication of a clock and refresh circuitry. With modern fast analogue to digital conversion and cheap logic ICs, shift register storage can be used to delay quite complex analogue wave forms. For instance, some high quality audio recording studios now use this method of generating echo.

Bussing

The first example above, of the sensors in a chemical factory leads onto a very important concept in computing; bussing. Six sensors might be connected to the central processor by a wire each, but if there were thirty-six, or three hundred and six, this would be impracticable. What happens is that two wires are used which run right round the whole site from sensor to sensor. One wire carries commands which order the sensors in turn to write their data onto the data wire. The computer knows that the data at its input comes from the sensor that has just been commanded to write. In this way sensors can be interrogated at different rates—one might, for instance, measure the level of raw material in a holding tank, which cannot change fast, once a day; another might measure a reaction rate which varies quickly and therefore needs

Fig. 300. Shift register converting serial data to parallel form.

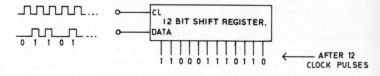

interrogating perhaps a hundred times a second. These two wires are called 'busses'. The same system of interconnection is used inside microprocessor chips and between them and their memories.

Memory

The array on p. 101 is a crude form of electronic memory. As we said there, it would be simpler to use a PROM chip (a programmable read only) than mess about with diodes.

The following are the usual forms of memory used:

1 PROM, or programmable read only memory, is one that can be set once by the user and is thereafter fixed.
2 ROM, or read only memory, is programmed by the factory either to the user's specification or with standard material. ROMs loaded with symbols (like the '2' on p. 100) can be bought to drive TV screen outputs for computers, radar setc etc; other versions translate morse into printer code, contain algorithms for calculators, etc.
3 EPROM, or erasable read-only memory, can be programmed by the user, erased by shining ultraviolet light on it, and re-programmed. They have little windows over the circuitry and are useful in prototyping computer systems.
4 RAM, random access memory, is used in computing, to store data, programme and output. The power of a computer system is limited in part by the size and speed of access of its RAMs. At the time of writing there is great excitement in the chip world about a 64-kb RAM (i.e. one which stores $2^{16} = 65\,536$ bits; with the perversity typical of electronics, this is called 64 kb when it's quite clearly 65.5 kb, because $2^{10} = 1024$, so 2^{10} is called a kilobit, and so on up).

There are two types of RAM: 'static' and 'dynamic'. The static type stores data in flip flops (p. 89). The advantage is that the data stays put as long as the power supply stays on. The disadvantage is that because two transistors are needed, with some extra gear per memory cell, the system is rather wasteful of space on the chip and is therefore expensive. The other system, 'dynamic', stores data on a small capacitor, which drives a CMOS source follower (p. 11). Naturally, the capacitor has to be small—about 20 pF—and charge leaks off it rather quickly (with an FET input impedance of 1 GΩ, $C \times R = 20$ ms). So a dynamic memory has to have circuits which read the data and recopy it back into the capacitors. This is called 'refresh' and is a great nuisance. But a lot of dynamic memory can be got on a chip, and since the cost of manufacturing a chip is roughly proportional to its area rather than the complexity of the circuits on it, the cost per bit goes down dramatically as memories get larger.

Microprocessors

This is no place to go deeply into these formidable beasts, but it might be useful to give a brief description. As a glance at any logic manufacturer's catalogue will show, more and more specialized circuits have been designed, built and put on the market in the last ten years. But as a circuit gets more specialized, so the market it can be expected to appeal to goes down. It became apparent that it would be better to make one hideously complicated circuit that could turn itself into any of the others when and as it was wanted, but would sell in huge volumes to all sorts of different markets. Having made this circuit—a forerunner is the arithmetic logic unit (ALU) offered by many manufacturers—and given it some memory, electronic engineers found they had something that was not much different from a proper computer which came in umpteen man-sized grey boxes. Hence the microprocessor and the microcomputer. And it is true that in terms of power and memory capacity micros costing only a small amount are rapidly reaching the specifications of computers that ten years ago cost over 1000 times more. At the moment micros are still logic devices and have to be programmed like any other logic chip. They lack civilization. Even big computers are obdurate, stupid beasts; micros are awful. Great things are claimed for 'home computers', but before one embarks on buying or building one, it would be as well to spend a little money on a user's manual for a typical microprocessor. You may well be appalled by the difficulty of getting it to do anything useful. I was.

POSTSCRIPT TO THE ABOVE

Having had a computer (a Research Machine 380 Z) in the house now for 6 months, I realise that the remarks above were somewhat pessimistic. One actually deals not with the computer but with its languages and operating system. BASIC is what we use and its quite painless.

One can also program the processor directly using machine code. This is tough. I haven't tried yet.

Part IV: Basic ideas and hardware

POWER SUPPLIES

Circuits need sustenance, and the problem of power supply is a perennial one, often irritating and sometimes quite hard to solve.

Broadly speaking a supply should:

1 Give a smooth voltage with no mains ripple, noise spikes or oscillations.
2 Give the same output voltage even if the input changes by quite a large amount—say ±10 per cent.
3 Have a low impedance, so that the output voltage does not vary with the current drawn, and ripple from one circuit is not passed on to others.
4 Be protected against short circuits so that inevitable accidents will not destroy it.
5 Protect the circuits supplied by automatic shut down of voltage and current.

The last two conditions may amount to the same thing.

In many ways the best source of electrical power is a battery. It is relatively cheap,* its internal resistance makes it practically short-circuit proof, it has no hum, little noise, doesn't pass on ripple from other circuits. Now that low power COSMOS devices are easy to get and use, small dry batteries can often be the best answer. For quite a long time I used two car batteries for a ±12 V bench supply and kept them charged with an old transformer and a silicon diode.

On the other hand a proper mains supply is a good thing to have. There are dozens of circuits around; Fig. 301 I find pretty well fool-proof. Mains is transformed down to 18 V. The current rating of the transformer fixes the maximum output of the circuit. 1 A would be reasonable. A bridge rectifier produces rough DC. R_1 prevents the transformer and rectifier burning out on switch-on when C_1 is empty. $18 \text{ V}/1 \text{ A} = 18 \Omega$ is the right value, and it has to dissipate $1^2 \times 18$ W, so it had better be a 20 W resistor. C_1 is as big as you can afford, and must be rated at at least 25 V. The voltage reference is set by the zener fed through a 10-kΩ resistor and smoothed by 0.01-μF and 10-μF capacitors in parallel, so that the base of T_1 is held at 15 V. The emitter goes to R_2. The collector is fed by the base of the pnp power transistor.

The action of the circuit is ingenious: T_2 supplies current until the voltage at the output is 0.7 V (the forward voltage drops across D_1) higher than the emitter of T_1. Diode D_1 then conducts, raises the emitter voltage, drops the collector current and therefore drops the current through T_2. Hence the output is stabilised at 15 V. If the output is shorted, and drops to 0 V, then D_2, which is normally reverse biased, starts to conduct, drops the base of T_1, cuts off T_1 and therefore T_2. Short circuit protection that works, and if D_2 is made an LED on the front panel, visual warning too. An important part of the circuit is output decoupling. This needs an assortment of capacitors in parallel: a big electrolytic to smooth out low frequencies, and because this type has very high internal inductance, due to its intricately folded 'plates', it must also be bypassed by smaller capacitors to decouple RF. A single one will not do, because it too can form a resonant circuit at some high frequency, so we must have at least two of different values.

The rest of the design work is simple enough.

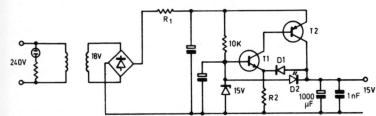

Fig. 301. Power supply to give 15 V with overload protection and short circuit indication.

---

* Actually battery power costs 1000 times more than mains power. But mains power is so cheap in the quantities we're interested in that its cost is irrelevant.

Suppose we measure T_2's β as 100. If the maximum output current is to be 1 A, R_2 should be 14.3/10 mA = 1.4-kΩ. If more than 1 A is drawn from the output, the base current of T_2 won't be enough to support it, the output voltage will fall, and soon short circuit protection will start. There is a voltage drop of 3 V across T_2 at a maximum of 1 A, so it has to dissipate 3 W. A BD131/7/9 will do fine, for they handle 6 W—with a decent heat sink.

For a negative supply, one just reverses the diodes and polarized capacitors, substitute pnp for npn, and vice versa.

One can now get IC voltage regulators which incorporate similar circuitry, and need only the addition of a couple of capacitors. They are, for some reason, more expensive than the general run of ICs, and one can often make up a supply for less. I have three of them mounted under my bench supplying ±15 V and +5 V. A neon mains tell-tale is next to the sockets, and each socket has its LED short-circuit light mounted above it, so one can instantly detect stupidities.

One sometimes wants to put electronic gear in cars. The normal 12 V supply is very suitable, with a simple filter to keep clicks out of the sensitive bits; see Fig. 302. If the car has positive earth, one either has to build

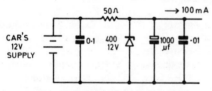

Fig. 302. Filter for use in cars.

a pnp version of the gear, or take care to insulate the car from the electronic chassis. It's always a good idea to put a big power diode in series with the + supply to prevent expensive mistakes.

One also sometimes needs to run mains powered gear away from home. There's no great difficulty about turning 12 V DC into 110 V (or 240 V AC). The basic circuit is shown in Fig. 303, known as an 'inverter'. The oscillator—a digital multivibrator would be fine— produces complementary square waves, the transistors

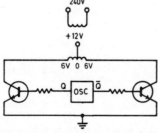

Fig. 303. Inverter for converting 12 V DC to 240 V AC.

draw current alternately from the ends of a centre tapped secondary of a 6 V–0–6 V mains transformer. 240 V appears across the primary. If it is important to have 50-cycle output, then the oscillator must run at that speed, but if not, the whole thing will work much better at 10–20 kHz. Obviously the transistors need to be able to pass the current appropriate to the power to be drawn. And the oscillator needs to be able to supply $1/\beta$ of it to the bases. If not, use a Darlington pair, say a 2N2926 with a BD139; see Fig. 304. The effective β is

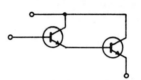

Fig. 304. Darlington pair to increase current gain.

$\beta_1 \times \beta_2$, and will be about 3×10^4. For a deeper discussion of inverter design, see *Semiconductor Circuit Design, I*, pp. 83–115.

ELECTRICITY

The 'working fluid' of electronics, as they used to say in the days of steam engines, is streams of electrons flowing in bits of metal—conductors. In general we're not interested in the electrons, but in the information the flow can be made to carry, by chopping the stream into pulses, or making it stronger and weaker in some sort of wavey way. The nature of electrons is not very important. There are a lot of them in the average bit of wire, they repel each other, and they flow from a negative pole of a battery to a positive. That's really all we need to know. They may well look like small éclairs for all we care.

There are two quantities we need to know about electricity: *Voltage* is the pressure it's at, like the pressure of water or gas in a pipe. The symbol is V and the unit the volt (V). To give an idea of the range of voltage we handle, 1 V you can just taste on the tongue—an odd salty sensation, you can feel 100 V on dry skin, and 240 V you can definitely feel for when given a good conducting path it will kill you. A black and white TV tube uses 10 000 V or ten kilovolt, which is written as 10 kV. A colour set uses 25 000 V; the national electricity grid in Britain is at 275 000 V with some sections at 400 000 V. Going the other way, sounds in a microphone produce a signal roughly of one thousandth of a volt or one milivolt which is written as 1 mV and the weakest useful radio signal on a receiver's aerial is about one millionth of a volt or one microvolt which is written as 1 μV.

The other essential unit is *current*, a measure of the quantity of electricity—or the number of electrons— passing a point per second. It's like the rate of flow of water in a pipe in pints per second. The symbol is I and the units Amperes or amps (A).

Most signal processing circuits, which is what electronics is largely concerned with, operate with modest voltages—±15—and draw currents of 10 mA or so. When the signal is ready, then it is amplified in current and voltage to the large flows needed for, say, radar transmitters, or motor drives or loudspeakers or TV tubes, or any of the hundreds of devices that turn the flows of electrons into effects that are felt by man's senses.

CONDUCTOR

This is the basic electronic element and is a piece of wire. Nominally it has no resistance, in practice a very low resistance, so that the voltage on it is the same everywhere.* The symbol is a line: there are two schemes for showing them connected or crossing; see Fig. 305. (a) is easier to read, as you can see but (b) is easier to draw.

A special conductor is the earth plane to which all current returns; see Fig. 306.

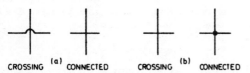

CROSSING (a) CONNECTED   CROSSING (b) CONNECTED

Fig. 305. Conductor conventions used in circuit diagrams.

OR   OR

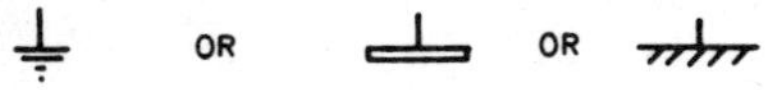

Fig. 306. Earth conventions used in circuit diagrams.

RESISTOR

A *resistor* is a device that impedes the flow of electricity. In the process it gets hot—an electric fire is just a heavy duty resistor—though in most electronic circuits this heating is too slight to detect.

The value of a resistor is measured in ohms (Ω), and is the voltage V across it, divided by the current through it.

$$\frac{V}{I} = R \qquad (4.1)$$

V is the voltage *across* the resistor—if one end is at 15 000 V and the other at 14 999, the voltage across it is the same as if one end were 1 V and the other 0. If you know any two of the three quantities, V, I, R, you can work out the third by using equation (4.1).

There could be an infinite range of possible values of resistances: to reduce the number that actually have to

be produced, manufacturers make a few standard ranges in what are called 'preferred values'.

Resistors go up in cost as their values are more precise. Those used in ordinary work are accurate within 10 per cent—if successive preferred values differ by 20 per cent, then it is possible in principle to find any intermediate value. So 'E12', the most usual range, runs 1, 1.2, 1.5, 1.8, 2.2, 2.7, 3.3, 3.9, 4.7, 5.6, 6.8, 8.2. They are made in decades, starting with 10 Ω and running up to 1 MΩ. An essential beginning to any serious electronic work is to have a supply of each value: three years ago I bought fifty of each and there are still plenty left except for the 10 and 12-kΩ which seem to get used up unusually fast. One can order 'development packs' from several houses.

Resistor values are coded in two ways: either by colour, or in writing. The most useful is the colour code, since you can read the value whatever position the resistor is in. Often number-coded resistors are face down in the box, or worse, face down on a circuit board, so it is difficult to read them. The colour code is broken down as shown in Fig. 307. Band 1 is the first

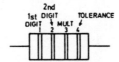

Fig. 307. Meanings of resistor stripes.

digit, band 2, the second, band 3 the multiplier and band 4 the tolerance. In practice you look first for band 4, which is either *gold* = 5 per cent, or *silver* = 10 per cent because it tells you which end *not* to start from.

TABLE 5

Colour	Digit	Multiplier
Black	0	0
Brown	1	10
Red	2	100
Orange	3	1000
Yellow	4	10000
Green	5	100000
Blue	6	1M
Violet	7	10M
Grey	8	100M*
White	9	1000M*

* Resistors with these values are not often found in practice since many insulators have lower resistance.

The code is less than logically perfect because although the multiplier gives the index of 10 ($100 = 10^2$), there is another 10 built into the two digits; see Fig. 308. This resistor is $22 \times 10^2 = 2.2$ kΩ with a tolerance of 10 per

---

* This may not be true at frequencies where the physical length of the wire approaches $\frac{1}{4}$ of a wavelength. A conductor will also have a small amount of inductance, again negligible except at UHF and SHF.

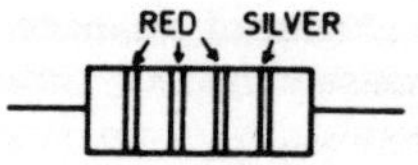

Fig. 308. 2.2 kΩ, 10% resistor.

RED   SILVER

cent which means it may be anywhere between 2 kΩ and 2.4 kΩ. However it is an easy system to work, and one soon is able to read resistors without consciously thinking about it.

The second system writes values in a Roman fashion: 10M2 means 10.2 MΩ, 5k6 means 5.6 kΩ, K33 means 330 Ω, 47R means 47 Ω. (Resistors made in Russia use this system except that R is E. So 82E means 82 Ω.)

The mechanical construction of resistors is important when one uses them for radio frequency (RF) work (Fig. 309). Some are made by depositing a

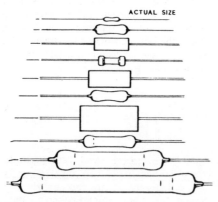

ACTUAL SIZE

Fig. 309. Various resistors, actual size. 1/20 W at top, 7 W at bottom.

conducting layer—perhaps a metal or a carbon film— on an insulating body, and then cutting a helical track in it until the right resistance is reached. The snag about this is that it turns the resistance into a coil which has inductance (see below) and makes it useless for direct exposure to VHF or UHF circuits. Other resistors are made from wound wire. One should be suspicious of any resistors with the slightest spiral pattern on their surface, or with bumps at the ends, as these usually betray metal end caps which can cause a lot of anguish.

A resistor at work consumes power (p. 110), gets hot, and how hot it gets depends on how much surface area it has to radiate this heat. If it gets too hot its value will change, it will affect nearby components, and eventually destroy itself or start a fire. Consequently it is most important to use resistors of a high enough power rating for the job in hand. Happily, again, transistor cuircuits use so little power that the standard rating is 0.33 W or 0.25 W—these are the cheapest. One can get 0.125 W and 0.05 W, which are much smaller and will do almost all jobs in most circuits, but they are more expensive. Unless otherwise stated, all

resistors in circuits in this book are 0.25 W. Two resistors in series are equivalent to a single resistor with a value equal to their sum; see Fig. 310. Two resistors in parallel are equal to a single resistor, the reciprocal of whose value is the sum of their reciprocals; see Fig. 311. The value of resistors in series is always *greater* than either of the pair; the value of resistors in parallel is always *less*.

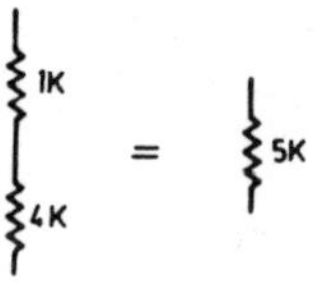

$$\text{1K} \quad \text{4K} \quad = \quad \text{5K}$$

Fig. 310. Resistors in series add their values.

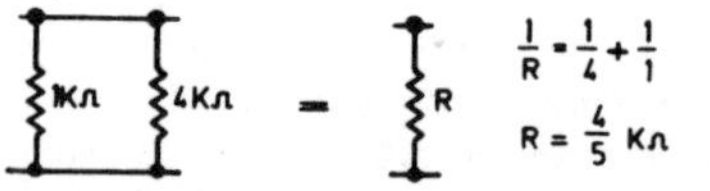

$$\text{1KΩ} \quad \text{4KΩ} \quad = \quad R \qquad \frac{1}{R} = \frac{1}{4} + \frac{1}{1}$$
$$R = \frac{4}{5} \text{ KΩ}$$

Fig. 311. Resistors in parallel add the reciprocals of their values.

Sometimes it is necessary to concoct a resistor with a particular, precise value which is not one of the preferred values (for example, the phase shifting circuit on p. 45). There are two points to remember:

1 As well as adding resistances in series, it is worth looking at subtracting them in parallel: sometimes two in parallel can do the work of three in series.

2 In a series combination usually only the *high* value resistor needs to be an expensive low tolerance type. For example, if we need $11.2 \text{ kΩ} \pm 1$ per cent, it can obviously be made up from a 10-kΩ resistor in series with 1.2-kΩ resistor. The error of the combination is the square root of the sum of the squares of the individual resistors. We want the final error to be less than ± 1 per cent of $11.2 \text{ kΩ} = \pm 112 \text{ Ω}$. So, only the 10-kΩ resistor needs to be 1 per cent accurate. That will contribute an error of, at most, $\pm 100 \text{ Ω}$. The 1.2-kΩ resistor can be 5 per cent accurate, with an error contribution of $\pm 60 \text{ Ω}$. The final error is then $\pm \sqrt{(100^2 + 60^2)} = \pm 116.6 \text{ Ω}$ or ± 1.04 per cent. In a parallel combination, remember that the *low* value resistor dominates so it has to be the accurate one, while the high value can often be a 5 per cent or 10 per cent type.

The main uses of resistances are to:

1 Alter or set up voltages.
2 Prevent currents rising above a desired maximum.
3 Deaden unwanted oscillations.

Fig. 312 is a potential divider and it is evident that here two 10-kΩ resistors divide 10 V by two to produce 5 V. Two 1-kΩ resistors would do the same, or indeed any two equal resistors. The lower the value of the resistors, the more current passes through them,

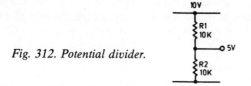

Fig. 312. Potential divider.

and the more we can draw off at the mid, or 'tapping' point, without noticeably altering the 5 V. By altering the relative values of R_1 and R_2 any voltage between 10 V and 0 V can be produced at the tapping point. Suppose we need to draw off 1 mA at 3.2 V; see Fig. 313. It is a good rule to make I, the current through the

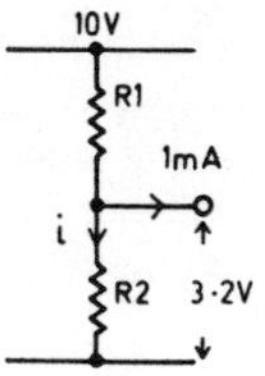

Fig. 313. Potential divider to give 1 mA at 3.2 V. See text.

divider, at least $10 \times$ the current drawn off. So $I = 10$ mA. This defines R_2: $3.2/10 = 320\ \Omega$. The current through R_1 is 11 mA so it is $(10 - 3.2)/11 = 6.8/11 = 618\ \Omega$. In practice, precise settings are seldom necessary, and one can ignore the 1 mA drawn off.

A potential divider works just as well with alternating voltages. Fig. 314 shows a common arrangement

Fig. 314. Potentiometer reducing AC.

for adjusting the audio volume of an amplifier. Here the potential divider is a variable device, called a *potentiometer*, which consists of a carbon or wire track of a fixed resistance, which may vary between 100 Ω and 10 MΩ, along which moves a *slider* to pick off increasing or decreasing voltages from it. The *value* of a potentiometer is the total resistance across it: you choose it by considering how much current is available to drive it, and how much current you need at the slider. There is no point connecting a 1-kΩ potentiometer to ground when the source has an impedance of 10 kΩ—it will completely flatten it. Nor is it much use employing a 100-kΩ potentiometer when the next stage needs at least 10 kΩ.

A *variable resistance* is usually the same piece of hardware but with one terminal ignored (see Fig. 315), or it is sometimes seen as wired in Fig. 316, which

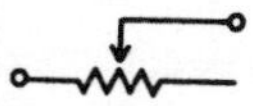

Fig. 315. Potentiometer used as variable resistance.

Fig. 316. Alternative wiring for Fig. 315.

reduces the total resistance and changes the rate at which the output alters.

There are three types of variable resistors:

1 Potentiometers (see Fig. 317), designed for continuous operation by a knob. They may turn or slide. They are available with linear or logarithmic tracks, the latter for volume control to give apparent linearity—the ear is logarithmically sensitive to loudness.

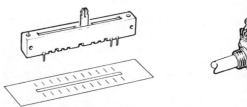

Fig. 317. Potentiometers ('pots') or variable resistors. Left: sliding; right: rotating.

2 'Pre-sets', or 'skeletons'—small variables designed for setting once on lining up a circuit; see Fig. 318. After that they are usually locked with a blob of paint.

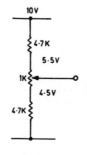

Fig. 318. Preset, 'skeleton', potentiometers, used for lining up circuit on first assembly.

3 Precision pre-sets and multi-turn variables: more highly engineered devices which need ten or more turns to cover the full range. Often a circuit that needs precision pre-sets to work right is doomed to upset for some other cause. A multiturn pot though would be useful for electronic tuning of a receiver. But the same effect can be got by two sets of ordinary pots (p. 83).

The range of a potentiometer can be limited by resistances in series—'end stops'. For instance, if we want to vary a voltage over a range of 1 V in a total of 10 V, we could use the circuit shown in Fig. 319. The output will vary from about 4.5 V to about 5.5 V.

Fig. 319. Potential dividers with end stops to keep variable voltage between 5.5 V and 4.5 V.

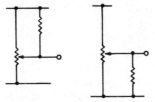

Fig. 320. Alternative methods of wiring potential divider to give different laws.

Also, the law of a potentiometer can be altered by resistance in parallel; see Fig. 320.

Another frequent use of resistors is to limit total current flow. If for instance we have a circuit component, as it might be a transistor, through which no more than a certain current must pass, we can safeguard it as shown in Fig. 321. Even if the circuit behaves at times like a piece of wire the current cannot exceed 10 V/100 = 1000 mA. This is better at the top (see Fig. 322) so the box can have a proper ground.

Fig. 321. Resistor as current limiter in negative supply.

Fig. 322. Resistor as current limiter: more usual use as decoupler in positive supply.

Fig. 323. Resistively coupled amplifiers.

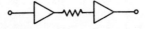

The last common use is between stages in a complex circuit; see Fig. 323. Here two amplifiers are 'resistively coupled'. The resistance used will have a low value compared to the input impedances, and an unwanted oscillation, produced by feedback from front to back of the amplifier chain, will pass through the resistance many times and be damped, while the wanted signal will go through it only once and so be hardly affected (p. 81).

POWER

Electrical power is just like mechanical power—it is a measure of the work that can be done in heating, or lifting weights or accelerating masses. In radio, the range of a transmitter is related to its power.

Power is measured in watts, mili- and micro-, symbol W, mW, μW, and is simply amps times volts:

$$W = V \times I \tag{4.1}$$

2 V across a resistor produces a current of 1 mA through it. What power is dissipated? Answer: $2 \times 1 \times 10^{-3} = 1$ mW, but, by Ohms law:

$$\frac{2V}{1\text{ mA}} = 2\text{k}\Omega \tag{4.2}$$

so we can eliminate either volts or amps in the first equation and insert resistance instead. The equations then become

$$P = \frac{V^2}{R} \tag{4.3}$$

or

$$P = I^2 R \tag{4.4}$$

The thing to remember is that if the *voltage* stays the same, the power dissipated increases as the resistance goes down. That is why an 8-Ω loudspeaker makes more noise than an 80-Ω one.

MULTIPLIERS

This is the point at which to set out all the multipliers in a table:

TABLE 6

	Power	Symbol
Pico-	10^{-12}	p
Nano-	10^{-9}	n
Micro-	10^{-6}	μ
Mili-	10^{-3}	m
Kilo-	10^{3}	K
Mega-	10^{6}	M
Giga-	10^{9}	G
Tera-	10^{12}	T

So 4.7 nF is four point seven nanofarads; 5 kW is five thousand watts (in some old books picofarads are called 'μ.μ.F').

TIME

Time comes into electronics a lot and is measured, as one would expect, in seconds; mili, micro, nano, pico (see p. 91 for time signals).

FREQUENCY

A basic idea in electronics is the *frequency* of an oscillation. Frequencies are measured in Hertz (Hz) which means one oscillation per second. A thousand is

1 kHz, a million is 1 megahertz or 1 MHz, a thousand million 1 gigahertz or 1 GHz.

Period is the inverse of frequency—the time between the crests or troughs of a wave

$$\tau = \frac{1}{f} \quad \text{or} \quad \frac{1}{\tau} = f$$

Wave length λ is period τ times the speed of light c:

$$\lambda = \tau \times c$$

$$\lambda = \frac{c}{f}$$

c is $3 \cdot 10^{10}$ cm/sec.

At any particular time t, one can write the voltage V of a sine wave oscillation as $V_0 \times \sin 2\pi ft$. Since $f = 1/\tau$:

$$V = V_0 \times \sin 2\pi \frac{t}{\tau}$$

Whenever t is a multiple of τ, the period V is $V_0 \times \sin 2\pi \times A$ where A is some whole number. And this, casting desperately back to school trigonometry, is 0. When t is a multiple and a half, also it's 0, when it's a multiple and a quarter, $V = V_0$; see Fig. 324. This means one can add and subtract and multiply waves from and by each other by using simple trigonometry.

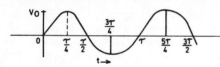

Fig. 324. Sine wave with period t and its fractions.

One often sees the wave equation as:

$$V = V_0 \times \sin \omega t$$

where ω is $2\pi f$.

Radio bands

The common name for the frequency bands are as follows: 0–50 Hz is sub-audio; and 50–15 kHz is audible, but 'audio' is often taken to extend up to 200 kHz even though it overlaps 'radio'.

For radio purposes:

1 Very Low Frequency or VLF is 3–30 kHz
(wavelength: 1 000 000–10 000 m);
2 Low Frequency or LF is 30–300 kHz
(wavelength: 10 000–1000 m);
3 Medium Frequency or MF is 3000–3 MHz
(wavelength: 1000–100 m);
4 High Frequency or HF is 3–30 MHz
(wavelength: 100–10 m);
5 Very High Frequency or VHF is 30–300 MHz
(wavelength; 10–1 m);

6 Super High Frequency or SHF is 300–3 GHz
(wavelength: 1 m–10 cm)
7 Extra High Frequency or EHF is 3–30 GHz
(wavelength: 10 cm–1 cm)

And there for the moment the art stops.

The rather odd choice of 3 as the basic factor is explained by the speed of light: $3 \cdot 10^{10}$ cm/s. This gives wavelengths in decades of metres and is also convenient because the ionosphere bounces waves between 10 and 100 m long—which neatly limit the HF band—over the horizon, thus making intercontinental radio possible.

ALTERNATING CURRENT

If you imagine a sine wave current whose voltage swing is V_0 flowing through a resistor R, the current at any moment is V/R and the power generated ranges between V_0^2/R and 0.

The average power is half the maximum power (i.e. $V_0^2/2R$) and this has the heating effect of a steady voltage V_d where

$$\frac{V_d^2}{R} = \frac{V_{max}^2}{2R}$$

or

$$V_d = \frac{V_{max}}{\sqrt{2}}$$

This is called the root mean square or rms value. AC meters are almost always calibrated in rms, so that while a meter reading of mains voltage is 240 V in Britain, or 110 V in America, the peak value is $\sqrt{2}$ times as much: 338 V or 155 V.

DECIBELS

We are often concerned with ratios and multiples of quantities. It is handy therefore to use logarithms, rather than ordinary arithmetic, and to do this we use the decibel system.

TABLE 7

dB	Ratio
0	1
3	1.413 ($\sqrt{2}$)
6	1.995
10	3.162
20	10
40	100
60	1000
80	10^4
100	10^5

Thus +23 dB is $10 \times 1.4 = 14 \times$ and −46 dB is 1/200th (very nearly).

Since the eye and ear are logarithmic too, one generally reckons that if two things are within 3 dB they're the same, and if one is 60 dB down (1/1000th of the other), we can ignore it.

CAPACITORS (OR CONDENSORS)

A capacitor is simply two plates of metal separated by a thin layer of insulation. Because electrons repel each other, an electron on one plate pushes one off the other and down the conductor leading away from it. If an electron is taken off the first plate, it leaves room for one to flow back onto the other. Thus, although a capacitor will not allow a steady flow of electrons, it appears to allow an oscillating flow. From another point of view, a capacitor is an electronic spring: it takes force (voltage) to squeeze electrons onto one of the plates, because of repulsion of electrons on the other plate.

The impedance of a capacitor to an oscillating current depends on the size of the device and the frequency of the flow. As both *increase*, the impedance, called *reactance*, measured in Ω, *decreases*. The reactance of a capacitor is called X_c

$$X_c = \frac{1}{2\pi fC}$$

Practical capacitors range from several thousand microfarads (μF) to 1 pF. There is little point making smaller capacitances than this since components mounted on a circuit board have mutual capacitances, called 'strays', of the order of pFs. Much of radio work revolves round small capacitances, and the unit, pF, is familiarly called 'puff'.

There are two important types: the ordinary, which is made of foil separated by an insulator, and the *electrolytic* which is rather like a battery, using a chemical action to pack more capacitance into a smaller package (see Figs 325 and 326). Both have a maximum working voltage which must be observed, but the first doesn't mind which terminal is positive—they are

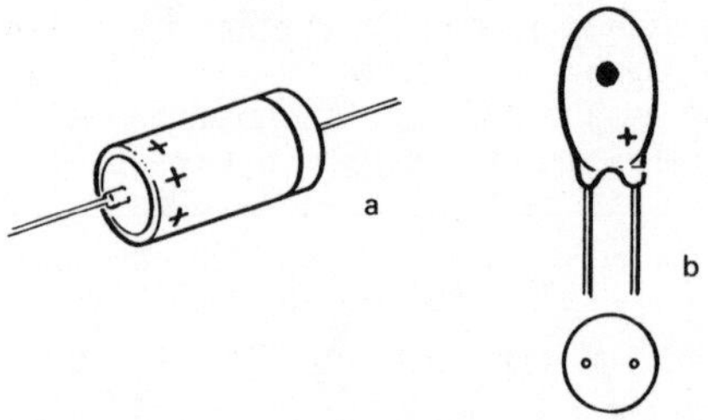

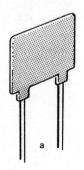

Fig. 326. Electrolytic capacitors: (a) Ordinary type: positive lead indicated by + signs (as shown) or ridge in case, parallel to end; (b) Tantalum bead: positive lead indicated by + sign, or is on the right when looking at spot. (Spot and + will not be found together.)

'non polarized'—while the electrolytic does. Higher values, starting at about 0.5 μF, tend to be electrolytic. Ordinary capacitors pass negligible direct current, but electrolytics do, and this gets worse as the capacitor gets bigger. A high quality variant is the tantalum capacitor—a sort of diode—which is very small and has negligible leakage, but is expensive. Non-electrolytics are made with a variety of insulators—polycarbonate, polypropylene, polyester, which have minor advantages for different purposes. All are suitable for audio frequencies, but tend to absorb energy at RF, so for that one should use silvered mica or ceramic discs and plates—which, however, are noisy at audio. Before using an electrolytic measure its resistance (the *black* lead of the ohmeter is usually positive). On first connection the resistance should be low, showing that current is flowing in, rising to a high value as it charges up.

Most capacitors have their value written on, either in picofarads or microfarads—it is easy to tell which by the size of the thing. Some are colour coded.

Fig. 327. Variable capacitor: symbol.

Small value variables are available, and these come in different forms. Again, as with resistances, there is the 'variable' type, controlled by a knob (see Figs. 327 and 328), and the 'trimmer', designed to be set once and left; see Figs. 329 and 330.

Fig. 325. Capacitors: (a) Silver Mica; (b) Disc ceramic; (c) Tubular ceramic; (d) Polyester: values given by colour bands. Band 1 gives 1st significant digit; Band 2 the second; Band 3 the multiplier; Band 4 the tolerance—black 20%, white 10%; Band 5 the working voltage—red 250 V, absent 30 V (obsolete). See p.107 for colour values.

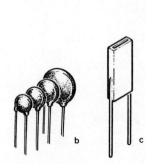

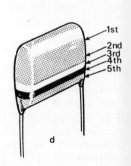

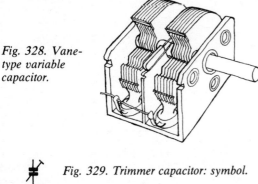

Fig. 328. Vane-
type variable
capacitor.

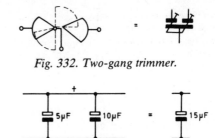

Fig. 332. Two-gang trimmer.

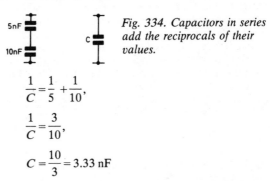

Fig. 333. Capacitors in parallel add their values.

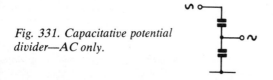

Fig. 329. Trimmer capacitor: symbol.

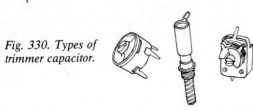

Fig. 330. Types of
trimmer capacitor.

I prefer the rotating to the screw-down type because there will be two settings for the desired maximum or minimum voltage. If there's only *one*, it shows the maximum capacitance is too small or the minimum too big. With the other type this may not be clear. If possible the *rotor* of a trimmer should be connected to ground, so that the stray reactance of a screwdriver, or the hand holding it doesn't alter the value of the setting. Variables can often be replaced for low voltage work by varicap diodes (p. 20) which are much smaller and more convenient, but more lossy and sometimes noisy at RF.

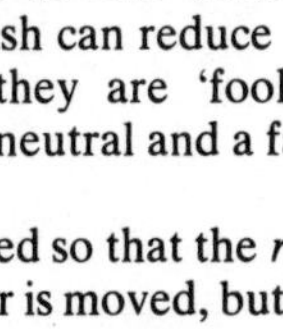

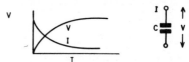

Fig. 331. Capacitative potential
divider—AC only.

Fig. 331 is the capacitative potential divider. Much the same considerations apply as to the resistive potential divider (p. 109). The foolish can reduce AC mains to any voltage this way: they are 'foolish' because it puts the chassis at mains neutral and a fault could be lethal.

There is a variable version designed so that the *ratio* of the capacitances alters as the rotor is moved, but the total stays more or less constant. The advantage of a capacitative potential divider is that it consumes no power: for this reason it is often used in radio work to match impedances without losing precious RF energy.

The variable divider must be distinguished from a double variable (see Fig. 332), where both sides increase and decrease together. The rule for combining

capacitors is the opposite to that for resistors; see Fig. 333. One can easily remember this by imagining that the two capacitors are made into one by joining their plates together sideways.

Capacitors in series are combined like resistors in parallel; see Fig. 334.

Fig. 334. Capacitors in series
add the reciprocals of their
values.

$$\frac{1}{C} = \frac{1}{5} + \frac{1}{10},$$

$$\frac{1}{C} = \frac{3}{10},$$

$$C = \frac{10}{3} = 3.33 \text{ nF}$$

Because the voltage across a capacitor depends on the quantity of electricity that has already flowed into it, it follows that when an empty capacitor is first connected across a supply, the incoming electrons find no voltage to oppose them. It can look like a short circuit and cause as much damage. The *current* into the capacitor is at a maximum when the voltage across its terminals is a minimum. As the capacitor charges up so the electrons in it repel those being driven in by the supply, and the current becomes less strong. When the voltage across the capacitor is equal to the supply, no current flows into it at all. If we draw a graph of current and voltage it looks like Fig. 335. If we put an alternating

Fig. 335. Curves of current into a capacitor and voltage
across it against time.

voltage across the capacitor the same thing happens: the current is at a maximum when the voltage is 0, and the current is 0 when the voltage is a maximum; see Fig. 336. The result is that the voltage peaks happen a

Fig. 336. Sine wave voltage and current in a capacitor: current leads voltage.

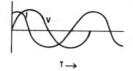

T→

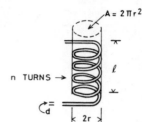

Fig. 339. The important dimensions of a coil: area A, length l, turns n, coil radius r, wire diameter d.

quarter of a cycle (or 90°, if we regard a whole cycle as 360°) *before* the current peaks. (In a resistor, of course, voltage and current are always in step.)

COIL

In many ways a coil (or an inductor) and capacitor are the electrical opposite of each other. A capacitor works because of the phenomenon of electrostatic repulsion; a coil works because of the electromagnetism of a flow of current. When a voltage supply V_s is connected across a coil, it finds a conductor clear to ground. A current tries to flow, but this creates a strong magnetic field which acts to resist it. This field slowly dies down so that more and more current is allowed to pass, until a steady current is reached, whose value depends on the impedance of the supply; see Fig. 337. Thus, while

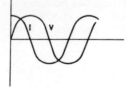

Fig. 337. Curves of current into a coil and voltage across it, against time.

a capacitor passes alternating current and blocks direct; a coil tends to resist alternating and passes direct.

The phase relationship between voltage and current is opposite to that in a capacitor so that if an alternating current is applied to it, the *current* peaks happen before the voltage peaks; see Fig. 338. The resistance offered

Fig. 338. Sine wave voltage and current in a coil: voltage leads current.

by a coil to alternating current is again called the reactance, X_L, when L is the inductance:

$$X_L = 2f\pi L \ \Omega$$

This increases as the frequency increases.

One should in theory be able to calculate L, the reactance of the coil in Henries, from its shape (Fig. 339). In practice this is hard because of end effects. But

it's worth remembering the form of the equation:

$$L = \frac{kAn^2}{l}$$

This means that reactance increases with the cross-sectional area A (or the square of the radius), with the square of the number of turns n, and decreases with length, l. If we wind a coil with n touching turns of wire which has a diameter d we obviously have

$$l = n \times d,$$

so that:

$$L = \frac{kAn}{d}$$

which means that under these conditions, inductance is proportional to the number of turns. (We could write it in terms of l:

$$L = \frac{kAl}{d^2},$$

but it's easier to count turns than to measure length.) This equation comes in handy during the essential process of wind-and-try through which most coils go in idiot electronics. For instance: suppose we want to resonate a 12 pF capacitor at 100 MHz. We've wound a coil that does the trick at 60 MHz. The inductance of the coil is L_1, say, and we want to know how to change it to L_2, the desired final value. Since the coil and capacitor resonate at 60 MHz, their reactances must be equal. So:

$$\frac{1}{2\pi \times 60 \times 10^6 \times l_2 \times l_C} = 2\pi \times 60 \times 10^6 \times L_1$$

or

$$L_1 = \frac{1}{(2\pi \times 60 \times 10^6)^2 \times 12 \times 10^{-12}}$$

By the same argument, at 100 MHz:

$$L_2 = \frac{1}{(2 \times 100 \times 10^6)^2 \times 12 \times 10^{-12}}$$

so that

$$\frac{L_1}{L_2} = \left(\frac{100}{60}\right)^2 = 2.78$$

(We could have left the capacitance out at the beginning.)

Suppose the number of turns on the 60 MHz coil is n_1, and we have to change this to n_2. Since L is proportional to n, we can say:

$$\frac{L_1}{L_2} = \frac{n_1}{n_2}, \quad \text{so that} \quad n_2 = \frac{n_1}{2.78}$$

So that if, for instance, the 60 MHz coil has ten turns, you know you need 3.6 for the final one. Actually, you'll need slightly more because end losses get more important as the coil gets shorter. The best shape for a coil is roughly 'square': as long as it is broad.

TRANSFORMER

A useful trick of the coil is that one can mount two or three or more on the same axis, in each other's magnetic field, and they will then induce voltages and current in each other; see Fig. 340. Although in circuit

Fig. 340. Turns and voltage ratios of a transformer. See text.

diagrams they are shown side by side, in real life they must be wound on the same former, often in amongst each other so that all the terms in the L equation are the same except the number of turns. The rule is that the voltages go in proportion to the turns; currents go in inverse proportion:

$$\frac{V_1}{V_2} = \frac{n_1}{n_2}, \quad \frac{I_1}{I_2} = \frac{n_2}{n_1}$$

Changing voltages becomes ridiculously simple: to bring mains at 240 V down to, say, 15 V you need a transformer with turns ratio 16:1. That's the ratio; just how *many* turns you need on each side is more difficult to calculate—but happily transformer manufacturers look after that. (At RF where home-made transformers are common, calculations of the numbers is quite easy, p. 63.) But if voltage is down, current is up. The primary or mains side may draw 10 mA; the secondary or 15 V side will give 160 mA (this is because the power-in must equal the power-out—neglecting losses).

Impedance is a useful idea when dealing with transformers. The impedance of L_1, Z_1 is V_1/I_1 and similarly $Z_2 = V_2/I_2$, so it isn't hard to work out that:

$$\frac{Z_1}{Z_2} = \frac{(V_1/I_1)}{V_2/I_2} = \frac{V_1}{I_1} \times \frac{I_2}{V_2}$$

$$= \frac{V_1}{V_2} \times \frac{I_2}{I_1} = \frac{n_1}{n_2} \times \frac{n_1}{n_2} = \frac{n_1^2}{n_2^2}$$

Fig. 341. Tapped-down coil, equivalent to transformer with turns ratio $n_1 : n_2$.

It is not necessary to have two coils to make a transformer: you can *tap down* on the original coil and produce the same effect; see Fig. 341. In principle this is slightly better than having two coils, because it reduces noise; in practice one sometimes wants to experiment with the number of turns in the secondary; and then it's easier to have a separate coil to wind and rewind (but see *Isolation* below). It may help to imagine the oscillations across a coil as having a wide range at the top, but 'thin' and of little driving force, growing less extreme but 'thicker' and more powerful towards the bottom, until when one gets almost to earth, the voltage swing is minute, but with great force; see Fig. 342.

Fig. 342. Voltage and impedance in a coil: both high at hot end, tending towards 0 at the cold end.

Consequently one can find any impedance between the highest and 0 by tapping at the right place in the coil.

Mains and audio transformers are wound on laminated iron cores, shown in Fig. 343. There may be

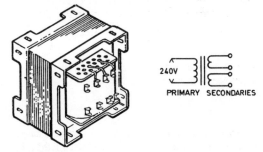

Fig. 343. Mains transformer with secondaries: reality and diagram.

several secondaries—to give different voltages. Since the voltage across a secondary is, as it were, floating, one end can be connected to ground, or to any other voltage in a circuit, and the other end will have its AC added to the first. Some secondaries have a *centre tap*, which can be connected to ground to give opposite + and − voltages. Or can one connect the inner ends of two equal secondaries together to give the effect of a centre tapped coil. But make sure you choose the ends so that the current flows through the two coils with the same rotation. If it goes right handed through the first, and left handed through the second, the net result will be nothing. In circuit diagrams, when it's important to get this right, a dot is marked by the ends of the coils that must all have the currents flowing in the same sense; see Fig. 344.

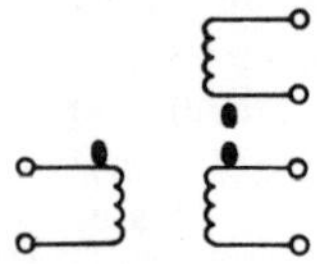

Fig. 344. Primary and secondaries with winding sense dots.

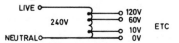

A great advantage of the transformer is *isolation*: the direct voltage on one winding is isolated from that on the others. There is a cheap type called the *auto-transformer* which reduces mains with a single winding; see Fig. 345. The disadvantage is that the chassis has to be at mains neutral which can become mains positive at any moment if there is a fault in the neutral supply. Be warned!

Fig. 345. A tapped down coil across the mains, called an 'autotransformer', can be a dangerous item.

A vast range of mains transformers are available, many of them—used—are cheap from surplus stores. It is always as well before using one of these to check continuity and interwinding resistance with an ohmeter: it may have been overloaded and the insulation destroyed inside.

To measure the turns ratio of an unknown transformer use the simple circuit shown in Fig. 346. The

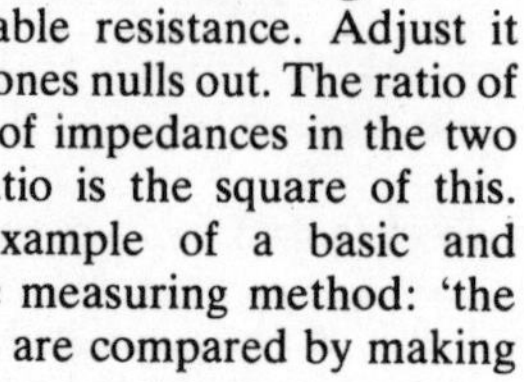

Fig. 346. Method of measuring turns ratio in an unknown transformer. See text.

transformer is connected so that the audio signal is in anti-phase across the variable resistance. Adjust it until the note in the headphones nulls out. The ratio of the resistances is the ratio of impedances in the two windings, and the turns ratio is the square of this. Incidentally, this is an example of a basic and extremely useful electronic measuring method: 'the bridge', where two voltages are compared by making them cancel each other.

Coil winding

Until recently, most audio filters relied on large and difficult to wind coils for their effect. Now, happily,

op-amps have made synthetic filters very simple, so this burden has been removed. However, it is still necessary to wind one's own RF coils, and this is how to do it.

Down to about 5 μH, coils have enough turns to need a former. This former needs to have special properties, otherwise much of the RF energy goes into cooking it. Polythene and thermosetting plastic (e.g. Bakelite) are good materials, and one can get 0.18 in. (5 mm) formers with up to six pins on the base and the inside screwed for a ferrite slug; see Fig. 347. When the

Fig. 347. Coil formers with screwed ferrite slugs for adjustment.

slug is fully in, it *doubles* the inductance of the coil—but make sure it's the right type of ferrite for the frequency. Less often a brass slug is used for adjustment—this, when fully in *reduces* the inductance to 0.8 of its old value.

Let's make a 15 μH coil. A glance at equation for L on p.114 shows that that there are two variables we can play with: the number of turns, n, and the length l. The area A is fixed by the former. The graph on p.125 shows that there are indeed a number of ways of setting about it. Coils work best when square; that is, when length and diameter are about equal. It's also best to avoid overlaying turns because they form capacitances between themselves. This internal capacitance shunts an external tuning one (p.118), and sets an upper limit to the possible Q of the coil. If you plan to use a slug for adjustment, then you want to aim at 15 μH when the slug is half in: we want to wind a coil two-thirds of the final value. This is 10 μH and we look along that line.

So we have a choice ranging from 0.18 in (5 mm) of 42 swg to 0.5 in (12.7 mm) (a bit over actually, but it wouldn't matter) of 34 swg. I prefer to count the turns rather than measure the length, so we convert these using the table as 38 T, or 48 T. It's difficult to wind such fine wire so the turns lie alongside each other and is better to wind on half a dozen, spaced well apart, then slide them down to lie evenly. When the coil is finished, a coat of nail varnish will hold the turns in place, but the wire can easily be pulled off. Strip the insulating varnish off the wire with the tip of a hot soldering iron, and solder it to the pins. Check the windings for continuity and mutual insulation with the ohmeter before putting the coil into a circuit. Some slugs have a slot for a screwdriver; others have a six-sided hole for an allen key—specially made in plastic or bronze to be non-inductive. When the slug is finally adjusted, lock it in place with a drop of candle wax. Some people put a bit of elastic band inside the former before they screw the slug in: this sometimes holds the slug too tight so the screwdriver breaks it. When winding a transformer, it's a good idea to put the secondary at the end away from the slug so that its reactance isn't altered by tuning the primary.

One end of a coil, or the centre tap, is often earthed, at any rate to RF. This is called the 'cold end'. The other, naturally, is the 'hot' end.

Higher inductance coils and transformers are wound on *pot cores* made of ferrite; see Fig. 348. Since the

Fig. 348. Pot cores (Siemens) for winding larger value inductances.

whole magnetic field is trapped by the ferrite, the inductance depends only on n^2 multiplied by a factor characteristic of the particular type. In choosing a pot core one has to remember the maximum number of turns that can be got into it, the current they have to carry, the frequencies for which the core material is suitable, and, of course, the desired inductance.

A common component in radio circuits is an *RF choke*, used to keep RF in one part of the supply. These are simply made by winding wire onto a high value non-inductive resistor and soldering the ends to the resistor leads. If possible, divide the turns into two or more windings so the self capacitances are in series and reduce each other; see Fig. 349. An RF choke

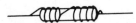

Fig. 349. RF choke wound on a high value resistor.

should have an impedance of at least $10\,\text{k}\Omega$ at the operating frequency—but watch out for resonance with the decoupling capacitor(s). For MF and LF they become somewhat large, and can be bought ready wound on ferrite cores.

Coils for VHF are so small they can be wound from quite thick wire to support themselves. To wind a coil spaced 'one diameter' (i.e. of the wire) take two pieces of wire, wind them together and then unscrew the two coils from each other (see the graph on p. 114).

IMPEDANCE

Any output produced by a circuit must have limits to the voltage and current it can supply. A simple way of looking at it is to imagine an ideal generator which produces an infinite current at the appropriate voltage, feeding through a resistor; see Fig. 350. This imaginary

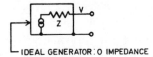

Fig. 350. The impedance, Z, of an output is like an internal resistor Z in series with an ideal generator.

Z resistor is the *impedance* of the circuit or device. If you connect another, real resistor of the same value across the output, the voltage will fall to half its value (see Fig. 351) and this is a crude way of measuring Z

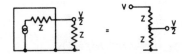

Fig. 351. Rough method of measuring the output impedance of a device: shunt it with different resistances until the output voltage is halved.

(not a perfect way, because the circuit may also have inductance or capacitance as well as resistance). This idea of impedance is a very broad and useful one. You can talk about the impedance of an aerial—a signal voltage of 5 V on a 50 Ω whip will deliver a power of $1/2 \times 5^2/50 = 0.25\,\text{W}$. You can talk about the impedance of a transformer (see p. 77), of supply rails—say a 15 V supply falls to 14 V when you draw a current of 1 A: the impedance is $(15 - 14)$ divided by $1 = 1\,\Omega$. A wire has an impedance—the twisted pair that connects your telephone to the exchange has an impedance of 600 Ω.

Impedance can obviously vary with frequency, depending on the inductances and capacitances involved. An obvious example is the supply rail quoted above: it may have a DC impedance of 1 Ω; at the operating frequency, one would hope that its decoupling capacitors would give it a much lower impedance than that. In engineering texts impedances are often written as complex numbers:

$$Z = R + iX$$

where R is a resistance, i is $\sqrt{-1}$, and X is the reactance of a coil or capacitor. There are complicated mathematical methods for combining complex impedances, and a simple graphical one, the Smith Chart. (For an introduction, see *Semiconductor Circuit Design III*, Chapter XVI.)

A circuit may well—and almost certainly will—have different input and output impedances. In an audio frequency op-amp (p. 22) the input impedance may be 1 MΩ and the output 10 Ω. The function of some circuits is just to lower impedance while keeping signal voltage the same (p. 11)—this obviously corresponds to an amplification of power.

Careful impedance calculations are only necessary in high power circuits. But it's always as well to bear at the back of one's mind these three ideas:

1 High impedances generally imply low power.
2 If circuit A is to drive circuit B without oscillation, then A needs to have a lower output impedance than B has input impedance. (Otherwise B gulps power, A runs down, B stops, A picks up etc, producing a characteristic oscillation called 'motorboating'. When you hear it, you'll understand why.)
3 If power transfer has to be a maximum, then input and output impedances should be equal. In ordinary life this problem only arises with the drive from an audio amplifier to its loudspeaker.

L AND C IN COMBINATION

Apart from electronic logic, the whole of this vast field rests ultimately in the behaviour of the three basic components: resistor, coil, capacitor. The 'active' devices—transistors, valves, diodes—serve as their auxiliaries: amplifying, switching, transferring their effects. If you have three devices, you can combine them two at a time in three different ways. In practice we do not have to bother about so many, because nowadays the language of electronics uses only combinations of capacitor and coil and capacitor and resistor. The other possibility, coil and resistor, would only have application in audio frequency work, and in this field coils have almost disappeared, so big do they have to be to work at low frequencies. In place of the huge chokes that used to be found in audio amplifiers, current technology uses synthetic chokes made from an operational amplifier and two or three resistors and capacitors (p. 26).

CAPACITOR AND COIL

This is the most spectacular combination, the one which was invented by Sir Oliver Lodge and makes the whole of radio possible.

If we look back at the equations for the reactance of capacitor and coil, we see that although they include the same terms, in the case of the capacitor the reactance is inversely proportional to frequency, while the reactance of the coil is directly proportional. This means that if you take any capacitor and any coil there is one frequency, and one only, at which their reactances are the same. At this frequency their voltage-current phase lags will be the same—though in

opposite sense, and if they are connected together they will resonate in a most satisfactory way. There are two ways of connecting them: in parallel and series. The parallel combination (see Fig. 352) acts as a resistance

Fig. 352. At resonance a perfect coil and capacitor in parallel behave like an infinite resistance or open circuit.

which strongly *resists* the frequency of resonance and passes frequencies higher and lower. It almost always connects the signal to ground, thus eliminating unwanted frequencies. Not only does it resist the resonant frequency, it also amplifies it, in the same way that small pushes will set a heavy pendulum swinging over a much greater arc, so a slight alternating voltage will cause a much higher resonant voltage to appear across the combination. The ratio of the two voltages is given by the Q or quality of the circuit—at medium frequencies, it is quite easy to get Qs of 200 or so.

The usefulness of this simple combination is that it will select just one frequency of the hundreds that may be buzzing in an aerial, and allow it to be amplified up to audibility without amplifying all the others with it. In practical radio receivers there are several such circuits in succession to give sharp selectivity, and they are tuned by altering the capacitor—either by using mechanically variable capacitors (see p. 113), or voltage-variable varactors (p. 20). The frequency of resonance is:

$$\frac{1}{2\pi\sqrt{(L \times C)}}$$

A high Q not only gives high amplification at the resonant frequency, it also gives sharper rejection of non-resonant frequencies; see Fig. 353. Of course a high Q circuit also has a high output impedance, so usually one can't take full advantage of the magnification.

The other, and less usual way of using a coil and capacitor in combination is in series. At resonance they have a *low* impedance; see Fig. 354.

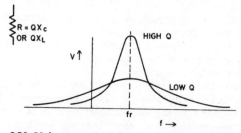

Fig. 353. Voltage-against-frequency curves for high and low Q resonant circuits.

*Fig. 354. Coil and capacitor
in series behave like a low
resistance at resonance.*

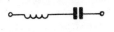

If there were no resistance in a parallel *LC* circuit, *Q*, voltage magnification and impedance would all be infinite. In practice, even if the circuit is not loaded, *Q* is limited by resistance *r*, usually in the wire of the coil (Fig. 355). Dielectric heating in the insulation of the

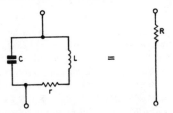

Fig. 355. A real coil and capacitor always have some resistance in series—usually contributed by the coil. This makes their equivalent resistance at resonance finite— but still high.

capacitor also plays a part at high frequencies. At very high frequencies, current flows only in the outer skins of conductors, in a layer so thin that resistances can become quite high. For this reason VHF coils are usually plated with silver to keep resistance down. At resonance, *R*, the dynamic resistance $= X^2/r$ where *X* is either X_C or X_L which are, of course, then equal. Usually we can't find *r* in any simple way. And, equally usually, we don't want to because we're not interested in the *unloaded Q* of the circuit. We want to know its *Q* in practice when it will certainly be loaded by more than *r*. Suppose we have an *LC* combination whose individual reactances at resonances are 1 kΩ, and they are loaded by a 10-kΩ resistor; see Fig. 356. The *Q* of

*Fig. 356. A resonant circuit
is usually loaded by other
driving or driven circuits.
See text.*

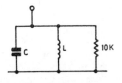

the combination is simply R/X which is 10 in this case (we can ignore *r* as much smaller than *R*). Why is this worth knowing? Because it tells us something very useful about the sharpness with which the circuit tunes. It turns out that *Q* is also the ratio of the bandwidth of the tuned circuit to its centre frequency. And the bandwidth is simply the difference of the two frequencies at which voltage magnification is 3 dB down on its value at resonance where $Q = f_r/f_b$; see Fig. 357. In Fig. 357, if f_r were 1 MHz, then f_b is 100 kHz, f_1 950 kHz and f_2 1.05 MHz.

When one has built an *LC* circuit, it's usually a good idea to test it to make sure it resonates at the right frequency. The obvious thing to do is to connect the

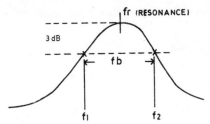

Fig. 357. Q is related to bandwidth as measured by the separation of the 3 dB points. See text.

signal generator across it and look at the output with the oscilloscope—or with a diode and sensitive voltmeter if the resonant frequency is higher than the oscilloscope will display. The snag about this is that the signal generator will have a low output impedance which—paradoxically—will load the tuned circuit. The oscilloscope's coax leads will also look like pretty big capacitors to the *LC* circuit, and will change its resonant frequency. In order to protect the—we hope—high *Q* tank circuit, we have to buffer it with a resistance and a small capacitance as shown in Fig. 358.

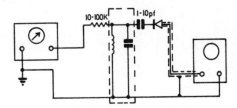

Fig. 358. Testing a tank circuit.

R should be about ten times the design load of the *LC* circuit, i.e.

$$R = 10 \times Q \times X_c$$

Most practical tuned circuits are loaded by inputs and outputs. Suppose we have a 50 Ω co-ax input and an FET amplifier that needs 40 kΩ for its best noise performance, and we want high selectivity with a *Q* of 100. We might have a circuit (see Fig. 359) in which all

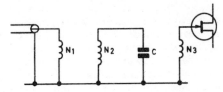

Fig. 359. Matching impedances at an amplifier input. See text.

three coils are wound on a ferrite core with a given A_L (p. 62). *C* is the starting point: the highest *Q* is given by the smallest *C*. 15 pF is a practical value—big enough not to be altered too much by strays. So:

$$X_c = \frac{1}{2\pi fC} = X_L = 2\pi fL$$

$$L = A_L \times n_2^2 \times 10^{-9}$$

Thus:

$$n_2 = \frac{1}{2\pi f(A_L \times 10^{-9} \times C)}$$

The load R that gives the tuned circuit a Q of 100 is found from the relation given earlier:

$$R = Q \times X_c$$

R is made up of the transformed loads of the input and output. In this case the output load is negligible because the FET has a minute input capacitance and huge input impedance. So:

$$QX_c = \left(\frac{n_2}{n_1}\right)^2 \times 50$$

But:

$$X_c = X_L = 2f \times A_L \times n_2^2 \times 10^{-9}$$

So:

$$Q \times 2fA_L \times n_2^2 \times 10^{-9} = \left(\frac{n_2}{n_1}\right)^2 \times 50$$

The 40 000 Ω that the FET wants to see at its input is the 50-Ω feeder transformed by $n_1 : n_3$

$$40\,000 = \left(\frac{n_3}{n_1}\right)^2 \times 50$$

$$n_3 = 28 \times n_1$$

WIRES

The straight lines in electronic circuit diagrams represent extremely important components: the wires between the terminals of devices that should be connected; while the paper represents an equally important component, the insulator between devices that should not be connected. Along with the problem of supplying these, goes the problem of supporting components against mechanical loads, screening them from unhappy effects on each other, and on occasion, of dissipating the heat they generate.

The problem of insulation and connection are common to all circuits. Insulation is either done by air, assuming it to be dry; by pouring plastic of some sort

over the component—'potting' it—which has the drawback that maintenance becomes almost impossible, and by the use of fibre, bakelite, glass fibre sheets. It is essential to support every component by soldering all its leads to something solid. To reduce mutual interference and stray reactances, it is important that these leads should be as short as may be. Transistor circuits are now almost always built on flat plastic boards, the components on one side and the wiring underneath.

Mutual interaction of the wires can be reduced by making them thin enough in the direction perpendicular to the board, so from this point of view it is convenient to use copper foil bonded to the board as conductor (Fig. 360). In many applications it doesn't really matter whether the conductors are foil or wire: one often uses foil because the boards can then be printed, which makes assembly much easier and more accurate. Since all the leads are on the underside, the component side can be completely covered with foil to act as a ground plane. Radio circuits at VHF and UHF particularly benefit from this treatment, since it absorbs unwanted radiation and promotes stability. But it does no harm at lower frequencies either, and for logic circuits, with their high frequency switching transients (p. 60) it is also useful. The foil earth plane gives a very low impedance return path for all parts of the circuit, and avoids mutual interactions that can happen in a narrow earth rail. Leads to earth are simply soldered to the foil, other conductors are taken through it—the copper having been cleared away from the edge of the hole with the tip of a larger drill twirled in the fingers.

If one starts out with two-sided foil board, the underside could be etched to make a printed circuit. But, to be honest, I have found that the business of printing and etching is hardly worth the trouble. It is more difficult to get it to work than the manufacturers of photoresist like you to think; and once it is done, it is relatively difficult to alter or repair the circuit. *ICs* in particular are difficult to unsolder from a printed circuit board because all eight or fourteen legs are held down at once. When they are wired underneath you can easily undo them, and if components are kept close together, most of the connections can be made using their own leads. The result looks neat and works well.

A half way stage between old fashioned tag strip and printed circuit board is the well-known Veroboard system. The insulating board is drilled with a square matrix of holes at 0.15 in. (3.8 mm) or 0.1 in. (2.5 mm) centres. On the lower side parallel rows are joined by copper strips. Components are mounted on the plain

Fig. 360. Circuit construction using a plastic board coated with copper foil on one side as an earth plane.

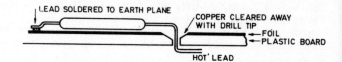

LEAD SOLDERED TO EARTH PLANE

COPPER CLEARED AWAY WITH DRILL TIP

FOIL

PLASTIC BOARD

'HOT' LEAD

side and the leads soldered beneath. A tool is sold to enlarge holes to break the strips where connections are *not* wanted. Ingenious in principle, I find that the intellectual difficulty of *breaking* conductors, rather than making them, together with the practical problems of avoiding solder bridges across the very narrow spaces between the strips is enough to make Veroboard rather unattractive. Also, one loses the advantage of a solid copper ground plane. If your ambition is to cram the maximum number of components into the smallest possible space, then 0.1 in. (2.5 mm) Veroboard with the copper cleaned off with a big hot soldering iron is the answer. Using the smallest resistors and transistors, it is possible to pack some eighty components to the cubic inch. But that way eye strain, instability and madness lie.

An indispensable tool for the coarse electronician—and the expert one too—is one of the variety of breadboards one can now buy; see Fig. 361. These plastic

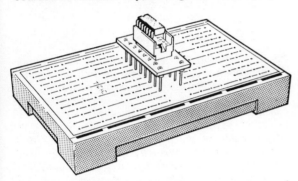

Fig. 361. A breadboard (reproduced by courtesy of Electrovalue Ltd.).

boards have holes for component leads, connected in rows by bronze foil blades underneath, so that circuits can be easily and quickly tried out. Special boards can be had to accept DIL ICs. I would never build any circuit without testing it on one of these first. The only snag is the relatively large inter-row capacitance which can prevent high frequency circuits working as they would on a proper board. See review of breadboards in *Wireless World*, November 1978.

SCREENING

RF circuits have to be screened from each other to prevent *pick-up* of stray radiation. A foil earth plane is half the battle; small walls of tinned steel salvaged from 1 gallon oil cans—which can be cut with stout scissors—can be soldered between amplifier stages, or made into boxes and put round coils. Screening is usually shown in circuit diagrams by dashed lines. In VHF amplifiers it's often called for to separate input from output; see Fig. 362.

Fig. 362. Screening input from output on an RF amplifier.

If the transistor has a metal can which is *not* connected to one of its leads, then turn it upside down and solder it to the ground plane. If it *is* connected, glue it on with a thin dab of Araldite, pressed well down—check for insulation after—to act as an earthing capacitor. The screen can be carried across the middle, dividing the leads. This is a counsel of perfection, though, and in most cases it will be enough to mount the device the right way up and carry the screen over it.

Even though an unstable circuit will often oscillate at a high RF frequency which won't show on an oscilloscope, instability can be detected. Characteristic signs are variable performance, sensitivity to hands and metal objects, bumps, clicks and dead patches while tuning. A cause of trouble is sometimes too long emitter leads or resonance in the decoupling capacitor. Or it may be an RF choke oscillating with some capacitor you wouldn't suspect. If VHF parasitic oscillation is a perisistent problem, it can be helped by ferrite beads slipped over wires carrying DC, emitter leads, output to IF stages etc.

RF and low level audio circuits should be mounted in metal boxes to prevent interference. It's easy enough to bend up a box with one side missing and bolt down to the ground plane—leaving holes for access to trimmers, slugs, etc. for the presence of the box will detune all the resonant circuits. Or one can get diecast boxes in various sizes, that can easily be drilled, sawn and filed to make the necessary openings. Mount the circuit on the *lid* for ease of access. Similarly RF and low level audio should be carried from circuit to circuit in screened cable. Microphone leads in particular should be screened, and there is a variety of cable to do this sort of job.

The idea is that the braided outer screen extends the earth plane and box of each circuit. A snag arises when the earth planes are connected by another route—say by a supply lead, or back through power supplies to mains earth. The braid and the 0 V supply may then form a loop which can have currents induced in it by stray magnetic fields, causing baffling persistent hum, RF pick-up and a multitude of maladies. One solution is to put a filter between the braid and one earth plane; see Fig. 363. R should be 50 Ω or so; C as big as may be. In severe cases experiment will be necessary with both.

Fig. 363. Method of earthing far end of screened cable through a filter to avoid ground loop.

CO-AX

RF currents should be carried in co-axial cable (co-ax), a specially made type of wire which has a braided screen round an inner conductor. The outer braid is always earthed, so RF on the inner is screened, and, as it were, piped safely from place to place. The line acts as a series of low Q, LC tanks, and looks like a pure resistance to the input and output when correctly matched. The characteristic impedance is determined by the ratio of the diameters of the inner and outer conductors; see Fig. 364. Commonly available co-ax is either 50 Ω or 75 Ω. Plugs and sockets of these

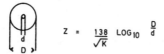

$$Z = \frac{138}{\sqrt{K}} \, LOG_{10} \, \frac{D}{d}$$

Fig. 364. Dimensions of co-ax, and formula for impedance.

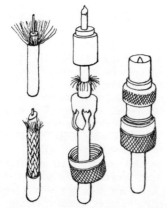

Fig. 365. How to connect a plug to co-axial cable: 1. Strip off outer insulation for length of plug to reveal woven outer screen conductor; 2. Fray out screen; strip inner insulator off central conductor leaving about $\frac{1}{4}$ inch; 3. Thread knurled ring and retaining clip onto cable, insert bared inner conductor down central tube of plug—which is embedded in a plastic block—and solder conductor to end of tube. Trim screen to diameter of retaining clip; 4. Screw knurled ring and plug body together to press retaining clip fingers into outer insulation and to squeeze screen between clip and insulating block.

impedances are also available, though except at the highest frequencies it doesn't really matter using the wrong one. See Fig. 365. If RF is to be carried in co-ax for more than a small fraction of its wavelength, the ends have to be properly teminated: usually with transformers; see Fig. 366. See p. 77 for the sums.

Another kind of wire used for RF is twin feeder, usually with 300 Ω impedance; see Fig. 367. This line is non-radiating because a positive current in one wire in

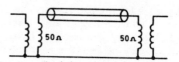

Fig. 366. Co-ax terminated in matching impedances.

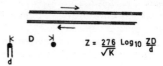

$$Z = \frac{276}{\sqrt{K}} \, Log_{10} \, \frac{2D}{d}$$

Fig. 367. Twin feeder for RF: dimensions and formula for impedance.

balanced by a negative current in the other; at a distance the two cancel to give no radio field; a third type is a strip conductor parallel to another or a ground plane; see Fig. 368. K in each case is the dielectric

$$Z = \frac{377}{\sqrt{K}} \, \frac{d}{D}$$

Fig. 368. Strip line RF feeder: dimensions and formula for impedance. Excess of lower strip—or ground plane (hatched)—does not alter the result a great deal.

constant of the medium round the conductors, and is 1 for air or a vacuum, 2.3 for polythene. The strip line is usually made by etching one side of double sided copper clad insulating board (see p. 120) and is used for 500 MHz up. One advantage is that by gradually tapering the top conductor, an impedance change can be made; see Fig. 369. Half a wavelength of any of

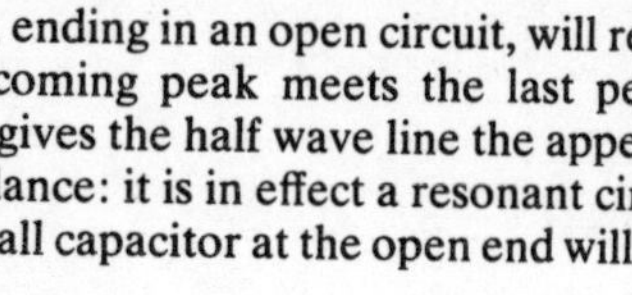

Fig. 369. Tapered strip line acts as an impedence transformer.

these lines, ending in an open circuit, will reflect RF so that an incoming peak meets the last peak coming back. This gives the half wave line the appearance of a high impedance: it is in effect a resonant circuit (see p. 118). A small capacitor at the open end will tune it; see Fig. 370.

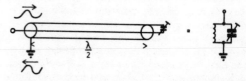

Fig. 370. Half wavelength co-ax as a resonator, tuned by small capacitance.

SWITCHES

Electronic instruments and devices use a good many switches: to change operating ranges, frequencies, to bring functions into play. They are classed by 'pole' and 'way'—a 3P 2W switch has three inputs which can each be switched to one of two outlets. Simple switches, up to 2P 2W, are often toggle type; see Fig. 371.

Fig. 371. Toggle switch.

More complicated ones are made up of wafers on a common spindle. Each wafer has twelve contacts, so the possibilities range from 1P 11W to 6P 2W. Wafers can be stacked or 'ganged', on the same spindle.

It is not a good idea to switch RF mechanically, particularly at the top of the HF band and upwards, but switch wafers are designed to be non-reactive and one can get special wavechange switches designed for the purpose. RF, particularly VHF, is best switched by using diodes controlled by DC (see p. 19) or, with high powers, special coaxial relays designed not to upset the impedance of a line.

Small switches are made in DIL shape to preset logic inputs 0 or 1. Another type, the micro-switch, is sensitive to small movements and can be used for instance to turn motors off when some moving object touches it at the end of its desired travel.

RELAYS

See Fig. 372. A relay is simply an electromagnet which, when energized, attracts a pole piece which in turn operates one or more contacts. If one wants to use an electrical signal to switch others of the same, a relay is the traditional answer. Although relays have a distinctly Victorian air, there are still billions of them in the world, mainly in telephone exchanges, and they are a simple, reliable way of rearranging electronic

Fig. 372. Relays: (a) Reed switches: the glass capsule is inserted into central hole of coil. When the coil (top) is energized its magnetic field makes the steel switch blades attract each other and form an electrical connection. Centre: two on/off reeds of different sizes; bottom: a two-way switch; (b) Conventional relay with two two-way contacts.

circuits. The current a relay needs is defined in terms of its operating voltage and resistance—a 6-V relay of 29.5 Ω draws rather more than 1 W. It is important to get the voltage right, and because the magnetic core which activates the relay is a massive choke, the surge voltages when it is turned on and off by transistor circuits can be difficult, so it is often necessary to shunt it as with capacitors and diodes; see Fig. 373. In this case the diode stops the collector going higher than the rail, which might make it exceed the max collector–emitter voltage for the transistor. Evidently the transistor must be able to sink 109 mA.

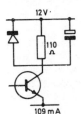

Fig. 373. Relay operated by transistor, with precautions against surge.

Faster switching is done by reed relays: two slips of steel overlap in a vacuum in a small glass tube. The tube is inside a coil; when current flows through it the contacts attract each other and make the circuit. These can operate much faster, and one can get coils with room inside for up to half a dozen reeds. These can be used for switching RF, though then only one reed should be used in a coil. In the 'off' position, there will still be some feedthrough because of the capacitance between the contacts. A permanent magnet can be used to close a reed relay: for instance mounted in a door with the relay in the jamb as part of a security system.

The traditional relay has a great advantage over more modern devices in that one can easily bolt different switch arrangements onto it: on-off, change-over etc., so that one component performs perhaps half a dozen tasks. The disadvantage is slowness and heavy power consumption in the solenoid.

Semiconductor switches

Naturally, everything a relay can do, a semiconductor can do too, but oddly, not always as easily. The appropriate device is a thyristor. This may be represented essentially by two transistors; see Fig. 374. With no

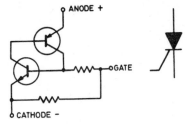

Fig. 374. Thyristor and equivalent circuit.

voltage on the gate, the device is open circuit and no current passes. When a voltage more positive than the anode is applied to the gate, it acts as a diode: it will pass forward current and resist negative. Once on it stays on, until the current through it falls to zero, then it switches off and stays off until a gate signal turns it on again. A more useful and more modern device is the Triac (see Fig. 375), which will trigger on positive *or*

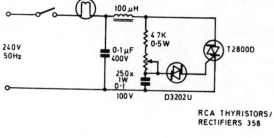

RCA THYRISTORS/
RECTIFIERS 358

Fig. 375. Triac.

LAMP CONNECTED DURING ▨

Fig. 376. Triac and bidirectional trigger diode in a lamp dimmer circuit (reproduced by courtesy of RCA).

negative gate voltages—with regard to terminal 1. The snag about these semiconductor relays is that many things one would like to switch them withdraw huge currents at turn-on. A tungsten filament draws twelve to fifteen times the current cold that it does when hot. Uncharged capacitors look like short circuits and inductive loads can react with heavy reverse voltage pulses. All of which are bad for semiconductors, but hardly affect contact switches. Still, problems exist to be overcome.

Switching AC is relatively easy because the triac switches off each time the voltage falls to 0. If we delay its switch on, we can make it pass only a part of the AC cycle in each direction, thus giving power control; see Fig. 376. The *D* device is a double diode, used to even out variations in the gate trigger-voltage of the triac. The rate of charge of the 0.1 µF capacitor is controlled by the 250 kΩ variable resistor, so that the triac fires earlier or later in the AC half cycle, so letting the lamp

draw more or less current from the mains. Because the switching times are short, the triac generates considerable RF energy which must be kept out of the mains by the choke and capacitor. The important parameters of a triac are: peak off state voltage; rms on state current; peak surge current; and fusing current to protect the device. If used correctly, triacs can be very useful, but unlike most of the circuits described in this book, they are not really suitable for trial and error design. Copy a published circuit, or master the principles. The RCA data book *Thyristors and Rectifiers* has comprehensive applications notes. Remember too that the device is usually mounted by one of its terminals which will be mains *live*, so be careful how you fix it.

Appendix 1

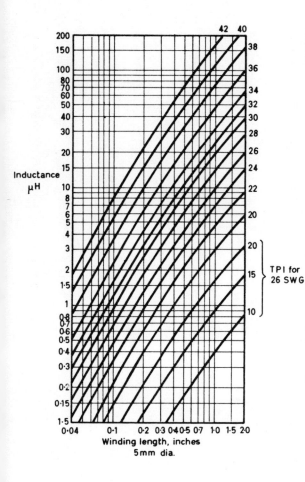

Winding length, inches
5mm dia.

Inductance curves for 5 mm formers. Use 'winding length' with the following table to get the number of turns:

Gauge swg	Turns per inch
20	26
22	33
24	41.5
26	50.3
28	61
30	72.3
32	83
34	96.2
36	116.3
38	114.9
40	178.6
42	212

Adapted from G. R. Jessop, *Radio Data Reference Book* (RSGB, London, 1972), with permission.

Remember that this gives the inductance *without* a slug. Since a ferrite slug fully in roughly doubles the inductance, wind for $\frac{2}{3}$ nominal value to get adjustment either side.

Appendix 2

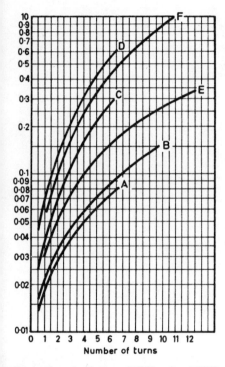

Number of turns

Inductance curves for small self supporting coils. 'CW' spacing means that the coils touch; '1 dia' spacing means that the turns are 1 wire diameter apart.

Curve	Internal coil diameter mm	Wire swg	Space	Lead length mm
A	3	24	1 dia	5
B	5	18	1 dia	10
C	10	18	1 dia	10
D	20	14	1 dia	15
E	5	22	CW	10
F	10	22	CW	10

'Lead length' gives the length of the lead included in the test coil whose inductance was originally measured. It is not very important.

Reproduced from *VHF & UHF Handbook* (RSGB, London, 1972), with permission.

Index